SARTRE
HIS PHILOSOPHY AND
EXISTENTIAL PSYCHOANALYSIS

SARTRE

HIS PHILOSOPHY AND
EXISTENTIAL PSYCHOANALYSIS

SECOND REVISED AND ENLARGED EDITION

by Alfred STERN

Professor of Philosophy and Languages
California Institute of Technology
Pasadena, California

A DELTA BOOK

A DELTA BOOK
Published by Dell Publishing Co., Inc.
750 Third Avenue, New York, N.Y. 10017
Revised and enlarged edition Copyright © 1967 by Alfred Stern
First edition Copyright 1953 by the Liberal Arts Press, Inc.,
under the title *Sartre, His Philosophy and Psychoanalysis*
Delta ® TM 755118, Dell Publishing Co., Inc.,
The hardcover edition of this book is published by
Delacorte Press, New York, N.Y.
Library of Congress Catalog Card Number: 66-22200
First Delta printing
Manufactured in the United States of America

TO THE MEMORY OF MY BELOVED PARENTS

Rose and Julius Stern

CONTENTS

2. Sartre's Existential Psychoanalysis

Foreword
TO THE SECOND EDITION

DURING THE FOURTEEN YEARS which have passed since the publication of the first edition of this book the international status of Existentialism has changed. The Extentialist night clubs in Paris closed, but the lecture halls of the world's universities were opened to Existentialism. From a sensational fashion Existentialism was converted into an object of serious scholarly, academic studies. This change is a guarantee for the survival of Existentialism as a part of modern Western philosophy. The second English edition of this book, which was also published in Spanish and in Japanese, is intended for those who wish to get familiarized with Sartre's Existential philosophy and its psychoanalysis, as one of the most stimulating manifestations of contemporary thought.

The revision and enlargement of the original text became necessary by the fact that, since the first printing of this book in 1953, Sartre's work has grown and much more material about its background has become available, especially through the publication of the first part of the philosopher's autobiography, *Les Mots* (1963; American edition: *The Words*, 1964), and the three volumes of Simone de Beauvoir's memoirs. Ample use of these sources has been made in the present edition, and also other material related to Existentialism was introduced. The new biographical sources now available helped the author to correct certain errors contained in the first edition.

Replacing the *Introduction* of the latter, the present edition contains a new first chapter under the title "Preliminary Remarks about Existentialism and Sartre the Man."

When referring to the "growth" of Sartre's work I do not only mean his plays *Lès Séquestrés d'Altona* (*The Condemned of Altona*) and *Nekrassov*, the first of which is of considerable artistic interest, but especially the publication in 1960 of the first volume of his large theoretical work, *Critique de la raison dialectique* (*Critique of Dialectical Reason*), in which Sartre definitely disproves the charge of antihistorical orientation leveled against his earlier form of Existentialism. Since in this latest of his works Sartre tried to clarify the relations between his philosophy and dialectical materialism, I have added a new last chapter titled "Postscript on Existentialism and Marxism."

According to its subject matter this book is divided into two large sections: PART I: *Sartre's Existential Philosophy*; PART II: *Sartre's Existential Psychoanalysis*.

The author wishes to express his thanks to the following publishers:

The AMERICAN-SCANDINAVIAN FOUNDATION and PRINCETON UNIVERSITY PRESS for excerpts from *Concluding Unscientific Postscript* (1941), by S. Kierkegaard, translated by F. Swenson, completed by Walter Lowrie.

HARCOURT, BRACE and COMPANY, INC., New York, for excerpts from *The Republic of Silence* (1947), by J.-P. Sartre, edited by A. J. Liebling; and *The Practice and Theory of Individual Psychology* (1929), by Alfred Adler.

Sanford Jerome Greenburger and BASIC BOOKS INC., New York, for excerpts from *The Individual Psychology of Alfred Adler* (1956), edited by H. L. and R. Ansbacher.

HENRY HOLT and COMPANY, INC., New York, for excerpts from *Creative Evolution* (1911), by H. Bergson.

ALFRED A. KNOPF, INC., New York, for excerpts from *The Reprieve* (1947), by J.-P. Sartre, translated by Eric Sutton.

LITTLE, BROWN and COMPANY, Boston, for excerpts from "We Are Looking at You, Agnes," in *We Are the Living* (1933), by Erskine Caldwell.

W. NORTON & COMPANY, INC., New York, for excerpts from *An Outline of Psychoanalysis* (1949), by S. Freud.

PHILOSOPHICAL LIBRARY, INC., New York, for excerpts from *What*

Is Literature? (1949), by J.-P. Sartre, translated by B. Frechtman.

RANDOM HOUSE, INC. (The Modern Library), New York, for excerpts from *Light in August* (1950), by William Faulkner.

SCHOCKEN BOOKS INC., New York, for excerpts from *Anti-Semite and Jew* (1948), by J.-P. Sartre.

GRUNE & STRATTON, New York, for excerpts from *Autobiography of a Schizophrenic Girl* (1951), by M. Sechehaye.

INTERNATIONAL UNIVERSITY PRESS, INC., New York, for excerpts from *Symbolic Realization* (1951), by M. Sechehaye.

WILLIAM SLOANE ASSOCIATES, INC., Publishers, New York, for excerpts from *Joan of Lorraine* (1946), by Maxwell Anderson.

THE UNIVERSITY OF BUFFALO PUBLICATIONS IN PHILOSOPHY, Buffalo, New York, for excerpts from *Philosophic Thought in France and the United States* (1950), edited by Marvin Farber.

Excerpts from other works in French, German, Spanish, and other languages have been translated by the author.

San Juan, Puerto Rico   ALFRED STERN

PART ONE

SARTRE'S EXISTENTIAL PHILOSOPHY

Didst Thou forget that man prefers peace,
and even death to freedom of choice in
the knowledge of good and evil?
FEODOR M. DOSTOYEVSKY,
The Brothers Karamazov

i
Preliminary Remarks about Existentialism and Sartre the Man

THE STRONGEST INFLUENCE brought to bear upon literature and philosophy during the first half of the twentieth century did not come from a writer or a philosopher but from a psychiatrist: Sigmund Freud and his psychoanalysis. Now literature and philosophy repay their obligation by creating a psychoanalysis of their own—that which Sartre calls "Existential psychoanalysis." We shall see whether this young discipline, which started after World War II, is able to influence psychiatry.

Jean-Paul Sartre is one of the most versatile minds of our time. Not only a dramatist of great talent, a remarkable novelist and brilliant essayist, he is also a disciplined professional philosopher and psychologist. We may even say that Sartre is basically a philosopher whose novels and plays are essentially different ways of artistically exemplifying a certain type of philosophy: Existentialism. Created a century ago by the Danish Protestant theologian Søren Kierkegaard, Existentialism was rediscovered at the beginning of the twentieth century by the Spanish thinker Miguel de Unamuno and developed in different directions by the German philosophers Karl Jaspers and Martin Heidegger, by the French philosophers Gabriel Marcel and Louis Lavelle and finally by Jean-Paul Sartre. The French term *existentialisme*, from which the English word is derived, was coined by Gabriel

3

Marcel. It roughly corresponds to the German *Existenzphiloso-phie*, although the representatives of the latter deny any community with their French counterparts, who, among themselves, are split into different factions.

According to certain remarks of Heidegger, Existentialism could be defined as a phenomenological description and interpretation of human existence. The latter should not be confused with life. One *has* one's life, but one *is* one's existence. A person may have a good or a bad life, much or little life. Existence, however, has no degrees. It is entire or it is not. It is this human existence which Existentialism tries to elucidate, by means of a phenomenological description and interpretation.

But what does the word "phenomenological" mean? It means that the examination of human existence is more than a simple psychological introspection into one's own existence. It is based on a method which consists in "bracketing" all real human existences in order to grasp the "essence" of human existence *as such*, as it shows itself (the Greek word φαινόμενον meaning that which shows itself or is brought to light).

The creator of the phenomenological method, the Austrian philosopher Edmund Husserl, still believed that by virtue of it he would be able to change philosophy into a "rigorous science" (*eine strenge Wissenschaft*). However, this illusion was destroyed by the Existentialist dissenters among his disciples. They showed that the phenomenological method can only be employed within the limits of the philosopher's own existence. With this it became obvious that philosophy cannot be a rigorous science, that philosophical truth cannot have the universal depersonalized character of scientific truth. Each philosopher can only give the truth of his own existence, which, however, always offers an essential aspect of human existence as such. Each man is thrown or cast into existence—to use an equivalent of Heidegger's term *ge-worfen*—and can see reality only from the angle of his specific existential circumstances. He can thus only give the truth of his own existential perspective. Yet, as the Spanish philosopher, José Ortega y Gasset, tried to show, each individual perspective requires the others, as its complements, and all perspectives together constitute absolute reality. This doctrine of Ortega, inspired by Leibniz, is called "Perspectivism." [1]

Being cast into certain circumstances each man has to *act*, in order to maintain himself in existence. These *actions* determine each man's outlook on the world. As Heidegger and Saint-Exupéry have shown, each in his way, the world reveals itself differently through the different utensils man applies in his actions. The Existentialist's world-view is not purely theoretical, but determined by his actions and his means of action. He does not recognize "things," but only obstacles and helps for his actions. While the traditional philosopher's approach to reality is that of a detached, objective observer, the Existentialist philosophizes as an *actor* in the human drama. This is perhaps the main reason why Existentialism finds so strong a resonance among nonphilosophers. In reading Existentialist philosophy or literature, the average educated person realizes the meaning of Horace's words *de te fabula narratur*—it is your story which is told.

Let us now talk about the man whose contribution to Existentialism stimulated a wider interest in this philosophy than did any other of its representatives: Jean-Paul Sartre. Some people may ask themselves why it should be necessary to know the man who propounded a certain type of philosophy. This is indeed not necessary if one considers the history of philosophy in the traditional way. Then the different thinkers appear only as names standing for certain possibilities of thought, inherent in the very structure of the mind which, with inner logical necessity must appear in time, as soon as certain cultural, social, scientific and psychological conditions have been fulfilled. To Existentialists this is, however, not the right approach. As we already know, they deny that philosophy can reach that type of depersonalized, objective truth, which was the ideal of Rationalism. In this respect there is complete agreement between such thinkers as Kierkegaard and Nietzsche, Jaspers, Marcel and

[1] More about this subject in my book *Philosophy of History and the Problem of Values*, The Hague, Mouton & Co., 1962. See also my article: *¿Ortega Existencialista o Esencialista? La Torre*, Puerto Rico, No. 15–16, Julio-Diciembre 1956, pp. 385–399.

others. It was perhaps the Spanish philosopher Miguel de Unamuno who expressed this idea most clearly when he wrote: "Philosophy is a human product of each philosopher, and each philosopher is a man of flesh and blood who addresses himself to other men of flesh and blood like himself. And, whatever he may do, he does not philosophize with his reason alone, but with his will, his feelings, with his flesh and blood, with his whole soul and his whole body. It is the *man* who philosophizes." [2]

Reason is a universal function of mankind, able to arrive at objective truths—i.e., truths which are independent of the individual particularities of the different knowing subjects. Body, will and feelings, however, are specific individual endowments of each existing subject, of each person. If they take part in the building-up of a person's philosophy, they give it a personal impress. Thus our interest in the person who philosophizes—in the present case, Sartre—is justified by the very nature of his philosophy, Existentialism.

Jean-Paul Sartre was born June 21, 1905, into a Parisian middle-class family. His father, an officer of the French navy, died of tropical fever when Jean-Paul was still a baby. Young Sartre never knew his father. "I left behind me a dead young man," he wrote, "who had not had the time to be my father and who, today, could be my son. Was it an evil or a good? I do not know. But I willingly accept the verdict of a prominent psychoanalyst: I have no Super-ego." [3]

Yet, there was a powerful father figure around Jean-Paul during the most important years of his childhood: his maternal grandfather, Charles (Karl) Schweitzer, an authoritarian Alsatian professor of German, in whose home the boy was raised. Schweitzer, an uncle of the celebrated African jungle doctor Albert Schweitzer, was a Lutheran, while the rest of the family was Catholic. Sartre wrote later: "I was a Catholic and a Protes-

---

[2] M. de Unamuno, *Del Sentimiento trágico de la Vida*, p. 31. In the Spanish original the literal expression is *"un hombre de carne y hueso,"* a man of flesh and bone. Amer. ed., *The Tragic Sense of Life*, New York, Dover Publications, 1954.

[3] J.-P. Sartre, *Les Mots* in *Les Temps Modernes*, No. 209 (Oct. 1963), p. 582. American edition, *The Words*, New York, Braziller, 1964.

tant, I added the critical spirit to the spirit of submission."[4] Thus, Sartre, like Gide, is a religious hybrid who became an atheist.

There is a well-known story about Pascal, reported by his sister Gilberte, that the boy begged his father to explain what mathematics were, and that when the father hesitated, the child is said to have discovered by himself several of Euclid's theorems. It was as if this future mathematical genius felt that numbers and figures would be fateful for him. One is reminded of this story when Sartre tells about his passionate longing, as a small child, to learn the art of reading. He caressed his books, acted as if he were able to read them, followed with his eyes and fingers line by line the sequence of those mysterious printed signs. Finally, with the help of a story he knew by heart, young Sartre taught himself the art of reading. It was as if this future literary genius felt that words, and especially printed words would become fateful for him. If he calls the first volume of his autobiography *Les Mots*, or *The Words*, it is because these symbols, the great invention of the human mind, never lost their fascination for him. As soon as he knew the alphabet, no book of his grandfather's library was spared from his reading fury— neither the Classics, nor the Romantics, nor the philosophers. But the *Grand Larousse*, the famous French encyclopedia, became his main teacher. The animals he saw in the zoo, the people he met in the streets seemed less real to him than the ones described in the encyclopedia. "As a Platonist by calling, I went from knowledge to its object; I found in the idea more reality than in the thing. It was in the books that I met the universe,"[5] Sartre confessed later.

One has called the Jews the people of the book, alienated from nature. "*En ce cas, je suis plus juif qu'eux,*" [6] Sartre writes —in this case I am more Jewish than they are. Time and again he admits that for a long time he took words for the quintessence of things, that he confused the world with the language by which it is described. Since Husserl's phenomenology and especially its application by Heidegger have likewise a tendency to see the

[4] *Ibid.*, p. 629.
[5] *Ibid.*, p. 601.
[6] *Ibid.*, p. 599.

world through the network of language, we may partly understand the strong attraction Sartre felt toward these thinkers.

At the age of six Jean-Paul began to write; not the ABC's, like other children, but novels, poems and dramas. He tried to rewrite the fables of La Fontaine in alexandrines. I never gave much credence to these stories reported by Marc Beigbeder, one of Sartre's first and most enthusiastic biographers.[7] Now Sartre admits himself, that he only wrote *"par singerie,"* by aping, to give the impression of being an adult, that he invented nothing, because all was a "deliberate plagiate."[8] He was not, indeed, a precocious writer, for he was thirty years old when his first book appeared.

An excellent student, Sartre was admitted to the famous Ecole Normale Supérieure in Paris, but failed in his first attempt to pass the *agrégation*. The following year, however, he passed this very difficult competitive examination with high marks. At the time Sartre was a member of a group of top students, nicknamed *les petits camarades* (the little comrades), which included the philosopher Politzer, who died in World War II as a hero of the Resistance, and Raymond Aron, today professor of philosophy and sociology at the Sorbonne, member of the Académie des Sciences Morales et Politiques and a political analyst of worldwide fame. It was Aron who advised Sartre to do his military service in the corps of meteorologists, where he became Sartre's superior and instructor. Thus, Sartre did not see any combat service in World War II and could devote most of his time at the front to writing.

Aron played an important role in Sartre's evolution in another respect. In the early thirties after a year at the French Institute in Berlin, where he had studied Husserl's phenomenology, Aron returned to Paris and joined Sartre and Simone de Beauvoir one evening in a Montparnasse night club for an apricot cocktail. Aron pointed to his glass and said to Sartre, "You see, my little comrade, if you are a phenomenologist, you can talk about this cocktail and it will be philosophy."[9] As Simone de Beauvoir

[7] M. Beigbeder, *L'Homme Sartre*, Paris, 1947.

[8] *Les Mots*, in *Les Temps Modernes*, No. 210, Nov. 1963, pp. 770–771.

[9] S. de Beauvoir, *La Force de l'Age*, Paris, 1960, p. 141.; American edition, *The Prime of Life*, Cleveland, 1962.

reports, "Sartre became pale from emotion, or almost," when he heard Aron's words; for years he had been longing for such a philosophy of the concrete which can grasp the world as it offers and shows itself to our consciousness. The next day Sartre bought Lévina's book on Husserl and, following Aron's advice, he applied for a year of study at the French Institute in Berlin. He wanted to concentrate on Husserl. Meanwhile Hitler had come to power in Germany. Sartre's application meant paradoxically that a non-Jewish French philosopher was going to the Third Reich to study a Jewish philosopher on the advice of another Jewish philosopher. In spite of the fact that for racial reasons Husserl was at that time no longer *persona grata* in Germany, his works were still available there. After a year's study Sartre returned to France as a consummate phenomenologist. Later, in 1936, he published, in the *Recherches Philosophiques* his *Essai sur la transcendance de l'Ego*, based on Husserl's phenomenology but giving sights already of deviation from the master's point of view. It is well known that Sartre's main work, published years later, bears the subtitle *Essai d'ontologie phénoménologique* (American edition, *An Essay on Phenomenological Ontology*).

During the greater part of the years between his graduation and the outbreak of World War II Sartre was a professor of philosophy at a Lycée in Le Havre, the French port which he was later to describe in his novel *La Nausée* (American edition, *Nausea*) under the name of Bouville, probably based on the French word *boue*, or mud. There he also met the *salauds*, or stinkers, the self-righteous bourgeois world of this province town by which he felt oppressed. Sartre has always felt much sympathy with the working class and was invited several times to become a member of the Communist Party. He refused, as he always has, because he was eager to preserve his intellectual independence. He wishes to study and to criticize Marxism when necessary, without being bound by a party line. He wishes to be a free "fellow traveler" rather than a disciplined party member. In cases of political conflict, however, he sides with the working class.

Although *nausée,* or nausea, later became a metaphysical category for Sartre, it is interesting to note that it was not he who made the word the title of his first novel, but his publisher, Gallimard. Sartre's original title was *Melancholia*.

Published in 1938, *La Nausée* (American edition, *Nausea*, 1949) made its author famous in France. The novel has as narrator a man who feels at certain moments that anxiety which has become a trade mark of Existentialism. Running desperately through the streets of Bouville he has the impression that "the houses with their gloomy eyes" watch him fleeing. Now Simone de Beauvoir reveals that Sartre himself suffered from this kind of hallucinatory anxiety at the time he wrote *La Nausée*. Making studies for his theory of emotions he had asked one of his friends, the psychiatrist, Dr. Lagache, to give him an injection of mescalin, a drug producing hallucinations. The effect, which was supposed to disappear after a few hours, lasted, however, for many months, and Sartre became the victim of a hallucinatory psychosis. "His perceptions got out of shape, the houses had grimacing faces with eyes and jaws everywhere." [10] Traveling on a train he saw an orangutan, suspended by the feet on the roof of the coach, pressing his grimacing face against the window-panes. Everywhere he saw crabs and polyps, and during a nightly walk through Venice a gigantic lobster trotted behind him, giving him not a moment of respite. "He was a prey of anxiety and he became frightened." [10] Finally, after several months, Sartre was cured, and the gigantic lobster took its leave forever.

What interests us in this experience is the fact that anxiety, which Existentialists such as Kierkegaard, Heidegger and Sartre himself consider a metaphysical condition, inherent in man's existence in the world, was in Sartre's own case, the result of something quite physical: a drug, a chemical compound.

Another fact concerning Sartre the man, which may reveal Sartre the philosopher, is his dislike for mathematics, science and especially engineering. He condemns our modern "engineer's civilization," and when he was once told that he resembled an engineer he considered it a "violent insult."

There is, furthermore, Sartre's Realism. Among the metaphysicians, he always preferred those who saw in the cosmos a synthetic totality of concrete things, like the Stoics and Spinoza.

[10] *Ibid.*, p. 217.

As a student he was impressed by Bergson's concrete way of studying duration. If he was attracted by Husserl's phenomenology it was partly because the latter had proclaimed the imperative *"zurück zu den Sachen!"*—back to the things! Sartre wishes to defend the reality of this world against the attempts of Idealism to dissolve it into perceptions of our senses and categories of our understanding. Affirming that the world coincides exactly with the knowledge man has of it, Sartre's Realism often lacks critical reflection. But in his most recent theoretical work, *Critique de la Raison dialectique*, of which only the first volume has appeared, Sartre's Realism became critical. There we can read, for example, such sentences as "one finds in nature only the dialectics which one has put into it," [11] and this means that the human mind is no longer considered a passive mirror.

Sartre's extreme sense of independence also expresses itself in his rejection of marriage. As Simone de Beauvoir, his companion for more than three decades, writes: "Sartre did not have the vocation for monogamy. . . . Between us, he explained to me . . . it is a question of a necessary love: it is appropriate that we may also know contingent loves . . ." [12]

Another manifestation of his sense of independence was the decision he took as early as his student days, never to encumber himself with possessions. He may have been impressed by the fact that the ancient Romans used the word *impedimentum* for both "luggage," which is a possession, and "obstacle."

"It seems to me," he said once, "that we are possessed by the things we possess." For many years Sartre lived in the Quartier Latin in a hotel room that was so tiny, that it amazed his visitors. It did not even have a book shelf. Now, wealthy and famous, he lives in a modest two-room bachelor apartment in the tenth floor of a Parisian apartment building.

During the years when it became obvious that Hitler was planning aggression against Germany's neighbors, many leftist intellectuals in France advocated peace at any price. Among them were the former pupils of the extreme pacifist philosopher Alain, who propagated the slogan, "France at war would be

---

[11] J.-P. Sartre, *Critique de la Raison dialectique*, Paris, 1960, I., p. 127.
[12] *Op. cit.*, pp. 26–27.

worse than a nazified France." Sartre's point of view was much more realistic. He knew that his country had no choice but to fight or to suffer the fate of Austria, annexed by Germany in 1938. Thus, when World War II broke out one year later, Sartre willingly joined the army and served as a meteorologist attached to the artillery. It was in the army where he developed his *morale de l'engagement*, or ethics of commitment, which consisted in accepting a given situation and trying to overcome it by a commitment to action.

In June 1940, when the French army surrendered, Sartre became a prisoner of war. In the German prison camp he was attached to the health service and worked as a male nurse. It was in this *Stalag* that Sartre started a kind of resistance movement by producing his first piece of *littérature engagée*, or literature committed to a definite project of action and liberation. For a Christmas celebration by his fellow prisoners he wrote and staged a play called *Bariona*, apparently about the mystery of the birth of Christ. In fact, however, it was a drama about the occupation of Palestine by the Romans and a veiled call to resistance against the invader, which his fellow prisoners understood well. They applauded enthusiastically.

After nine months in the camp Sartre was released by the Germans for reasons of health and returned to occupied Paris. He was immediately reinstated as professor of philosophy at the Lycée Pasteur and was later put in charge of the preparatory courses for the Ecole Normale Supérieure at the Lycée Condorcet. In addition, he taught a course in the history of the theater at Dullin's school of dramatic art and engaged in intense activity as a writer.

He was then thirty-six and a man of firm moral principles. His imperative was not to bend under the yoke of the invader and not to make any concessions, either to the Nazis or to their French collaborationists. This must have made his teaching task very difficult, for as a professor he was a civil servant of the Vichy government, and his highest superior, the Minister of National Education, Abel Bonnard, insisted that teachers propagate the ideas of the so-called National Revolution, sponsored by the Nazis. Bonnard was such a radical collaborationist that after the liberation of France he was sentenced to death by default.

In his writings of this period Sartre was beyond reproach. He first tried to start an intellectual resistance movement, *"Socialisme et Liberté,"* to prepare a doctrine for the future, but he had to give it up. The Communists, who constituted the strongest and best organized group of the French Resistance, distrusted him, because he had been released by the Germans. Thus Sartre decided to resist by means of a *théâtre engagé.* He wrote his powerful tragedy *Les Mouches (The Flies).* Under the guise of a title reminiscent of Aristophanes' comedies and of characters borrowed from Aeschylus, Sartre protested in the play against the feelings of guilt and remorse for the sins of the Third Republic and its parliamentary democracy, with which Pétain and the Nazis tried to infect the French people, so that they would accept the occupation as a just castigation. When the play was given on a Parisian stage, Orestes' cry for "freedom!" had the force of an explosion. The collaborationist press and the German *Pariser Zeitung* criticized this masterpiece of Sartre's harshly, but it was praised in the clandestine leftist journal *Les Lettres Françaises.* The Communists no longer distrusted Sartre. He was invited to take part in the intellectual resistance and to publish articles in the clandestine press, especially in *Les Lettres Françaises.* Sartre did it most efficiently, contributing thus to the creation of a philosophical doctrine of the Resistance, based on his Existentialist ethics. We shall discuss it in a special chapter of this book.

Sartre's good relations with the Communists did not survive the occupation, for after the liberation of France they attacked his philosophy and person violently, and he counterattacked. There were reconciliations, followed by fights, more reconciliations, and so on.

In the summer of 1944 Sartre's work for the two Resistance groups, to which he belonged, brought him into serious danger. A member of one of these groups had been arrested and, under torture, had given the names of his fellow resistants, among them that of Sartre. The latter was warned by Camus, who belonged to the Resistance group *Combat,* and Sartre had to flee from Paris. He returned, however, to the capital at the approach of the liberators. During the days of the heroic fight of the Parisian population led by the underground leaders against the Nazis, Sartre was a reporter for Camus' newspaper *Combat*, which now operated in the open. He was present when General Leclerc's armored division entered Paris through the Avenue d'Orléans, under the jubilant sound of all the church bells, and when General de Gaulle walked down the Champs Elysées, acclaimed by thousands of enthusiastic Frenchmen.

During the occupation Sartre published some of his best work; in addition to *The Flies*, there were *Huis Clos* (*No Exit*), also produced on the Parisian stage; the film script *Les jeux sont faits* (*The Chips Are Down*); and his main philosophical treatise, the gigantic volume *L'Etre et le Néant* (*Being and Nothingness*), in which he developed his Existentialist doctrine in a systematic way. The book was published in 1943 in occupied Paris, but did not make much of an impression at the time; it sold very slowly.

Sartre's output was amazing during that period of moral depression and of physiological deficiency resulting from rigorous food rationing by the German occupation. Although calories may be indispensable for thought, they do not seem to determine either the quality or the quantity of its contents.

It is well know that Sartre wrote much of his work surrounded by the odor of coffee and cigarettes, the sound of clicking china and glassware, the comings and goings in a Left Bank café. Here friends and students gathered to discuss basic problems of existence over apéritifs and demitasses. What the Academy was for Plato, the Lyceum for the Peripatetics, the Café de Flore was for Existentialism, for a long time. This café on the Boulevard Saint-Germain will perhaps one day enter the history of philosophy. After the liberation it became the center of what the Argentine philosopher Emilio Estiú called "*existencialismo turístico*," tourist Existentialism. One of our philosopher's severest critics, Father Troisfontaines, sees Sartre as an individual uprooted from the traditional values of religion, family, home, and the like. By way of summary, he calls Sartre "*l'homme au café*"—the café intellectual.[13]

[13] R. Troisfontaines, *Le Choix de J.-P. Sartre*, Paris, 1945, pp. 51–52.

So deeply is the café atmosphere rooted in Sartre's mind that he even draws upon it in demonstrating metaphysical theories in his most erudite work *Being and Nothingness*. For instance, in explaining the two basic concepts of being and nothingness, he writes: "When I enter the café in order to look for Pierre, there takes place a synthetic organization of all the objects of the café, so that they become the background against which Pierre is given as that which is supposed to appear. And this organization of the café into a background is the first 'naughtization.' " [14]

Sartre had previously shown that "this café itself, with its customers, its tables, its benches, its mirrors, its lights, its atmosphere of smoke and noise of voices, of clashing saucers and footsteps, is a wholeness of being." Pierre, however, is not here; "he is absent from the whole of the café. Thus his absence congeals the café," and Pierre becomes "the nothingness on the background of the naughtization of the café." [15]

From this café example Sartre deduces his dubious metaphysical principle, in which he agrees with Heidegger, that "non-being does not come to things by the judgment of negation, but, on the contrary, the judgment of negation is conditioned and upheld by non-being." [16]

Similarly, when Sartre attempts to establish his thesis that classical logic with its principle of identity is invalid for the human personality, "which is what it is not and is not what it is," he demonstrates it in terms of the *garçon de café*, who only "plays at being a café waiter." [17]

Finally, in his novel *Le Sursis* (*The Reprieve*), Sartre describes his young protagonist, Boris, a philosophy student at the Sorbonne, who reflects in the following "profoundly" philosophical fashion upon the possibility that he will be called in the draft of World War II:

> The number of times that I will go to a café after today can be calculated: Suppose that I go twice a day, and that

[14] J. P. Sartre, *L'Etre et le Néant*, Paris, 1943, p. 44; American edition, *Being and Nothingness*, New York, Philosophical Library, 1956.
[15] *Ibid.*, pp. 44, 45.
[16] *Ibid.*, 46.
[17] *Ibid.*, 97-99.

I am called up in a year: that makes 730 times. 730 times!
That's not very often. . . . People who could look forward
to 10,000 to 15,000 evenings at cafés! [18]

So we see that Sartre even measures a human lifetime by the
number of visits to cafés. A modern Protagoras, he likes to
consider the café the measure of all things.

Yet Sartre's café complex has very serious sociological reasons.
We already know that our philosopher had to live, after his
return from the German prison camp, in a tiny hotel room on
the Left Bank. During the grim years of the occupation of Paris
by the German army there was no heating in hotel rooms and
almost none in private apartments. The only places where writers
were able to defreeze their stiff fingers, in order to be able to
hold a pen, were the cafés. Simone de Beauvoir describes how
she, Sartre and most of their friends had to spend every free
hour at the Café de Flore, the second floor of which was converted into a kind of a writing room, where dozens of intellectuals did their work. How should this place not have become
a second home for Sartre, more important than the place where
he only slept?

Besides, in cities like Paris and Vienna the café has been for
almost three centuries a place of important intellectual develop-
ments. In his history of *La Régence* Jules Michelet described
the influence of the Parisian cafés on the evolution of the ideas
of the *encyclopédistes*. Rousseau, Diderot, d'Alembert and others
used to discuss their philosophical doctrines at the Café Procope,
a few steps from the Café de Flore, and these doctrines had
a tremendous influence on the French Revolution. Philipp Frank
reports that the Logical Empiricism of the Viennese Circle
(*Wiener Kreis*) grew out of discussions held in a café of the
Austrian capital by some of Ernst Mach's disciples. Something
similar happened with Alfred Adler's Individual Psychology.
Excluded from the lecture halls of the University of Vienna,
this theory was developed in the regular meetings held in a
Viennese café by Adler and some of his pupils. At the end, this
theory became so powerful that it was able to force its way into

[18] *Le Sursis*, Paris, 1945, p. 215; American edition, *The Reprieve*, New York:
Alfred A. Knopf, 1947, p. 272.

the Medical Center of Columbia University in New York. There is thus nothing extraordinary in the fact that Sartre's Existentialism started and developed in one or two Parisian Left Bank cafés, before it could cross the thresholds of the Sorbonne and other great universities all over the world.

Since the liberation of France, Sartre's life and his activities have received so much publicity that they need not be discussed here. Let us only mention that during all these years Sartre has been a *philosophe engagé*, fighting colonialism, neo-fascism and social as well as political injustice everywhere, by means of his powerful pen and his eloquent spoken word.

There is only one of his acts which still puzzles many people: his rejection of the 1964 Nobel Prize for Literature. This decision of his was, however, only another manifestation of his sense of independence, especially regarding the great struggle between the capitalist and the communist blocs. In one of his plays, *The Respectful Prostitute*, he had attacked the persecution of the Negro in the U. S. South, while in another, *Red Gloves*, he had criticized the ways in which the Communists sacrifice the individual, when it is to the advantage of the party. In both cases he maintained the independence of his judgment. After the liberation of France Sartre had been a neutralist, but this situation has been modified. In rejecting the Nobel Prize he declared: "My sympathies go undeniably toward Socialism, that is toward that which one calls the Eastern bloc, but I was born and raised in a *bourgeois* family. Therefore I cannot accept any distinction by the high cultural authorities, neither of the East nor of the West . . . I would be just as unable to accept the Lenin Prize if someone should wish to award it to me." [19]

Sartre also complained that the Nobel Committee consistently overlooked such outstanding writers and poets as the Russian Sholokhov, the Frenchman Aragon or the Chilean Neruda, because of their leftist political orientation.

Sholokhov has since been awarded the Prize for Literature. One may ask oneself whether Sartre's spectacular gesture might not have contributed to this decision of the Swedish Academy.

---

[19] "Jean-Paul Sartre reçoit le Prix Nobel. . . et le refuse," *France-Amérique*, New York, 1er Novembre 1964, p. 8.

In 1964 Sartre contended that the Prize had become a distinction reserved for *bourgeois* writers of the West or Eastern rebels against the East, such as Pasternak. Therefore, he felt that with his acceptance of this distinction he would have given the false impression of having been "won back" by the West, an interpretation given to the acceptance of the Nobel Prize by Camus. This great French writer, who, in his youth, had even been a member of the Communist Party has, in one of his last books, *L'homme révolté (The Rebel)*, moved so far to the right that he not only rejected the Russian Revolution but even the great French Revolution of 1789. Sartre wanted to draw a clear line between himself and his former friend, who had been awarded the highest literary honor *apparently* for having become *"bien pensant"*—a conformist.

Finally, Sartre declared in another interview: "I do not think that an academy or a prize has anything to do with me. I consider that the greatest honor I can have is to be read." [20]

Pythagoras and Plato distinguished between the lovers of wealth, the lovers of honor and the lovers of wisdom, the philosophers. These three categories have not always been clearly separated in the history of philosophy. But one must admit that a writer and thinker who is able to refuse, unhesitatingly, more than fifty-three thousand dollars and the highest literary honor in the world, has proved to be a man of strong principles, a pure lover of wisdom, a true philosopher.

[20] "Playboy Interview: Jean-Paul Sartre," *Playboy*, May 1965, p. 76.

ii
EXISTENCE OR BEING?

Is IT NOT ODD that philosophy should try to explain the nature
of existence to man? Is it not like trying to explain the meaning
of swimming to fish or of flying to birds? Existence is even more
natural to man than flying is to birds, for birds do not fly all
the time, but man always exists, as long as he is alive, even when
he sleeps. How should he not know what existence is? Why
should he need to have philosophy explain it to him? Even the
most uneducated man knows existence by virtue of his permanent, most intimate, inward and outward experiences.

However, as soon as man tries to conceptualize his existence,
he runs into difficulties. Will philosophy and especially a philosophy of existence help him to overcome these difficulties? That is
what we shall try to find out.

Although existence is as old as mankind, a philosophy of
existence or Existentialism, is a rather young branch of human
knowledge. Traditional classical philosophy dealt only with
"being" (ὄντα, ens, être, Sein, essere, ser, etc.), sometimes replacing this term with the word "existence" (existentia, Dasein), but
using them interchangeably without any conceptual difference.
In the medieval scholastic distinction between *essentia* and
existentia the latter term was used as a synonym for "being,"
at least from the fifteenth or sixteenth century on.

During the last two centuries the philosophical concept of
being has become more and more abstract and, consequently,
more and more empty. In vain Leibniz tried to remind philosophers that we could not possibly "have the idea of being if we
were not beings ourselves and thus would find being in our-

selves." [1] It was German Idealism which, forgetting this reminder from Leibniz, evaporated being into such cloudy altitudes of speculation that it lost almost all connection with our individual being here and now, our human "existence." In Kant's philosophy being is no longer "a real predicate, that is, a concept of something which would be added to the concept of a thing. It is only the positing of a thing or of certain determinations in themselves." [2]

But it was Hegel who reached the climax in this process of the dehumanization of being when, in his *Logic*, he declared:

> Being, pure being without any further determination . . . is pure indeterminateness and vacuity . . . . Nothing, pure nothing . . . is complete emptiness, without determination or content. Nothing . . . is the same lack of determination as pure being . . . Pure being and pure nothing are, then, the same. [3]

Foreseeing that this unusual equation would arouse serious psychological objections, Hegel wrote:

> If being and nothing are identical, say the objectors, it follows that it makes no difference whether my home, the air I breathe, this city, the sun, the law, mind, God, are or are not. Now in some of these cases the objectors foist in special and private aims or the utility a thing may have for a particular person, and then ask whether it be all the same to that person if the thing exist and if it do not. As to that, indeed, we may note that the teaching of philosophy is precisely what frees man from the endless crowd of finite aims and intentions by making him so indifferent to them that their existence or non-existence is to him a matter of no moment. [4]

One can easily see that this haughty attitude of Hegel's idealistic philosophy toward individual existence, with all its pain,

---

[1] G. W. von Leibniz, *Nouveaux Essais sur l'Entendement humain*, I (1765), p. 23.

[2] I. Kant, *Kritik der reinen Vernunft*, III, Hauptstück, p. 472.

[3] G. W. F. Hegel, *Wissenschaft der Logik*, ed. G. Lasson, I, pp. 66–67.

[4] *The Logic of Hegel*, Oxford, 1874, p. 140.

anxiety, sorrow, and uncertainty, would provoke a kind of anti-idealistic revolution. It came from a man of dynamic temperament, endowed with a sharp analytical mind, a caustic eloquence, and an extraordinary capacity for moral suffering—Søren Kierkegaard, the Danish Protestant thinker who had deeply experienced Moses Mendelssohn's dictum: "If we start from ourselves . . . existence is a common word for acting and suffering." [5]

Kierkegaard's writings are a violent protest against all idealistic evasions of real issues into impersonal, objective, timeless schemes and eternal truths. He not only defended subjective truth but affirmed that "truth is subjectivity." Having gone through all the tragic antinomies and grim oppositions of individual existence with the terrifying "either-or" decisions it imposes, Kierkegaard rejected Hegel's solvent "mediation" of these oppositions by means of an automatic dialectical process which deals with timeless ideas and hollow generalities. Throwing the acid of his irony against Hegel's system, Kierkegaard wrote:

> Can the principle of mediation also help the existing individual while still remaining in existence himself to become the mediating principle, which is *sub specie aeterni,* whereas the poor existing individual is confined to the strait-jacket of existence? Surely it cannot do any good to mock man, luring him on by dangling before his eyes the identity of subject and object, when his situation prevents him from making use of this identity, since he is in process of becoming, in consequence of being an existing individual. How can it help to explain to a man how the eternal truth is to be understood eternally, when the supposed user of the explanation is prevented from so understanding it through being an existing individual, and merely becomes fantastic when he imagines himself to be *sub specie aeterni?* What such a man needs instead is precisely an explanation of how the eternal truth is to be understood in determinations of time by one who, as existing, is himself in time, which even the worshipful

[5] *Morgenstuden*, Berlin, 1785, I, p. 81.

Herr Professor concedes, if not always, at least once a
quarter when he draws his salary.[6]

These bitter words were written in Copenhagen, in 1846,
fifteen years after Hegel, professor at the University of Berlin,
had died of cholera. His reputation was still bathed in glory,
and Kierkegaard's protests found little echo. Nowadays Existentialists renew the same attacks with more success, when they
reproach classical philosophy for having "de-existentialized being" and thus emptied it of its "existential explosive." [7] These
are the words of a prominent Catholic Existentialist, Etienne
Gilson, formerly of the Collège de France.

All Existentialists, today as always, criticize the practice of
traditional philosophy that determines being in a general way
while remaining indifferent to the question of whether or not
such being exists. Thus, a classical philosopher seems to act like
a geometrician who deals with the relations of geometrical forms
or figures without being concerned with the problem of whether
there actually exists in nature something which corresponds to
these ideal constructions. But an individual is something other
than a mutilated species, since the individual exists while the
species does not.

Attacks of this type caused a sharpening of the antithesis
between being and existence, so that today we may characterize
them in the following manner:

Being is universal, abstract, timeless, and unlimited by
space. *Existence* is individual, concrete, limited to a definite, very short time, and confined to a restricted spatial
environment.

Being is "everywhere" and "always." *Existence* is only
"here and now" (*hic et nunc*).

Being embraces everything and everyone. *Existence* is
always one's own—my own, your own.

Being is unaware of itself. *Existence* is self-conscious and
understands itself.

[6] S. Kierkegaard, *Concluding Unscientific Postscript*, Princeton, N.J., Princeton University Press for the American-Scandinavian Foundation, 1941,
pp. 171–172.
[7] "Limites existentielles de la Philosophie," *L'Existence*, Paris, 1945, pp. 69–87.

Being is objective, determined, and logically necessary; for whatever I think I have to think its being, at least as a possible thought. *Existence* is subjective, completely fortuitous, sheer fact, free, without any necessity.

Being is the synthesis and identity of the subject and the object; thus it represents fullness. *Existence* is the insurmountable separation of the subject from the object, the permanent non-coincidence and tension between subject and object, even when this object is the subject's own personality; *existence* is the unbridgeable abyss between knowing and being which Rationalism had in vain tried to bridge with the words of Parmenides: τὸ γὰρ αὐτὸ νοεῖν ἐστίν τε καὶ εἶναι,[8] thinking is the same as being. *Existence* is also the separation between the lack provoking the subject's wishes and the objectives which would satisfy them. Thus *existence* is characterized by a "lack of being," a kind of emptiness.

Although none of the Existentialists formulated the oppositions between being and existence in such definite terms, they all were aware of them and most of them defended the rights of existence against being.

The extreme subjectivity of existence places it almost beyond the reach of philosophy. While being is always objective, existence is subjective in such an exclusive way that it can never become object—not even to itself. This is one of the stumbling blocks of Existentialism as a philosophy of existence; for by its very nature philosophy is conceptualization, and concepts necessarily are objective. Since existence is always subject and can never become object, it seems that there cannot be any philosophy of existence. As merely a subjective, emotional condition, existence is even beyond the reach of explanation, because explanation is made up of objective concepts. In trying to objectivize existence, concepts denature it, thus changing it into something else, namely, another variety of abstract being.

Existentialist philosophers, then, find themselves somehow in the situation of Saint Augustine who, when asked: "What is

[8] H. Diels, *Die Fragmente der Vorsokratiker*, Berlin, 1951, 19–3, p. 231.

time?" answered: *Si nemo ex me quaerat scio; si quaerenti expli-care velim, nescio.*[9]

It was probably for this reason that Kierkegaard did not create any kind of systematic philosophy and did not want to create any. He only expressed subjective Existentialist feelings in a rather artistic form. Therefore some modern thinkers—like Nicolai Berdyaev—consider Kierkegaard and the similarly unsystematic, subjectivistic, and artistic Nietzsche to be the only true Existentialists. "Only in subjectivity," Berdyaev says, "can we know existence, and not in objectivity. In my opinion this central idea has disappeared in Heidegger's and Sartre's ontology."[10]

It is, indeed, very strange that Heidegger's most important work has the title *Sein und Zeit* (*Being and Time*) and that Sartre's basic theoretical book is called *L'Etre et le Néant* (*Being and Nothingness*). Alternative titles like *Dasein und Zeit* (*Existence and Time*) and *L'Existence et le Néant* (*Existence and Nothingness*) would obviously have been more appropriate. The reason for the titles chosen is that both Sartre and Heidegger want to offer an "ontology," a theory of being. In recent years Heidegger totally abandoned his existential analysis in order to devote himself exclusively to a passionate, almost hysterical search for "being" (*Sein*), allegedly hidden behind the beings (*das Seiende*), which reminds us of the man who declared himself unable to see the forest, because of the many trees which hid it. All these efforts are directed toward an ontology. However, Berdyaev is right in saying that "in an ontology, existence disappears . . . because it cannot be objectivized." We may also agree with Jean Wahl, professor of philosophy at the Sorbonne, when he writes: "We have to know whether existence is not something which has to be reserved to solitary meditation. . . . Perhaps we have to choose between Existentialism and existence?"[11]

Confronted with this choice, Sartre, Heidegger, Jaspers,

<hr />

[9] "If no body asks me, I know; but if I wished to explain it to one who should ask me, I do not know." *S. Augustini Confessionum* Liber XI, Cap. XIV.

[10] Quoted in J. Wahl, *Petite Histoire de l'Existentialisme*, Paris, 1947, p. 67.

[11] *Ibid.*, p. 61.

Gabriel Marcel, and Jean Wahl have—evidently—chosen Existentialism, for otherwise they would be just as unknown as the millions who are confined to solitary meditation on existence. If thus these Existentialist philosophers have somehow become unfaithful to the true meaning of Existentialism, their sacrifice has not been in vain, since it has brought them fame, and, in the case of Sartre, even wealth. And this makes existence much more bearable, even to Existentialists.

iii
Existence as
Being-in-the-World

THE READERS of Heidegger's and Sartre's philosophical writings certainly have noticed the great number of hyphens linking as many as four to seven consecutive words. These hyphens are not just typographical caprice but have a basic philosophical meaning in Existentialism. One may even designate Existentialism as "a philosophy of hyphens."

The most frequent of these expressions is "being-in-the-world" (Heidegger's *in-der-Welt-sein*), or "man-in-the-world" (Sartre's *l'homme-dans-le-monde*). What is the philosophical meaning of these words compounded by hyphens?

In order to understand, we must remember that, unlike being, which is timeless and unlimited by space, existence is *now* and *here*. Consequently, the existing man is always a man now and here; in short, a man in the world. To emphasize the essential necessity and indissoluble character of this association between man and his world, Heidegger links by hyphens the words designating man's existence and his world. "The compound expression 'being-in-the-world' ", he writes, "shows already in its coinage that with it a unitary phenomenon is meant." [1]

From a common sense standpoint this position looks like a truism; and yet, philosophically, it has important implications. In ethics, it means a defiance of the classical concept of man as such, independent of space and time and subject to one unitary

---

[1] M. Heidegger, *Sein und Zeit* (4th ed.), Halle a. S., 1935, p. 53; American edition, *Being and Time*, New York, Harper, 1962.

type of moral requirements—the idea of man which is the basis of traditional humanism and humanitarianism. For epistemology, it means a defiance of the classical concept of a subject which, being timeless and spaceless, is a subject without a world; and this subject without a world has always been the starting point of idealism as well as of realism. Heidegger writes:

> The clarification of the being-in-the-world showed that there is not at first a mere subject without a world, that it is never given. And thus it is finally neither at first an isolated ego, given without the others.[2]

Since existence is being *now* and *here*, or "being-in-the-world," Heidegger concludes that the world of the existing man is always that which he shares with other men. This being-in-the-world means also "being-with-others" (*Mitsein* or *Mitsein-mit-Anderen*).

These are the basic theses of modern Existentialism, outlined by Heidegger in 1927, in his famous book *Sein und Zeit*. It should, however, not be forgotten that thirteen years before Heidegger the Spanish philosopher José Ortega y Gasset wrote, in his *Meditaciones del Quijote*, "*yo soy yo y mi circunstancia*," I am I and my circumstance; and that seventeen years before the German thinker, Ortega described our existence as a "*convivir*" and "*coexistir*" or living and existing together (*Adán en el paraíso*, 1910).

With the basic position of being-in-the-world and being-with-others, Existentialism places itself beyond realism and idealism, both of which, starting from a subject without a world, need to have the world outside the subject demonstrated afterward. If this demonstration is considered possible, we speak of "realism"; if it is considered impossible, we speak of "idealism."

"The scandal of philosophy," Heidegger says, is not that this demonstration is still missing, but that it is being expected and tried again and again. "Existence, well understood, is opposed to such demonstrations, because it *is* already in its being all that which ulterior proofs think necessary to demonstrate." [3]

Only from this approach can we understand the French Existentialist Lévinas when he describes Existentialism by saying:

[2] *Ibid.*, p. 116.
[3] *Ibid.*, p. 205.

> The novelty Heidegger adds to our thousand-year-old
> knowledge . . . when stating "being-in-the-world" or "be-
> ing-for-death" or "being-with-the-others" is that these prepo-
> sitions "in," "for," "with" are the root of the verb . . . ;
> that they articulate the event Being. . . . We may say that
> Existentialism consists of feeling and thinking that the verb
> "to be" is transitive.[4]

Sartre adopts all these basic positions of Heidegger's Existentialism as a starting point. His teacher Laporte, late professor
at the Sorbonne, warned him against the kind of abstraction by
which we think of as isolated certain things which are not made
to exist alone. Another of Sartre's masters, Edmund Husserl,
taught him that, unlike the abstract, the concrete is a "whole"
which can exist isolatedly, by itself. Sartre concludes:

> The concrete is man-in-the-world with this specific union
> of man and the world which Heidegger, for example, calls
> "being-in-the-world." . . . It suffices to open the eyes and
> to question in all naïveté this wholeness which is "man-in-
> the-world."[5]

Thus in Existentialism, Descartes' *cogito, ergo sum* ("I think,
therefore I am") is reversed and replaced with a plain *sum*
("I am," in the sense of "I-am-in-the-world"), followed by cognition: *sum, ergo cogito*. This formula, *sum, ergo cogito*, was
coined many years before Heidegger by Miguel de Unamuno[6]
and constitutes the clearest expression of Existentialism.

While Descartes' *cogito* places modern philosophy on the
foundation of the primacy of cognition, Existentialism tries to
place it on the foundation of the primacy of existence. For
Heidegger, "cognition is nothing but a mode of existence as
being-in-the-world."[7]

Although Sartre, as a Frenchman, refuses to take part in
Heidegger's violent anti-Cartesian campaign and affects to remain
faithful to Descartes' *cogito*, he modifies it, under the name

---

[4] Quoted in Wahl, *Petite Histoire de l'Existentialisme*, pp. 85–86.
[5] *L'Etre et le Néant*, p. 38.
[6] M. de Unamuno, *Del Sentimiento trágico de la Vida*, p. 39.
[7] *Sein und Zeit*, p. 61.

cogito préréflexif, in such a way that he can deny Descartes' primacy of cognition and thus fall in line with Heidegger. For instance, he declares:

> Consciousness is the knowing being as far as it *is* and not as far as it is *known.* This signifies that we have to abandon the primacy of cognition if we want to found this cognition itself.[8]

After having declared that Descartes' primacy of cognition is an "illusion," Sartre states that it is a nonreflective consciousness which makes reflection possible. "There is a prereflective *cogito* which is the condition of the Cartesian *cogito.*"[9]

With the prereflective consciousness, existing by itself, Sartre believes himself to have found an "absolute."[10] Thus in spite of his rejection of Descartes' primacy of cognition and in spite of his own insistence on the primacy of existence, Sartre thinks that he has preserved the Cartesian subjectivity as a starting point of philosophy, and that he has taken a middle road between Heidegger and Descartes. As we shall see later, Sartre draws the most important ethical conclusions from his basic ontological position that our mind is only secondary to our existence, as a simple manifestation of the latter.

But, for the moment, let us go back to Sartre's affirmation (inspired by Husserl's phenomenology) that it suffices "to open the eyes and to question in all naïveté" this concrete wholeness which is man-in-the-world. What is the answer to this question according to Sartre's philosophy?

"Being," he writes, "will be revealed to us by some immediate means of access, like nuisance, nausea, etc."[11] Whereas Heidegger's "existence" is revealed as "sorrow" (*Sorge, cura*), Sartre reveals existence as "nausea." Those who read his novels, in which, according to Marcel Thiebaud, "kisses are given between diarrheas and declarations of love made between vomitings," will not be astonished to see the physiological state of nausea promoted to the rank of a metaphysical category.

---

[8] *L'Etre et le Néant,* p. 17.
[9] *Ibid.,* p. 20.
[10] *Ibid.,* p. 23.
[11] *Ibid.,* p. 14.

The Revelation of Existence: Contingency, Absurdity, Anxiety

We spoke of the intrinsic difficulty of explaining existence in terms of objective concepts; because existence, being basically subjective, cannot be objectivized without being denatured. Heidegger, having at his command nothing but the objective, abstract concepts of the philosopher, was unable to unveil existence in its most immediate emotional character. His "sorrow" is a category, not a suffering.

Sartre, on the other hand, is not only a philosopher but an artist, endowed with imagination and intuition. Thus he can try to represent subjectively in novels and dramas things which the objective concepts of the philosopher cannot grasp. Consequently, it is not astonishing that Sartre's most impressive characterization of existence is not to be found in his great theoretical treatise *L'Etre et le Néant* but in his early novel *La Nausée*. Let us translate from this novel a passage in which the central character, Roquentin, an historian, intuitively grasps the meaning of existence and describes it as follows:

> It took my breath. Never, before these last days, had I felt the meaning of to "exist." . . . Ordinarily existence hides itself. It is there, around us, in us, it is we, one cannot say two words without speaking of it; and, finally, one does not touch it . . . If somebody had asked me what existence is, I should have answered in good faith that it is nothing,

just an empty form which came from outside to add itself to things, without changing their nature in any respect.[1]

And now, behold! at one blow it was there, it was as clear as day: Existence had revealed itself suddenly. It had lost its inoffensive aspect of an abstract category: it was the very dough of things. . . . The diversity of things, their individuality was nothing but an appearance, a varnish. This varnish had melted. What was left were monstrous soft masses in disorder, naked in frightening nudity. . . .

Existence is not something which can be thought from a distance: it must invade you bluntly, it must sit down on you, weigh heavily upon your heart like a big, motionless animal.[2]

This is *how* Sartre's character experiences existence. But as *what* is it revealed to him? Three words describe it: *contingency*, *absurdity*, and *anxiety*. Roquentin suddenly feels that everything, including himself, is superfluous, gratuitous, supernumerary (*de trop*), because, logically, existence can no more be justified than can nonexistence.

Nietzsche had already asked: "Is my existence as compared with my nonexistence something which can be justified?" [3] Sartre, without referring to his great predecessor, bluntly retorts: No! Those who do not share his opinion, but try to justify their existence as necessary, are relegated by Sartre to a new philosophical category and denounced as *salauds* (filthy stinkers).

Here is another portion of Sartre's *La Nausée* in which Roquentin states these ideas more explicitly:

The essential is contingency; I mean that by definition existence is not necessary. To exist is simply to be there; the existing beings appear but can never be deduced. I believe there are people who have understood it. They tried to overcome their contingency, inventing a necessary Being which is the cause of itself. But no necessary Being can

---

[1] This is obviously an allusion to Kant's definition of existence which we quoted previously.

[2] *La Nausée*, Paris, 1938, pp. 166–172; American edition, *Nausea*, trans. by Lloyd Alexander, New York, New Directions, 1949, 1959.

[3] F. Nietzsche, *Gesammelte Werke*, Munich, 1925, XVI, p. 252.

explain existence: contingency is not a false appearance which can be dissipated; it is the *absolute* and, consequently, the perfect gratuitousness. Everything is gratuitous —this garden, this town, I, myself. When we realize this, then it turns our hearts, everything begins to float . . . *that is nausea*; that is what *les salauds* . . . try to hide from themselves with their idea of *rights*. What a poor lie! *Nobody has rights!* These men are entirely gratuitous, just as other men. . . .[4]

The term *salaud* (filthy stinker) is not just an angry expression of Sartre's hero in a moment of overwhelming nausea, but a category maintained by the philosopher in his theoretical works also. In *L'Existentialisme est un Humanisme,* for example, Sartre gives the following definition: "Those who will try to show that their existence is necessary, although it is the very contingency of man's appearance on earth, I shall call them *salauds.*"[5] In *Nausea* Roquentin concludes by saying: "Every existing being is born without reason, prolongs itself by weakness, and dies by fortuitousness."[6] Maurice Maeterlinck, the great Belgian poet, expresses a similar idea in *Pelléas et Mélisande* when he speaks of his young heroine in beautiful prose full of melancholy: "She was born . . . without any reason . . . in order to die; and she dies without any reason." We have here a poetical expression of that age-old truth which Heidegger voiced later when he said that without any reason man is cast into a world where his being is "essentially sorrow" and "being toward death."[7] Lord Byron and others wrote in similar vein.

Sartre concludes that our being-in-the-world and the being-of-the-world are absolute absurdity. He even goes as far as to establish an equation between the absolute and the absurd. Where Spinoza says *Deus sive natura* ("God or nature"), Sartre says *l'absolu ou l'absurde* ("the absolute or the absurd").[8]

---

[4] *Op. cit.,* p. 171.
[5] *L'Existentialisme est un Humanisme,* Paris, 1946, pp. 84–85; American edition, *Existentialism,* trans. by B. Frechtman, New York, Philosophical Library, 1947.
[6] *Op. cit.,* p. 174.
[7] *Sein und Zeit,* pp. 180, 266, *passim.*
[8] *La Nausée,* p. 169.

The absurd is that which cannot be deduced logically. Thus Sartre has to include all nature in his absolute absurdity.

Sartre is an inhabitant of a large city and a café habitué. He has apparently no real relation to nature, no love for or understanding of nature. In none of his novels can any impressive description of nature be found. His only reaction toward nature is dread. His character Roquentin, looking down from the heights above a city called Bouville, thinks that the townspeople are foolish to feel that they are protected from the nature which surrounds them.

"I see this nature, I see it," Roquentin says to himself. "I know that nature's submission of itself to us is laziness, I know that it has *no laws.* . . . It has nothing but habits, and tomorrow it may change some of them." [9]

Sartre-Roquentin imagines some consequences of such a possible change. For instance, a mother may suddenly see that her child's cheek has cracked and exposed a third eye which laughs; or some day we may discover that our clothes have changed into living beings; or somebody suddenly feels something scrape his mouth: "He will go to a mirror and open his mouth; and his tongue will have become an enormous live centipede . . . etc."

Here Sartre was obviously influenced by Kafka, whom he venerates. In *The Metamorphosis* Kafka describes how Gregor Samsa, a commercial traveler, awakens one morning in his room and finds himself changed in his bed to a monstrous, gigantic insect, with a little head and a big brown belly, divided by bowed corrugations; and how he tries in vain to regain contact with his family, which has remained human. Kafka exegetes explain that this story illustrates man's complete isolation as a punishment for his hidden wish to escape his responsibilities toward human society. Sartre and Simone de Beauvoir think that Gregor Samsa set between himself and his familiar surroundings such a distance that human order broke down for him, leaving him foundering in a strange darkness. In any case, the symbolization of this idea is so absurd that it explains why, twenty years after his death, Kafka has come to be regarded as an Existentialist. For Existentialists not only discover the absurd

[9] *Ibid.*, p. 204.

where it is, but also invent it where it is not. The absurd has apparently become their *raison d'être*, although Existentialism, by definition, denies any raison d'être.

Sartre's reaction toward the gratuitousness and absurdity of existence is nausea. Observing his fellow men, Roquentin cries out: "I should like to vomit!" [10]

Inasmuch as vomiting is the climax of nausea, we can understand why, in most of his novels, Sartre describes the vomiting of different persons. Simone de Beauvoir, disrespectfully called "la grande Sartreuse," develops a similar theme in several of her novels. Sartre himself describes with phenomenological accuracy these repugnant physiological processes and their results. Sometimes, in a paroxysm of perversion, the vomitings of Sartre's characters are linked to sexual desires, as in his story *"Intimité,"* (*Intimacy*) or his novel *L'Age de Raison* (*The Age of Reason*), in which we read the following description of a "love scene" between the professor of philosophy Mathieu Delarue and one of his drunken students, the young girl, Iwich: "A slightly bitter smell of vomit escaped from her mouth, so pure. Mathieu passionately inhaled that odor."[11]

It would be difficult to find elsewhere in literature a more perverse and repugnant description, but Sartre's novels abound with even more repulsive examples.

Saleté poisseuse (sticky filth) is the name Roquentin gives existence,[12] and Sartre's other metaphors for the characterization of existence swarm with images similarly "viscous." Vomit also is viscous. The metaphysical meaning of viscosity in Sartre's philosophy will be revealed later by Existential psychoanalysis.

Existence is linked to a physiological body; consequently, our body is, for Sartre, a main object of nausea. Here is what he says about this in his Being and Nothingness: "A discrete and insuperable nausea perpetually reveals my body to my consciousness." The reason is that our body, too, is sheer fact, without any logical necessity. "It can happen that we seek pleasure or physical pain in order to free ourselves from it, but as soon

[10] *Ibid.*, p. 160.

[11] *L'Age de Raison*, Paris, 1945, p. 255; American edition, *The Age of Reason*, New York, Alfred A. Knopf, 1947; Bantam Books, 1959.

[12] *La Nausée*, p. 176.

as pain or pleasure exist for consciousness, they . . . manifest its [the body's] facticity and contingency, and it is on the ground of nausea that they reveal themselves." [13]

Christian Existentialists consider this incarnation a paradoxical scandal. Sartre's Existentialism, which, like Heidegger's, never overcame its theological heritage, seems sometimes to emphasize this scandal of incarnation by delving into the most repugnant details of carnal manifestations; but the accompanying morbid pleasure indicates that Sartre, after all, is not averse to enjoying that "scandal."

It would be erroneous to believe that Sartre's nausea is the result of a specific physiological predisposition. To him nausea is something metaphysical. Sartre insists that we must not take "the term 'nausea' as a metaphor drawn from our physiological disgusts; on the contrary, it is on metaphysical grounds that all concrete and empirical nauseas begin and produce vomiting. (Nauseas produced by the sight of rotten meat, fresh blood, excrements, etc.)" [13]

Nausea and anxiety are closely related. In his essay *Was ist Metaphysik?* (*What Is Metaphysics?*) Heidegger describes anxiety in a way which closely resembles Sartre's nausea. In anxiety, Heidegger says, we feel a kind of "floating" sensation (*Schweben*), because reality "slips away from us." Anxiety reveals nothingness[14] and basically the nothingness of death.[15]

When nauseated, Sartre's Roquentin has likewise the impression that "everything begins to float," and "nothing seems real." [16]

Heidegger insists that anxiety (dread, *Angst*) must not be confused with fear (*Furcht*). Following Kierkegaard, Freud clarified this difference when he wrote: "I think that anxiety is related to the subjective condition, abstracting from any object, while in fear the attention is precisely directed toward an object." [17]

---

[13] *L'Etre et le Néant*, p. 404.
[14] *Was ist Metaphysik?* Frankfurt a.M., Klostermann, 1960, p. 32; American edition, *Existence and Being*, Chicago, H. Regnery, 1949, 1951.
[15] *Sein und Zeit*, p. 266.
[16] *La Nausée*, pp. 105, 171.
[17] Freud, *Vorlesungen zur Einführung in die Psychoanalyse*, Vienna, F. Deuticke, 1916, p. 417.

Similarly, Heidegger emphasizes that anxiety represents the essential impossibility of defining the "what" which causes it. Thus anxiety is endowed with a certain character of "indefiniteness and objectlessness." [18] We shall see later how in Sartre's philosophy anxiety is linked to his basic concept of freedom.

The diffuse anxiety related to no definite object, but vaguely linked to man's feeling of forlornness and isolatedness as an individual confronted with the nothingness of death, predominates also in Roquentin's nausea:

> I ran along the docks . . . the houses, with their gloomy eyes, watched me fleeing. I repeated to myself anxiously: Where shall I go, where shall I go? Everything may happen!" [19]

But we cannot run away from ourselves, from the only certainty we have in this life: each of us will have to go alone through the somber door of death. "We shall die alone," as Pascal says.[20] And Camus reminds us again that life is nothing but a terrifying apprenticeship to death.

[18] Freud, *The Problem of Anxiety*, New York, W. W. Norton, 1936, p. 147.
[19] *La Nausée*, p. 106.
[20] *Pensées*, III, 211.

First Critical Intermezzo

ROQUENTIN'S NAUSEA still was not philosophy, but only a subjective intuition and emotional interpretation of existence as sheer contingency, absurdity, and anxiety. However, our philosophies, as conceptual systems, greatly depend upon our subjective intuitions of existence—a fact which may explain, in part, the diversity of those systems.

The same nature can be interpreted emotionally in quite opposite ways, as a comparison between Sartre and Chateaubriand, for instance, will show. To Sartre, a tree's root is a "voracious claw rending the earth, extorting from it its nourishment," and defiantly, in order to play with the world's absurdity, his Roquentin kicks the root violently with his heel.[1] Thus, we see that in Sartre's intuitive interpretation of existence even innocent plants are voracious monsters, revealing the world's repugnant absurdity. For Chateaubriand, even monsters reveal divine providence. "It seems to us," he writes, "that God has allowed these productions of matter in order to teach us what creation would be without him. It is the shadow which sets off lights." [2]

Here are two possible interpretations of the same nature: the one that a man chooses depends greatly on his emotional reactions. Criticism can only begin where reason finds a working point—in rational arguments.

As far as reason is concerned, one has to admit that the great rationalistic systems have not succeeded in deducing material

[1] *La Nausée*, pp. 169, 177.
[2] *Oeuvres de Chateaubriand*, Paris, 1857, I, 3, p. 149.

facts by merely logical operations; and the failure of Hegel's and Schelling's systems of philosophy of nature dooms such attempts forever. In fact, there remain in nature a large number of merely empirical elements, which have no logical necessity and may truly be called contingent.

At the end of the nineteenth century Emile Boutroux wrote his book on *The Contingency of the Laws of Nature;*[3] and Boltzmann's kinetic theory of gases gave another blow to determinism. In 1927 the physicist Heisenberg stated that "the mechanics of quanta has definitely established the invalidity of the law of causality."[4] There are still laws of nature, but, as Louis de Broglie says, "They are no longer causal laws but laws of probability."[5]

In spite of these blows to determinism the laws of nature still offer sufficient regularity to make possible certain predictions and to exclude certain possibilities, especially as far as the macrocosm is concerned.[6] As a practical matter, in most cases the probability of our new statistical laws of nature hardly differs from certainty. There exist in our society powerful professional groups whose activities rest entirely on the regularity of our physical laws: the physicists, chemists, engineers, geologists, industrial workers, etc. Since this is so, it is a great exaggeration to speak, as Sartre does, of a total contingency of nature and a complete absence of physical laws.

We may speak of contingency in an absolute sense, because the whole of physical laws cannot be deduced logically from the whole being. Their being is no more necessary than the being of the whole universe. Even so rationalistic and theistic a thinker as Whitehead had to admit the contingency of the presence,

---

[3] E. Boutroux, *De la Contingence des Lois de la Nature*, Paris, G. Baillière, 1874.

[4] W. Heisenberg, "Über den anschaulichen Inhalt der quantentheoretischen Kinematik und Mechanik," *Zeitschrift für Physik* (Berlin, 1927), Vol. 43, p. 197.

[5] L. de Broglie, "Déterminisme et Causalité dans la Physique contemporaine," *Revue de Métaphysique et de Morale*, XXXVI, 4 (Paris, 1929), p. 441.

[6] See A. Stern, "Causalité, Incertitude et Complémentarité," *Revue de Synthèse* (Paris, 1937), pp. 133–148, and A. Stern, "Science and the Philosopher," *American Scientist*, vol. 44, No. 3 (July 1956), pp. 281–295.

called **God**, of a rationalistic selective principle in reality. According to Whitehead, this principle simply is there, since itself is the only reason for anything being there and being what it is. Besides, there is another contingency in Whitehead's highly rationalized reality, since the universe might have been different without being less rational. It, seemingly, might have been morally more satisfactory. Consequently, if there is this universe and none other, this is contingent.

Nevertheless, I believe that if there is no absolute necessity, there is enough relative necessity left between the parts of our reality to guarantee the regular recurrence of phenomena in nature. In saying that nature has no laws, only habits which may change tomorrow, Sartre obviously throws out the baby with the bath.

Another of Sartre's affirmations is that all of us are superfluous and that persons who try to hide this from themselves, pretending that they are necessary, are *salauds* of "bad faith" (*de mauvaise foi*). This concept of bad faith will be analyzed more thoroughly, because it has a basic meaning in Sartre's philosophy. In his Existential psychoanalysis we will see that he tries to detect in various forms of human activity hidden attempts of men to justify themselves in contradiction to what they know to be true.

In his novels Sartre has tried repeatedly to show that all of us are superfluous and that nobody is really necessary. This sometimes leads him to the most inhuman statements. Just before the outbreak of World War II, Mathieu, the hero of the novel *Le Sursis* (*The Reprieve*), had the following conversation with his brother Jacques. The first speaker is Mathieu:

> "Peace or war! That does not make any difference . . ."
>
> "No difference? Tell this to those millions of men who are preparing to be killed!"
>
> "And so what! They have carried their death in themselves since their birth. And when they have all been slaughtered to the last, mankind will still be as full as before; without a gap; without one missing."
>
> "Minus twelve to fifteen million men."

Mathieu, the Existentialist professor of philosophy, answers that "this is not a question of numbers"; with or without those men the world will continue to go "nowhere." [7]

Some of Sartre's characters recognize that they are superfluous. Henri, a Frenchman in the Resistance caught by the fascists and condemned to death, says to his friends:

> I am not missed anywhere, I do not leave any empty spots. The subways are crowded, the restaurants full, the heads crammed to bursting with little problems. I slipped out of the world and it remained as full as an egg.[8]

However, there are other people who are not great enough to recognize their superfluousness. They believe they are necessary to their families, their countries, their professions, and claim rights in this world. They are told by Sartre that they are "stinkers" and that "nobody has rights." [9]

We think that, here again, Sartre overshoots the mark, placing absolute measures on relative things. To be sure, for the whole of the universe nobody is necessary and nobody will be missing when an individual disappears. But every son will be missing to his mother, every loved one to his beloved.

Is a father a "stinker" simply because he thinks that he is necessary to his wife and children, since nobody will take care of them if he dies? I do not think so. A George Washington was necessary to his nation to win its independence, and a Georges Clemenceau was necessary to his country to drive out the invader. If these men had the conviction of their necessity, were they therefore "stinkers"?

Of course, one may ask whether America's independence and France's freedom are absolutely necessary for the whole universe, including all planets and fixed stars, and this question, certainly, cannot be answered. But one cannot deny that the independence of these nations is relatively necessary for the continuance of civilization, and civilization is relatively necessary to mankind.

---

[7] *Op. cit.*, p. 168.

[8] *Morts sans Sépulture*, Paris, 1949, p. 47; American edition, *The Victors* in *Three Plays*, New York, Alfred A. Knopf, 1949.

[9] *La Nausée*, p. 171.

Although it is impossible to prove the absolute necessity of the existence of mankind, existence is relatively necessary to mankind. For if mankind had not felt this necessity, it would have already finished with existence, according to Schopenhauer's recommendations.

As we shall see later, in discussing Existentialist ethics, Sartre rejects all given, constituted values as limitations of our liberty, and grants everybody the freedom to invent his own system of values, without any possibility of having it legitimized by any supra-individual authority. Of one of his characters, Sartre says: "There would be neither right nor wrong unless he invented them." [10] It is strange that a philosopher, who denies in this way all bases for value judgments that are objectively valid, would utter so frequently the most offensive value judgments, with the most apodictic certainty, on the moral behavior of other people, and claim universal validity for such "philosophical categories" as "coward" and *salaud*. Only by examining Sartre's theory of freedom and his philosophy of values can we understand the confusing fact that the same philosopher who wants to teach workers that not Marxism alone but only Marxism allied to Existentialism leads to true social revolution can, by proclaiming that "nobody has rights," implicitly condemn the men who gave France the *Droits de l'Homme et du Citoyen* and America the Bill of Rights.

If Sartre's characters find existence unbearable because it does not offer absolute necessity, they show only that they are incurable philosophical absolutists. It seems to me that this is the real moral disease of Existentialists. Their philosophy must be called irrationalist because it considers that the universe is not subjected to rational laws and is therefore not logically deducible. Existentialism is irrationalist also because it ascribes to emotional states such as anxiety, sorrow, and nausea a power superior to that of reason, refuting the claims of reason and defeating the efforts of reason. And yet the Existentialist temperament is definitely and primarily rationalist. In my opinion there are two kinds of rationalists: The first consists of those who, like Descartes, Spinoza, and Hegel, believe in the possibility of deduc-

[10] *L'Age de Raison*, p. 249.

ing the relations of the material world as if they were formal relations of logic or mathematics; the second group is formed by those who—like the Existentialists—do not believe in that possibility and yet uphold stubbornly their claim for such a world, demonstrated *more geometrico,* a world deducible with absolute necessity. Since they cannot have such a world they escape into sickness, their metaphysical disease which they call "nausea." Most Existentialists seem to be frustrated rationalists. "I want everything or nothing" ("*Je veux tout ou rien*"), Albert Camus writes in his *Myth of Sisyphus,*[11] apparently without realizing that he only repeats the outcry of Ibsen's Pastor Brand, whose search for the absolute in religion was so tragically doomed to failure.

Even before Ibsen, Balzac demonstrated that the search for the absolute is doomed in other fields: in art, by the failure of his hero Frenhofer *in Le Chef-d'Oeuvre inconnu (The Unknown Masterpiece)*; in science, by the ruin of his hero Balthazar Claës in *La Recherche de l'Absolu (The Quest of the Absolute)*; and in family life, by the tragedy of his *Père Goriot (Father Goriot).* They are all forerunners of Ibsen's Brand, who is a fictionalized portrait of Søren Kierkegaard, the founder of Existentialism. In my opinion Kierkegaard was the prototype of a philosophical absolutist and of a frustrated rationalist. He fought Hegel, but like Hegel he would have wished to have a world where "everything which is real is reasonable and everything which is reasonable is real." Recognizing the impossibility of such a world and such a reason, Kierkegaard revolted against both.

Kierkegaard's battle cry was best expressed in the title of his famous work *Either-Or!* Either God or the dragons, either everything or nothing! To accept the "absolute paradox" which he

[11] *Le Mythe de Sisyphe* (Paris, Gallimard, 1942), p. 118 (American edition, *The Myth of Sisyphus and Other Essays*, New York, Alfred A. Knopf, 1955). As I have shown elsewhere, Camus was not an Existentialist in a technical sense, since he believed in a human nature and in natural rights. He himself rejected this label. Yet, having arisen during that crisis of existence brought about in France by the Nazi occupation, Camus' problems are basically existentialist. See A. Stern, "Considerations of Albert Camus' Thought," *The Personalist*, Vol. XLI, No. 4 (Autumn 1960), pp. 448-457.

saw in Christ, he crucified reason. In the conflict between Christianity and modern civilization—upon which Feuerbach insisted —Kierkegaard was ready to sacrifice modern civilization in order to maintain Christianity in its absolute purity. Finding modern society not ready to accept this "either-or," Kierkegaard engaged in lifelong revolt against society, democracy, and his own Church, its bishop, and all Christian institutions, including marriage, because according to his claim for absolute purity, procreation seemed to be "sinful."

In the same way, Sartre's Roquentin is in a state of permanent revolt against the world, only because this world is not as it should be according to his absolute postulates. The fact that Kierkegaard was a theist and that Sartre is an atheist is of minor importance; what they have in common is something much more essential: the claim of the absolute in a relative world, and the attitude of revolt against a world which does not comply with their absolute claims.

Camus, author of *The Stranger*, a character whose life is a rejection of the world and of the links between things and their human significance, states explicity that the only coherent philosophical attitude of man in an absurd world is revolt. "This revolt gives its price to life," he says, and he finds in this revolt a new kind of "grandeur." [12]

I cannot find it. There was grandeur in Prometheus' attitude, because it was more than revolt. By bringing men the fire from Olympus he caused a revolution. But revolt against existence as a natural condition has to remain sterile, because we cannot change existence. The true philosophical attitude toward that which we cannot change is acceptance. There is the true wisdom. Revolt against the unchangeable existential condition of man is a childish attitude, not an adult one.

If we recognize that we cannot have a world logically deducible, a world of absolute necessity, we have to accept the fact wisely and not adopt the attitude of a child who cries because he cannot have the moon.

Bertrand Russell said that the chief thing philosophy in our

[12] *Ibid.*, p. 78.

age can do for us is "to teach us how to live without certainty, and yet without being paralyzed by hesitation." [13]

There is no doubt that, in the last analysis, Existentialism, too, teaches that man has to accept his existential condition. We find this postulate in Heidegger, in Sartre and—most forcefully—in Jaspers[14] and Simone de Beauvoir. For Existentialists, however, this acceptance presupposes a radical conversion, a "resolute decision," while for most non-Existentialists it is a self-evident, almost automatic reaction. It may be that the authentic Existentialists truly overcome their nausea, but most of them keep on vomiting as long as they exist in this world devoid of purpose, where, according to Sartre, "all human activities are equivalent," none more important than any other.

[13] *A History of Western Philosophy*, New York, Simon and Schuster, 1945, p. XIV.
[14] See especially K. Jaspers, *Tragedy Is Not Enough*, Boston, The Beacon Press, 1952, p. 105.

How to Overcome Nausea

THE TRAGIC ABSURDITY of existence is not a new discovery. In modern times Leopardi, Schopenhauer, Nietzsche, Dostoyevsky, and Unamuno have probably been those who most profoundly felt it. Many attempts have been made to conquer this condition.

Sartre's Roquentin overcomes his nausea by escaping into the imaginary world of art. Sitting in an obscure tavern at Bouville he hears an American jazz song played on a record, with the refrain, "Some of these days you'll miss me, honey." And, strangely enough, listening to this vulgar song, he recovers from his nausea, because in the melody he finally attains something "which does not exist." He decides to give up history, since "it speaks of that which has existed, and one existing being can never justify the existence of another existing being."[1] He will dedicate himself to art; he will write fiction, a kind of story where "behind the printed words, behind the pages one must guess something which does not exist, which would be beyond existence." [2]

It is Sartre's view that art and especially literature confer some necessity upon this deplorably contingent world of ours, a necessity which reflects upon the artist or writer and justifies him.

Schopenhauer already had found relief from the suffering of existence in the pure contemplation of Platonic ideas in art or in the revelation of the thing-in-itself in music. And Nietzsche

[1] *La Nausée*, p. 228.
[2] *Ibid.*

stated that "only as an aesthetic phenomenon, existence and the world are eternally justified." [3]

This seems also to be Camus' position, when he says that the work of art illustrates the "renouncement of thought . . . and its resignation to nothing but an intelligence which fabricates appearances and covers with images that which has no meaning." And he adds that if the world were understandable, there would not be any art.[4]

However, for none of these thinkers did the escape into the imaginary "non-existing" world of art become a permanent refuge and a true means of salvation from the sufferings of existence. In the pure contemplation of Platonic ideas in art Schopenhauer found only temporary relief, and he decided that salvation from existence, true "redemption," could only be found in the negation of the will to live.

Similarly, Nietzsche overcame his period of "illusionism," in which he had placed the "artist's gospel" with its beautiful lies above the dreadful truth of the scientist. He finally created the ideal of the "superman," the man who is strong enough to confront truth, without needing to cover it with the beautiful veil of illusion.

Camus, too, warns against seeing in art a shelter against the absurd. Art in itself, he says,

> is an absurd phenomenon. . . . It does not offer any escape from the evil of the spirit. It is, on the contrary, one of the signs of this evil. . . . But, for the first time, it causes the spirit to leave its confines and confront other spirits, not in order that it may lose itself in them, but in order to point, with a precise finger, to the road without escape, where we must travel.[5]

Thus, without succumbing to its illusions, Camus clings to art, giving to emptiness its colors, but without forgetting for a single moment that it is emptiness.

Here is the point where Sartre's ways deviate from those of Camus. Sartre goes beyond art. His Roquentin, overcoming

[3] F. Nietzsche, "Die Geburt der Tragödie," in *Gesammelte Werke*, III (1920), p. 46.
[4] *Le Mythe de Sisyphe*, p. 135.
[5] *Ibid.*, p. 132.

nausea through evasion into the nonexisting world of art, symbolizes only one station in the Calvary of existence. Art is only a temporary refuge from the absurdity of existence. The novelist Sartre, who in 1938 published *Nausea*, becomes the systematic philosopher and metaphysician who, in 1943, publishes his gigantic treatise *L'Etre et le Néant*.

Theoretical philosophy has, therefore, become a means to dispel nausea, but not for the first time in the history of philosophy. Considered from the standpoint of their psychological motives, the philosophical systems may be divided into those belonging to the *theorogone* type and those belonging to the *pathogone*.

Theorogone philosophy is motivated by observation of the world and the wish to explain what has been observed. (The antique θεωρός was an observer or a spectator at public games.) In this sense the philosophies of Aristotle, Descartes, Bacon, Hume and Kant may be designated as theorogone.

Pathogone philosophy, on the contrary, is motivated by the suffering which existence in the world imposes upon us, and the wish to overcome it (from the Greek πάθος, suffering). In this sense the philosophies of Epicurus, Pascal, Spinoza, Schopenhauer, Nietzsche, and Unamuno may be considered as pathogone.

If Sartre's philosophy should have to be classified on this basis, it certainly would have to be ranged among the pathogone systems. It is nausea—his kind of suffering from the world's absurdity—which motivates Sartre's philosophical system.

A comparison between Sartre's and the most representative pathogone philosophy ever produced in history—that of Spinoza—will clarify the peculiar character of the former.

Wishing to overcome man's suffering from existence, Spinoza tried to demonstrate away contingency, absurdity, and anxiety. His means were rationalism and determinism. According to Spinoza a reconciliation with destiny becomes possible if it appears not as an arbitrary force, but as the necessary manifestation of universal reason. Confronted by that which is logically and absolutely necessary, every resistance becomes senseless, and so does every wish to influence destiny by our desires. Thus our anxiety in the presence of contingency disappears, as well as the delusive hope to change the world according to our personal desires.

In the presence of that cosmic necessity, which belongs to Spinoza's universe, there is only one right attitude: that of comprehension; not a comprehension from the angle of individual, subjective imagination, but a logical comprehension, based on reason, or, as Spinoza says, a comprehension *sub specie aeternitatis*, under the aspect of eternity. In the serene regions of reason the individual's vision is diverted from the mean interests of everyday existence and directed toward the whole. The small discords of existence are then dissipated in the great harmonies of a universe full of reason, *Amor Dei*, the love of God and Nature, preached by Spinoza, becomes *amor fati*, a love of our destiny, since for Spinoza our suffering is nothing but an error arising from the limited prospect of individual life, of existence.

Sartre's pathogone philosophy is of a quite different type. For, unlike Spinoza's, Sartre's philosophy does not try to demonstrate away the contingency, absurdity, and anxiety of existence. On the contrary, Sartre's philosophy tries to demonstrate the necessity of contingency, absurdity, and anxiety. His means are opposed to those of Spinoza: not rationalism and determinism, but irrationalism and freedom.

But is it not somehow self-contradictory to establish the necessity of contingency, to prove logically the absurdity of existence, to rationalize that irrational condition which is anxiety?

That is exactly the reproach made to Sartre by some of his friends, especially by Albert Camus. "In a world where everything is given and nothing explained," Camus writes, "the fecundity of a value or of a metaphysics is a senseless concept." [6] And he states that in this absurd world we have not to try to "explain" or to "resolve," but merely to experience and to describe.

Another of Sartre's critical friends, the Surrealist Hubert Juin, writes: "It is true that anxiety annihilates the rational, and it is this, too, we are reproaching in Sartre. . . . Anxiety is not ink. It is the night, and when one emerges from the night, one does not write *Being and Nothingness*. One acts like Heidegger and re-descends." [7]

It is, however, a fascinating spectacle to see how Sartre ration-

[6] *Ibid.*, p. 186.
[7] H. Juin, *Jean-Paul Sartre ou La Condition Humaine* (Bruxelles, 1946), p. 79.

alizes the absurd and how he proves the necessity of contingency, for he is doing it with the most brilliant philosophical crafts- manship. It is even more fascinating to observe how he tries to evade the depressing consequences of his philosophy of despair in favor of a kind of optimism, which I should not qualify as heroic like Nietzsche's, but which I should, instead, regard as an optimism of defiance, an optimism "in spite of."

Sartre's doctrine teaches that man can rid himself of his nausea by recognizing his freedom, by which act he can give meaning and value to existence. But being responsible for his choice of meanings and values in a world in which he is the only moral lawgiver, the authentic man, who overcame his nausea, will always have to suffer from a tremendous "ethical anxiety." There is freedom in Sartrian existence, but anxiety is its price. And it is a high price, that few people are ready to pay. There are strings attached to Sartre's optimism.

Overcoming nausea means freeing oneself from the oppression of the absurd. Thus one can understand that in the years follow- ing the liberation of France, when the possibilities of meaningful action grew, Sartre gradually de-emphasized the concept of absurdity. In 1952 this evolution led to the end of the friendship which, for several years, had linked Sartre and Camus. The occasion of the polemic and the subsequent break between the two writers was Camus' dissatisfaction with a review published about his book *The Rebel* in *Les Temps Modernes*, the literary magazine directed by Sartre. The polemic reveals that Sartre no longer shares Camus' concept of the absurd, nor his rather abstract revolt against existence. Declaring that, although not being a Marxist, he believes in the "profound truth" of Marx's philosophy, Sartre reproaches Camus for his hostility toward history and concludes that, in refusing to participate in history —especially in the struggle of the proletariat—Camus ceases to share the aims of his contemporaries and cannot see anything but "absurdity" in all human actions.[8]

Thus, philosophically Sartre's break with Camus meant a turn- ing of his back on the world's absurdity and the beginning of a reconciliation between his Existentialism and history.

---

[8] See *Les Temps Modernes*, No. 82 (Aug. 1952), pp. 317-353.

Existence and Essence

Existence is the first basic concept of Existentialism, *essence* is the second. If existence is the "here" and "now" of being, essence is the "what" of this being. In this sense medieval scholasticism had already defined essence as the *quidditas* of things, a somewhat barbaric noun derived from the Latin pronoun *quid*, meaning "what." Heidegger, who is fond of barbaric expressions, used, after Scheler, the corresponding German term *Washeit*, or *Was-Sein*, in order to define essence.

Now the basic thesis of Existentialism is that *man's existence precedes his essence*. In other words, his being "here" and "now" precedes his being "something."

This thesis, however, characterizes the French Existentialists mainly. In a book published after World War II, Heidegger points out the differences between his and Sartre's philosophies, insisting that in his own main work, *Being and Time*, the relation between essence and existence has never been determined. He finds the name Existentialism adequate for Sartre's philosophy, but does not use it for his own.[1]

The religious Existentialists affirm the aforementioned thesis of man's existence preceding his essence, because human existence defies all prevision. Therefore, as Etienne Gilson says, they consider essences to be objects of an inquiry which is always open, instead of starting with them and deducing from them that which ought to exist. Existence is *real*, but the essence is only *possible*, it is a possibility of being, which, as Louis Lavelle

[1] M. Heidegger, *Platons Lehre von der Wahrheit, mit einem Brief über den Humanismus*, Bern, 1947, pp. 72–73, 79–80, 87.

pointed out, man can never completely realize, for total confidence between existence and essence is reserved to God.[2]

Sartre and his atheistic followers also affirm the thesis that man's existence precedes his essence; because, if God does not exist, there is no suprahuman consciousness that could think the human essence. Practically, this means that "man exists first, springs up in a world and is defined afterwards."[3] What he will be defined to be, will be his essence, according to Thomas Aquinas. (*"Essentia proprie est id quod significatur per definitionem."*)[4]

It seems to me that Sartre's basic Existentialist thesis implies a logical difficulty, for it is impossible to *be* without being *something*. We have already mentioned that Sartre had been warned by Professor Laporte against the kind of abstraction by which we think of certain things as isolated which are not made to exist isolatedly. Existence and essence seem to be such things. However this may be, according to Sartre's theory, we have to accept the postulate that man is first "here and now" before being something.

But what is it that man will be? He will be what he will have made of himself. And thus he will be responsible for what he is. He is not determined by any previously given essence or human nature, since, according to Sartre's atheistic assumption, there is no God, no suprahuman consciousness that could preconceive it. Thus, man is free, in the sense of not being predetermined—free and responsible for what he makes of himself.[5]

---

[2] L. Lavelle, *De l'Acte*, Paris, 1946, pp. 95, 332, et al.

[3] J.-P. Sartre, *L'Existentialisme est un Humanisme*, p. 21.

[4] *Summa Theologica*, I. 29, 2 ad 3.

[5] Sartre's and Heidegger's philosophies have often been considered as atheistic in the same sense. Heidegger, however, insists now that his philosophy is neither theistic nor atheistic. (See Heidegger, *op. cit.*, p. 103.) One of his most competent interpreters, Karl Löwith, writes about this: "To be sure, in *Sein und Zeit* God is not mentioned. Heidegger had been too much of a theologian to be, like Rilke, still able to tell stories about the good Lord. But with the "Being" surpassing man's thought, the whole (or sane) and the holy (*das Heile und das Heilige*), God and the Gods have again become possible also for him, while earlier, death alone seemed to be the highest authority over a free existence." (*K. Löwith, Heidegger, Denker in dürftiger Zeit*, Frankfurt, 1953, p. 7.)

During his whole existence man is making himself, creating himself an essence which becomes complete only at the moment of his death. Armand Salacrou, who strongly influenced Sartre, said: "Without a moment of rest man is a creator of things which are definitive." [6] The sum of these definitive things created by man is his essence. In this sense Sartre adopts Hegel's statement: "*Wesen ist, was gewesen ist.*" ("Essence is what has been.")

Thus Sartre can derive man's liberty from the Existentialist thesis that his existence precedes his essence. For not being determined by a previously given essence, by any concept of human nature conceived in God's mind, man is free. He exists only in the measure in which he created himself; "he is nothing but the sum of his acts," and there is no reality but in action.[7] Thus, in spite of its atheism, Sartre's Existentialism is no materialism, at least not in the form in which it is presented in his earlier basic works, especially in *Being and Nothingness*. Only in his subsequent theoretical work, *Critique de la Raison dialectique* (1960), did he make a desperate attempt at reconciling his antimaterialistic Existentialism with dialectical materialism. It is interesting to note that the definition of man as the sum of his acts appears before Sartre in Hegel's *Philosophy of History* and in Malraux' *La Condition humaine (Man's Fate)*.

We see now how the atheistic, indeterministic metaphysics of Sartre's Existentialism corresponds to his basic emotional intuition of the universe. For not being determined by any concept of essence or human nature in God's mind, man's existence lacks necessity; it is completely contingent and gratuitous.

In this sense man is the opposite of the artifact, the object created by man. If, for instance, a sculptor creates a statue or an engineer builds an apparatus, the concept, the "what," the essence of the statue or apparatus, precedes its existence in the mind of the sculptor or engineer. Every part of the statue or of the apparatus will be absolutely necessary to the whole, and the whole of the artifact will be necessary, too, because it will be determined by its pre-existing concept in the human creator's mind. Consequently, in the artifact nothing is contingent, noth-

---

[6] A. Salacrou, *L'inconnue d'Arras*, Paris, Gallimard, 1936, p. 18.
[7] J.-P. Sartre, *L'Existentialisme est un Humanisme*, p. 55.

ing is gratuitous, nothing *de trop*. On a theistic assumption, man *is* such an artifact. But for the atheist Sartre, man is derivable from nothing, he is "supernumerary for eternity." This is so because Sartre rejects also the idea that man possesses a "human nature," which could be found in each individual, so that each existing man would only be a particular example of a universal conception, the conception of "man."

We have to ask whether, from this standpoint, the difference between man and nature is that between freedom on the one hand, and deterministic necessity on the other. However, on Sartre's atheistic assumption, nature is not an artifact either. And we saw how, in his *Nausea*, he condemned nature as well as man as gratuitous.

Consequently, the basic difference between man and nature must consist of something else. That which makes the difference between human consciousness and inanimate nature is the most important thing in Existentialist philosophy: it is *nothing*, or to be more precise, *nothingness*. This problem is discussed in the next chapter.

Being and Nothingness

What is "being"? What is "nothingness"?

These are the most dynamic questions in modern Existentialism, as they were in ancient Greek philosophy, from the Ionic and Eleatic thinkers on. The most enlightened discussion of being and nothingness was offered in Plato's dialogue *The Sophist*. After Hegel and Schopenhauer had renewed the discussion, Heidegger took it up, especially in his essay *What Is Metaphysics?* and in his books *Being and Time* and *An Introduction to Metaphysics*. Finally, being and nothingness became the driving forces in the development of Sartre's work bearing this title.

Logically, both of these questions are hopeless. As far as being is concerned, Pascal, three centuries ago, in his treatise *On The Geometrical Spirit* made fun of those "scientists" who try to define a word by the word itself, saying for instance: "Light is a movement of luminous bodies," as if one could understand the word "luminous" without understanding the word "light." And Pascal continued with the very important statement:

> One cannot attempt to define being without falling into that same absurdity; for one cannot define a word without beginning by saying *it is*, whether one expresses it or simply implies it. Thus, in order to define being it would be necessary to say *it is*, and consequently to use the defined word in its definition.[1]

[1] Pascal, "De l'Esprit géométrique," *Pensées et Opuscules*, ed. Brunschvicg, Paris, 1946, Op. III, p. 169; American edition, *Pensées, The Provincial Letters*, New York, The Modern Library, 1941.

To this penetrating argument of Pascal's I should like to add another: Every definition is the determination of a concept by indicating its higher genus and the *differentia specifica*. But since being is itself the supreme genus, it is evidently impossible to find a higher genus in which it would be included; therefore any definition of being becomes logically impossible.

As far as nothingness is concerned, it is evident that any definition of it would have to say "Nothingness *is* . . . this or that." But this would be a *contradictio in adjecto*, by which the verb affirms what the noun denies. Any such sentence belongs to those which, according to Carnap, are "grammatically correct and, nevertheless meaningless."[2] In thinking "nothingness" I am thinking something which I call nothingness, but which *is* something, at least an abstract concept, but mostly a concrete image.

Plato's "stranger" already realized that

> it is impossible rightly to utter or to say or to think of non-being (μὴ ὄν) without any attribute, that it is a thing inconceivable, inexpressible, unspeakable, irrational.[3]

Thus we have to agree with Plato's conclusion "that it is no easier to define the nature of being than that of non-being."[4]

To be sure, symbolic logic has the means to distinguish four different meanings of the verb "to be": identity (symbol: "$=$"), membership in a class (symbol: "ϵ"), entailment (symbol: "C") and existence (symbol: "E"). It would thus be possible to say that "nothingness is a member of the class of pseudo-concepts," using for "is" the symbol "ϵ," which would not imply "E," existence. But this would still not give ontological status to "nothingness."

However, instead of realizing that logic reduces the questions, "What is being?" "What is nothingness?" to the absurd, Heidegger drew the opposite conclusion when he stated that by its

[2] R. Carnap, *Scheinprobleme in der Philosophie* (Berlin, 1928) , p. 28; American edition, *The Logical Structure of the World and Pseudoproblems in Philosophy* (Berkeley, Calif., The Univ. of California Press, 1964) .

[3] *The Sophist*, 238 C; likewise *Theaetetus*, 189 B; *The Republic*, V. 476, E–477, 478 B–C *passim*.

[4] *The Sophist*, 245 E–246.

inability to answer these questions, logic is reduced to the absurd. And with solemnity he proclaimed the dethronement of logic and reason,[5] suggesting somehow the classic case of the lunatic who considers himself sane and everyone else crazy.

It is well known how Heidegger solves his problem. Being and nothingness are not revealed by reason, but by an irrational fundamental experience (*Grunderfahrung*), manifest in moods (*Stimmungen*) such as boredom and anxiety. And he concludes with the following two statements: "Boredom reveals Being in the whole," "Anxiety reveals nothingness." [6]

Sartre does not go so far as to dethrone logic, although as an Existentialism his philosophy too is basically irrationalist and prerationalist; for to him the cognitive mind is only a mode of human existence, something secondary. Vainly struggling to define being, Sartre finally states these three definitions: "Being is. Being is itself. Being is what it is." [7]

With these definitions Sartre, unwillingly, confirms Pascal's statement that one cannot define being without falling into the nonsense of defining this concept by means of the concept which one has to define. In using the word "is" to define "being," Sartre obviously commits the fallacy of *petitio principii*, since he presupposes as defined that which he has to define. He cannot be blamed, for since being is the highest genus, he cannot possibly find a higher one in which it would be included. The only thing for which Sartre can be blamed is for having tried to define being, following the erroneous path of his master Heidegger.

In the seventeenth century the French writer Boileau wisely said: "*Ce que l'on conçoit bien s'énonce clairement.*" [8] In Sartre we find a considerable clarity of expression, and his ideas are well conceived, to the extent to which the irrationalist matter of Existentialism allows one to reach rational clarity and logical

---

[5] M. Heidegger, *Was ist Metaphysik?* Bonn, 1960, 8. Auflage, p. 30; American edition, *Existence and Being*, Chicago, Henry Regnery & Co., 1949, 1951, p. 372, *passim*.

[6] *Ibid.*, pp. 30–32.

[7] *L'Etre et le Néant*, p. 34.

[8] "What is well conceived is clearly expressed," *L'Art poétique*, in *Oeuvres complètes de Boileau*, Paris, 1872, X, p. 303; American edition, *The Art of Poetry*, French and English (Boston 1892).

conceptualization. Heidegger, however, surrounds his ideas with "that sort of luminous intellectual fog" which, according to Mark Twain, "stands for clearness among the Germans." [9] Is it that Heidegger did not refine his thoughts to full clarity, or did his intellectual presumption push him to use a German vocabulary of his own invention, so that he would not have to share that of other people?

However this may be, Heidegger made of Existentialism almost an esoteric science. Before becoming exoteric and a living force in our society, Existentialism had to be refracted through the lucid crystal of a Latin mind, that of Jean-Paul Sartre.

When this thinker states that "Being is what it is," one would suppose that he only expresses a presumptuous truism in the style of Heidegger. However, Sartre, with some success, denies the tautologic character of the statement, "Being is what it is," since the being of man which he distinguishes from being as such and which he designates by Hegel's term "being-for-itself" (*l'être-pour-soi*), is what it is not and is not what it is. Sartre's "being-for-itself" is human consciousness, while the being he designates with Kant's term "being-in-itself" (*en-soi*) is that of the phenomena of the inanimate world.

What does Sartre mean when he says that the being-for-itself, or in other words, *man*, is not what he is, while the being-in-itself, or nature, is always what it is? He simply means that man is not a "café waiter" or a soldier or a professor in the same sense as a mountain is a mountain. Café waiter, soldier, or professor is the subject which I have to be, which I imagine, and from which I am separated as the subject is separated from the object—"separated by nothing," says Sartre; "but this nothing isolates me from it, so that I cannot be it. I can only play at being it."

Being originally mere existence without an essence, man *is* not but *makes* himself; and he continues to make himself until he dies. Thus, as long as he is alive, man never coincides with himself, never coincides with the idea he has of himself. As we already know, man's existence is real, but his essence is only

[9] *A Tramp Abroad*, New York and London, Harper & Brothers, 1879, 1921, II, p. 293.

a possibility of being toward which he is striving, without ever totally realizing it, because for a living man new possibilities always arise. Thus a living man can never coincide with himself. Sartre defines man as the "lack" (*manque*) of this coincidence.[10]

Thus, man, "the being-for-itself," is full of negation. Being not what he is, man, according to Sartre, is not subjected to the principle of identity—unlike the "being-in-itself," nature, which, being what it is, does not include any negation and is "as full as an egg." [11]

Man is far from being as full as an egg; he is a "hollow which is always future" (Paul Valéry's *"creux toujours futur"*) and "the being by which nothingness comes into the world." [12] And nothingness comes into the world mainly by man's questioning, for a question always implies the possibility of a negative answer. But while for our logical conception, negation is nothing but a quality of our judgment, for Sartre's and Heidegger's ontological conception negation has its origin in nothingness, which is a kind of metaphysical power that acts by "naughting" (Sartre's *néantiser* and Heidegger's *Nichten*). "Nothingness . . . is the foundation of negation as act, because it is negation as being," Sartre says,[13] although it is obvious, logically, that if nothingness *is* negation as *being*, it is being and no longer nothingness.

We are familiar with Heidegger's preposterous statement, *"Das Nichts selbst nichtet,"* [14] which Sartre transcribes, *"le néant n'est pas, il se néantise."* [15] To translate this nonsense one would have to say, "Nothingness is not, it 'naughts' itself." Thus these authors try to escape from the contradiction of saying "nothingness is." However, it is difficult to find any action either done or suffered by a subject which would correspond to the verb "to naught." This explains why "to naught" does not exist in English, just as the French language does not have the verb *"néantiser,"* and the German does not have *"nichten."* Besides, even in order to "naught" itself, nothingness would have to "be."

10 *L'Etre et le Néant*, pp. 98–100, 516, *passim*.
11 *Le Sursis*, p. 52.
12 *L'Etre et le Néant*, p. 60.
13 *Ibid.*, p. 54.
14 *Was ist Metaphysik?*, p. 34.
15 *L'Etre et le Néant*, p. 53.

In his last attempt to save a desperate situation, Sartre tries to find his salvation in the passive voice by saying: *"Le néant n'est pas, il est été,"* or *"il est néantisé."* This is a new linguistic monster which must be translated by the nonsense, "nothingness is not, it *is* been," or "it is naught." However, Sartre does not seem to realize that even in order to undergo an action it would be necessary to be something and not a mere nothing. How right was Parmenides, who declared, twenty-four hundred years ago, that one can neither know nor express that which is not: "Never let this thought prevail, said he, that non-being is; but keep your mind from this way of investigation."[16]

Heidegger and Sartre did not heed the warning of Parmenides and were drawn into a whirlpool of contradictions.

The fact that nothingness resists every rational attempt to comprehend it does not mean for Existentialists that it does not exist. As already mentioned, we have, according to Heidegger, an *emotional* proof of the reality of nothingness: it is our anxiety. And Sartre shares his opinion, although he puts more emphasis on Kierkegaard's freedom as the source of anxiety. But, as we shall see later, freedom will also be defined as a manifestation of nothingness.

Since the time of Kierkegaard, anxiety, because of its object-lessness, has constituted the Existentialists' decisive argument against reason. Benjamin Fondane, varying Heidegger's words, says: "Anxiety reveals to us nothingness, which universal reason tries to conceal from us." [17]

However, the Existentialists do not realize that deducing from anxiety that nothingness is its cause is a logical inference, and hence an act of that odious reason they condemn so scornfully. Moreover, this inference is a logical operation which does not imply any certainty, since it is a conclusion from the effect to the cause. When we see a house burning we cannot infer from this effect a single possible cause of it, but only many different possible causes. The same is true of the conclusion from the effect of anxiety to its presumable cause, nothingness. Freud, for example, saw in the state of anxiety a reproduction of the

---

16 Plato, *The Sophist* 237; see also H. Diels, *Die Fragmente der Vorsokratiker*, Berlin, 1934, I, "Parmenides," Fragments 2, 6, 7, 8.
17 "Le Lundi existentiel," *L'Existence* (Paris, 1945), p. 35.

trauma of birth;[18] and one may easily imagine other inferences of more or less probability.

Sartre says that when questioning "a being as to its being and its manner of being . . . there remains always a possibility that it reveals itself as a nothingness." [19] But when taking this for an *absolute* nothingness, he disregards entirely the clear distinction which Schopenhauer has established between *absolute* nothingness (*nihil negativum*) and *relative* nothingness (*nihil privativum*). Here is what Schopenhauer says: "Every *nothing* is thought of as such only in relation to *something* and presupposes this relation, and also this something." Consequently, Schopenhauer is right in concluding that, logically, and considered more closely, "no absolute nothing, no proper *nihil* is even thinkable, but everything of this kind, when considered from a higher standpoint . . . is always merely a *nihil privativum*." [20] Thus, logically, the Existentialists have no right to consider the not-being or not-being-here as an absolute nothingness.

As a matter of fact, nothingness is only a grammatical noun expressing a logical relation between a particular subject and a particular predicate, and not at all a designation of a substantial being. Identifying linguistic forms with the structure of things expressed by these linguistic forms, Existentialists follow the fallacious path of their teachers, the phenomenologists. Seeing the whole of reality through the network of language, Existentialists have transformed the grammatical substantive "nothingness" into a metaphysical force which acts by "naughting," and can be "present" or "absent" like a thing.

Hypnotized by Heidegger, Sartre operates with the concept of "nothingness" as if his great compatriot Bergson had never written those classical pages in which he reveals nothingness as a "pseudo-idea, a mere word." We speak of "nothing" when we expect to encounter a certain thing and find another in its place, be it mere air. The word "nothing," then, expresses only the

---

[18] *The Problem of Anxiety*, New York, W. W. Norton & Co., 1936, pp. 93, 123, *passim.*

[19] *L'Etre et le Néant*, p. 59.

[20] A. Schopenhauer, *Die Welt als Wille und Vorstellung*, Leipzig, 1892, I, 4, pp. 523–524; English edition, *The World As Will and Idea* (London, 1907–9) .

disappointment of an expectation, a feeling rather than a thought. Bergson showed that "nothing" concerns the absence not so much of a thing as of a utility.

> If I bring a visitor into a room that I have not yet fur-
> nished, I say to him that "there is nothing in it." Yet I
> know the room is full of air; but, as we do not sit on air,
> the room truly contains nothing that at this moment, for
> the visitor and myself, counts for anything. In a general
> way human work consists in creating utility; and as long as
> the work is not done, there is "nothing"—nothing that
> we want.[21]

As for "absolute nothingness," Bergson showed that suppress-
ing a thing consists in replacing it with another, and that
thinking the absence of one thing is only possible by the repre-
sentation of the presence of some other thing. But if annihilation
signifies substitution, "the idea of an annihilation of everything
is as absurd as that of a square circle . . . since the operation
consists in destroying the very condition that makes the operation
possible." [22]

According to the American physicist and logician P. W. Bridg-
man, a question has meaning if it is possible to find operations
by which an answer can be given. As Bergson showed, there are
no such possible operations in the case of nothingness. Consequently, the problem of nothingness is meaningless.

However, Sartre believes in nothingness and uses this concept
for his distinction between human consciousness and the world.
There exist, he contends, many realities, such as distance, absence, alteration, repulsion, regret, and distraction, which are
not only objects of man's judgment, but are suffered, opposed,
fought, and feared by human beings. They are "inhabited by
negation in their inner structure, as a necessary condition of
their existence." Sartre calls them *"négatités,"* which should be
translated as "negatities." Here again, Sartre was strongly influenced by Heidegger, who wrote:

21 H. Bergson, *L'Evolution créatrice*, p. 322; American edition, *Creative Evolution*, New York, Henry Holt & Co., 1911, pp. 297–98.
22 *Ibid.*, p. 301; American edition, p. 283.

The permeation of *Da-sein* by nihilating modes of behavior points to the perpetual, ever-dissimulated manifestness of nothing, which only dread reveals in all its originality.[23]

But while in Heidegger there is also much emphasis on the fact that our existence (*Da-sein*) is suspended in nothingness (*die Hineingehaltenheit in das Nichts*, as expressed in one of Heidegger's barbaric neologisms), Sartre is more interested in the nothingness within being.

If nothingness can be given, it is not before and not after being, nor in general, outside being, but in the very womb of being, in its heart, like a worm.[24]

With the *question*, the basic negativity is introduced into the world. But a question presupposes a human being who asks and is basically a human process. The same holds for all the other negatities we mentioned before, so that it is through man, the being-for-itself, that nothingness comes into the world. His main activity is to "naught." This verb "to naught" (*néantiser*) constitutes one of the most obscure concepts in Existentialism. In Heidegger's "*Nichten*" it is almost mystical. In Sartre it becomes a little clearer. In one of his earlier works, *L'Imaginaire*, Sartre is already saying:

To imagine, to posit an image means . . . to hold the real at a distance, to free oneself from it, in short to deny it. . . . It is by placing himself at a convenient distance from his picture that the impressionist painter will disengage the whole of the "forest" from the multitude of little touches which he has put on his canvas. . . . Thus to posit the world as a world, or to naught it, is one and the same thing.[25]

Here the verb "to naught" seems to be a synonym for "to deny," in the sense of "to abstract from." The same seems to be true in the passage where Sartre describes how he enters a café

[23] "What Is Metaphysics?" *Existence and Being*, London, 1949, p. 373; American edition, Chicago, Henry Regnery & Co., 1949.
[24] *L'Etre et le Néant*, p. 57.
[25] *L'Imaginaire*, Paris, 1940, 1956, pp. 233–34; American edition, *The Psychology of Imagination*, New York, Philosophical Library, 1948.

to look for his friend Pierre. He looks at all the tables, but he cannot find him. Sartre speaks, in this case, of a *"néantisation"* ("naughtization") by which all the objects and persons in the café who are not Pierre "are engulfed in the fullness of the background" where Pierre is supposed to appear.[26]

However, Sartre denies the abstract character of the proposition, "Pierre is not in the café," while admitting the abstract character of such statements as "Wellington is not in the café."

It seems that the difference between these two statements lies in the fact that the absence of Pierre has an Existential meaning for the friend who looks for him, while that of Wellington is a mere thought.

Thus, if we try to establish an analogy between the process of abstraction and Sartre's "naughtization," we have to keep in mind that the former is a logical process, while the latter seems to be an *Existential attitude.*

Gabriel Marcel says that "néantiser" means *"entourer d'une région de non-être,"* that is, to surround something with a region of nonbeing. Sartre himself speaks of a "muff" of nonbeing, created by "naughtization." If I think my past, I "naught" it in the sense that I place between it and myself a thick layer of emptiness, or nonbeing. But this does not mean to annihilate it, as Heidegger has already said.

"Naughtization" is a human process. And man is the being by which nothingness, in the form of negatities, comes into the world. Being never what he is, being always separated by a region of nonbeing from what he has to be according to his idea, being always in the making of himself, man never coincides with himself, but is "full" of negation, an ever-questioning and denying hollow projected toward the future. Consequently man, the being-for-itself, is the opposite of nature, the being-in-itself, which, free from negation, coincides with itself, is what it is, and is the only object of the principle of identity.

For Sartre, the negation, which is the prime property of consciousness, arises from the formation of a sort of "vacuum" within the plenitude of being. In this sense he distinguishes "the mere in-itself," or nature, from "the in-itself surrounded by that

[26] *L'Etre et le Néant,* p. 45.

muff of nothingness, which we have designated by the name for-itself," [27] or consciousness.

Thus that which makes the basic difference between human consciousness and inanimate nature is, in Sartre's philosophy, really Nothing, or, to be more precise, the "nothingness" which is in the heart of man.

[27] *Ibid.*, p. 716.

Freedom and Anxiety, Choice and Project

In CHAPTER 7 we have shown that human freedom follows from the Existentialist assumption that man's existence precedes his essence. This means that man is not determined by any previously given essence or human nature, since, according to Sartre's atheistic assumption, there is no God, no suprahuman consciousness that could preconceive man's essence. Thus man is free, in the sense of not being determined.

But this is not the only reason for Sartre's considering man as free. In his principal metaphysical treatise he tries to demonstrate that man's freedom coincides with the nothingness which is in his heart and compels him to *make himself into* something, instead of *being* something. This latter theory completes the former. Since man has not gotten anything on his way and "nothing comes to him from outside or from inside," [1] man can get an essence, create himself an essence, only by "engaging" or "committing" himself, in this way or that.

A man who, like Sartre's Mathieu in *The Age of Reason* and *The Reprieve*, is never able to commit himself remains always inessential. Only through engagement can we become essential and fulfill our freedom. Man is free to act, but he must act to be free and become essential.

Since, according to Sartre, there is no reality but in action and man "is nothing but the sum of his acts," [2] he exists only to

[1] *L'Etre et le Néant*, p. 516.
[2] *L'Existentialisme*, p. 55.

the extent that he realizes his project and thus himself. When Mathieu's friend Brunot, a Communist, invites him to become a member of the Communist Party, Mathieu hesitates. He does not want to commit himself, lest he lose his freedom. Then Brunot says to him: "You are free. But what is freedom good for, if not to commit oneself? . . . You are floating, you are an abstract, an absent one!" [3]

Orestes, in Sartre's great tragedy *The Flies*, had been taught by his tutor that the best thing for a man is to be free for all commitments, but never to commit himself. At first, on arriving at Argos, Orestes enjoys this situation of a man who is committed to nothing—to no religion, no family, no country, no task. "There are men," he says, "who were born committed: they have no choice, they are cast on a road. . . . I am free, thank God!" [4]

Orestes is not only a pupil of his tutor but also a disciple of France's famous writer André Gide, who, between the two World Wars, proclaimed his dogma of man's permanent *"disponibilité,"* i.e., his condition of being always available, free from actual and for possible commitments. It was Gide who preached the rupture with all obligations—social and others—the refusal of any choice, and who proclaimed only *one* ideal: that of enjoying what he called *"la plénitude de l'instant"*—the fulness of the instant. No wonder that, after France's surrender in 1940, some writers—like Massis and Talvart—put the blame for the weakening of the country's moral forces on Gide's confessed "immoralism" and his religion of nihilism, with which he had infected thousands of his enthusiastic young French followers.

Born during the years of France's expiation for these sins, under the German occupation, Sartre's Existentialism vigorously rejected Gide's religion of *"disponibilité"* and of man's irresponsible refusal of choice and commitment. Already before Sartre the Spanish philosopher José Ortega y Gasset had declared: *"Una vida en disponibilidad es mayor negación de si misma que la muerte"*—a disposable life is a greater negation

3 *L'Age de Raison*, p. 123.
4 *Les Mouches*, Paris, 1943, p. 24; American edition, *No Exit and Three Other Plays* (*The Flies, Dirty Hands, The Respectful Prostitute*), New York, Alfred A. Knopf, 1947, 1955; Vintage Books, 1960.

of itself than death.[5] Both Ortega and Sartre insist on the moral necessity for man to commit himself by choosing a project and assuming the responsibility for his choice.

Thus we see that Sartre's Orestes soon becomes tired of his *"disponibilité"* and inessentialness, of his lack of commitment, for he exclaims;

> Oh, if there were an act, you see, an act which would give me citizen's rights among them (the people of Argos)! If I could only take possession of their memories, their terrors, their hopes, in order to fill the emptiness of my heart, be it by a crime, be it by killing my own mother.[6]

Existentialism has to preach commitment because only by commitment can man, this empty shell, build up his essence. But since *any* kind of commitment fulfills this condition, there seems to be a complete moral equivalence of all possible commitments. Orestes is quite satisfied to become committed, even by killing his own mother, Clytemnestra.

This secondary essence, which man has not inherited but which is his own work and is petrified in his own past (Hegel's *Wesen ist, was gewesen ist,* "Essence is what has been"), would likewise determine him and thus hamper his freedom, if he were not able to separate himself from his past by "nothingness." Thus Sartre defines freedom as "the human being putting his own past out of action by secreting his own nothingness." [7]

If man were considered as fullness, it would be vain to search in him afterward for a region of liberty, just as it would be absurd to look for emptiness in a receptacle which previously had been filled to the brim. "What is important in a vase is the emptiness of the inside." Thus freedom is the nothingness in man's heart which compels him to make himself; it is man's possibility of secreting the nothingness which isolates him and thus of "naughting" everything which is given, including his own past.

In a kind of synthesis of the doctrines of Kierkegaard and

[5] J. Ortega y Gasset, *Obras completas,* t. IV, p. 239.
[6] *Les Mouches,* p. 26.
[7] *L'Etre et le Néant,* p. 65.

Heidegger, Sartre declares that it is by *anxiety* that man becomes conscious of his freedom. This anxiety is understandable in the light of man's situation in a universe interpreted by Existentialism. Being undetermined by any previously given essence or human nature, each individual is what he makes of himself and, consequently, is responsible for what he is.

Man exists at first and "projects" himself toward a future, toward his own possibilities. Thus he is his own project, that which he has projected himself to be.

That is what Sartre, after Kierkegaard, Ortega, and Heidegger, designates as "man's choosing himself," and for him "freedom is freedom of choice." [8] As Kierkegaard said, the richest personality is nothing, until it has chosen itself, while the poorest personality is everything, once it has chosen itself.

If we object that we are not conscious of choosing ourselves, Sartre replies that this consciousness expresses itself indirectly, by the joint feelings of anxiety and responsibility.

The Existentialist thesis that man chooses himself is certainly one of those which arouses the strongest opposition of some inveterate prejudices. Most people would agree with Somerset Maugham's declaration that "a man is not what he wants to be but what he must be." [9]

However, Sartre insists that our choice must not be confused with our will. For what we want to be is a conscious decision and usually subsequent to a more original project. If I want to become a professor, to write a book, to get married, etc., all of this is only a manifestation of a more original choice, "much more spontaneous than that which we call will." [10] Kant had already taught that "man must make or must have made himself into whatever he is or is to become in a moral sense: good or evil. Either condition must be an effect of his free will; for otherwise he could not be held accountable for it and could therefore be neither good nor evil." [11] Similarly, Schopenhauer

---

[8] *Ibid.*, pp. 561, 563, *passim.*

[9] *The Moon and Sixpence*, New York, Modern Library, 1935, p. 28.

[10] *L'Existentialisme est un Humanisme*, p. 24.

[11] I. Kant, *Religion innerhalb der Grenzen der bloszen Vernunft*, I., S. 48. American edition, *Religion Within the Limits of Reason Alone*, New York, Harper, 1960.

insisted that only if a man is his own work are his deeds really entirely his and can be ascribed to him. And when Schopenhauer continues by saying that "every man is what he is through his will," [12] we have only to replace the word "will" with the word "choice" in order to get Sartre's doctrine.

The difference is mainly terminological, since for Schopenhauer "will" is no more a conscious decision than is Sartre's choice. "I say," Schopenhauer writes, "that a man is his own work *before* all knowledge, and knowledge is merely added to enlighten it." Sartre would be able to subscribe entirely to this thesis, but he never refers to the father of modern pessimism, with whom he shares so many ideas.

The same happens with José Ortega y Gasset, whose ideas reappear in many essential parts of Sartre's doctrine, without being identified as such. Eight years before the publication of Sartre's *Being and Nothingness*, for example, Ortega wrote the following:

> There is in man . . . the inescapable impression that his life, and with it his being, is something which has to be chosen. The fact is amazing; because it means that, unlike all other entities in the universe, which have a being that is given to them ready-made and by virtue of which they exist, i.e. because of which they already are what they are, man is the almost inconceivable reality which exists without having a being irremediably being prefixed, who consequently, is not yet what he is but must choose for himself his own being. How will he choose it? Because he will imagine in his mind many types of possible lives. . . . he will, doubtless, notice that some of them attract him more . . .[13]

Obviously, this is Sartre's doctrine. In *La Rebelión de las masas* (*The Revolt of the Masses*), his most famous book, published thirteen years before Sartre's *Being and Nothingness* (1943), as well as in *Historia como sistema* (*History as a System*) (1935),

---

[12] *Die Welt als Wille und Vorstellung*, II, 4, p. 694.
[13] J. Ortega y Gasset, "La Misión del Bibliotecario" (1935) in *Obras completas*, Madrid, 1951, tomo V, p. 211.

Ortega insisted on the moral necessity of man's "engagement" in, or commitment to, a definite project, not only individually but also collectively. Sartre never recognized his intellectual debt to the great Spanish thinker.

It is interesting to note that with their doctrine of the individual's responsible choice of his self, the Existentialists, as well as Kant and Schopenhauer, have a venerable ancestor: Plato. In the tenth book of his *Republic*, the father of occidental spiritualism tells us his myth of the souls in the other world. Before being reborn they are told by a prophet of Lachesis to choose the patterns of their future lives (βίων παραδείγματα). "Let him who draws the first lot have the first choice, and the life which he chooses shall be his destiny. . . . The responsibility is with the chooser—God is blameless (θεὸς ἀναίτιος)."[14]

Does this Platonic myth not seem to contain Existentialism in a nutshell? But as far as the theory of values, and of essences in general, are concerned, Existentialism is—as we shall see later —the most radical anti-Platonism.

If man is what he is through his choice and choice is based on freedom, the responsibility arising from freedom becomes obvious; and this responsibility explains the anxiety linked to our consciousness of freedom. But in Sartre's philosophy this responsibility is even greater than one would suppose, because by his choice man not only engages himself but engages all men, mankind in its entirety. If, for instance, I choose to remain unmarried or to become a thief, I engage the whole of mankind to celibacy or crime; for by my individual choice I create a certain image of man I have chosen and am therefore responsible for myself and for all men.[15]

"We are responsible to all for all." This sentence of Dostoyevsky's, which Simone de Beauvoir has chosen as the motto for her novel *Le Sang des Autres* (*The Blood of Others*), is the essence of the great Russian's ethics. Not only did he put it into the mouth of the Elder Zossima in *The Brothers Karamazov* but he emphasized it as his deep personal conviction in his *Diary of a Writer*. Sartre shares his conviction and tries to give

---

[14] Plato, *The Republic*, X, 617E.
[15] *L'Existentialisme*, p. 27.

it a philosophical foundation by saying: *I am responsible for myself and for all men, because by choosing myself I choose man as I want him to be.*

There are moments in which man must ask himself: "Am I the one who has the right to act in such a way that all mankind adjusts itself to my acts?" [16]

This tremendous responsibility, resulting from our freedom of choice, is simply the responsibility for the values of mankind. We shall have to examine now the peculiar form which the problem of values takes in Existentialism.

[16] *Ibid.*, p. 31.

FREEdom aNd ValuES:
SarTRE aNd NiETzschE

THE PROBLEM OF VALUES is a part of the problem of essence, that is, of general concepts or categories and universal norms. According to the classic tradition created by Plato, all concrete things exist only because they participate in universal ideas or essences. The Platonic conception was modified by Aristotle, the creator of traditional logic, but he, too, maintained the primacy of general ideas over individuals, stating that there is no science except of the general. In this sense traditional philosophy and science, influenced by Plato and Aristotle, have always been mainly a search for general concepts, universal categories and norms—in short, a search for essences. Thus traditional philosophy is based on the primacy of the universal, objective essences over the concrete, individual existents. We may therefore say that traditional philosophy is *essentialist*.

Existentialism, on the other hand, proclaims the primacy of the individual, concrete, subjective, single existent over the general, objective essence; and considers that an individual existent is more than a mutilated general concept, since it exists, while the general concept does not exist. A norm is also a general concept or an essence; but since Existentialism denies the primacy of the essence over existence, of the general over the individual, it necessarily must deny that any individual value we express in our valuations is determined by a general norm. For, according to Existentialism, the essences are not given before the existents but after them. This means that in evaluating we are not determined by any previously given essence or norm, by anything outside ourselves. We judge subjectively, without any objective support, and are responsible for our judgment or evaluation.

For Sartre the problem of values is conditioned by this basic anti-essentialism, by his atheism, and by his theory of freedom. He thinks that if God does not exist, man does not have presented to him any values or hierarchies of values to guide him, legitimize his conduct, or justify his preferences or repulsions and the significance he ascribes to things. Consequently, man has to choose in complete aloneness the ways of his conduct and the significance he will ascribe to things, with the entire responsibility for the choice of these values resting on his own shoulders. Without values of universal validity, guaranteed by the authority of a suprahuman being, there is no universally binding ethics. Each man has to act without a universal ethics to back him up; he has to act on his own responsibility, without excuse or justification, in complete solitude and dreadful freedom.

This ethical consequence of Sartre's metaphysics is a recurrent theme of his novels and plays. There is, for instance, Mathieu, the professor of philosophy, who finds himself in a dilemma:

> He was free, free for everything, free to act like an animal or like a machine, free for accepting, free for refusing, free for shuffling. . . . He could do what he wanted to do, nobody had the right to advise him. There would be neither right nor wrong unless he invented them. . . . He was alone in a monstrous silence, free and alone, without help, without an excuse, condemned to decide without any possible recourse, *condemned forever to be free.*[1]

And, in a similar way, another of Sartre's characters, Orestes, in the tragedy *The Flies*, exclaims:

> Suddenly freedom dashed upon me and penetrated me. . . . There was no longer anything in heaven, neither "good" nor "evil," nor anybody to give me orders. . . . I am con-

[1] *L'Age de Raison*, p. 249.

demned to have no law other than my own. . . . For I am
a man and each man has to invent his own way.[2]

Man is *condemned to be free*—this is the same formula Sartre
adopts in his theoretical work.[3] Some years before him Ortega
y Gasset said basically the same thing, when he declared: *"soy
por fuerza libre, lo quiera o no"* [4]—I am *forcibly free*—whether
I like it or not. Some may find these formulas an exaggeration,
for, according to a widespread belief, man loves freedom passionately. Only a profound psychologist like Dostoyevsky was
able to recognize that "nothing has ever been more unbearable
for a man and a human society than freedom." [5] If a man is
free, he is really "condemned" to be free. Sartre's "moral anxiety" (*angoisse éthique*), the consciousness of man's freedom in
choosing values, is explained by the individual responsibility
this choice implies. "My freedom is the only foundation of
values," Sartre writes, "and nothing, absolutely nothing justifies
me in adopting this value rather than that, this hierarchy of
values rather than another." [6]

From the standpoint of Existentialism, the French disciples
of Sartre who joined the underground, were no more justified
in choosing the values of French democracy and fighting for
them in the FFI than the German disciples of Heidegger were
in choosing the values of Nazism and fighting for them in the
SS. "Every time," Sartre writes, "a man chooses his engagement
and projects in all sincerity and lucidity, whatever this choice
may be, it is impossible to prefer another to it." [7]

Placing the difference between "good" and "evil" in an inner
criterion—that of sincerity—Extentialist ethics has to admit a
kind of moral equivalence of all projects, because a Nazi can
be as sincere as a democrat, a murderer as sincere as a benefactor
of mankind.

[2] *Les Mouches,* pp. 100–101.
[3] *L'Etre et le Néant,* p. 515, *passim.*
[4] J. Ortega y Gasset, "Historia como Sistema," *Obras Completas,* tomo VI,
p. 34.
[5] F. Dostoyevsky, *The Brothers Karamazov,* New York, Modern Library,
1929, p. 262.
[6] *L'Etre et le Néant,* p. 76.
[7] *L'Existentialisme,* pp. 79–80.

This is certainly one of the greatest danger spots of Existentialism. Sartre tries to moderate this extreme moral individualism, according to which everybody has his own ethics, by stating, "We should always ask ourselves: What would happen if everybody would do the same?" And he adds that only by a kind of "bad faith" can a man evade this reflection when acting. The man who lies and excuses himself by declaring that not everybody acts the same feels uneasy because the fact of lying implies a universal value ascribed to the lie.[8]

Sartre's principle has a certain similarity to Kant's categorical imperative. In order to determine the rightness or wrongness of an action, Kant bids us to ask ourselves whether the idea of the proposed action would at the same time be willed as a universal law. But in Kant, rightness and wrongness have an independent, absolute validity, because they are backed up by a universal duty, imperatively demanded by a universal practical reason. In Sartre's philosophy, however, there are no standards of rightness and wrongness before each man sets them up by his individual choice, according to the Existentialist principle that the individual existent precedes the general essence; and, even after the individual choice, the resulting moral standard exists only as long as we have not overthrown it by a new "naughting" free act, a new choice. For, to Sartre, my freedom is the only foundation of values, and since *I am my freedom*, I am the being by which values come into being. Therefore I cannot be justified, because, besides the values which I have set up by my free choice, there are no other values which would justify me in my act of choosing values. Consequently, "I am the foundation without a foundation" of values, and this explains my ethical anxiety. The latter becomes even more acute when we realize that values cannot be established without being, at the same moment, put in doubt, since I keep the possibility of overthrowing, at any moment, the hierarchy of values I have chosen and of replacing it with another.

Thus Sartre's freedom has no limits other than itself, because "we are not free to cease to be free."[9] The *jump* into freedom is indeed a jump into limitlessness and gives us a feeling of

8 *Ibid.*, pp. 28–29.
9 *L'Etre et le Néant*, p. 515.

anxiety, similar to that which we might have should we jump
into an apparently limitless space.

> I have not and cannot have recourse to any value when
> I am confronted with the fact that it is I who maintain
> the values in being: nothing can protect me against myself
> —cut from the world and from my essence by the nothing-
> ness I am, I have to achieve the sense of the world and of
> my essence: I make the decision concerning that sense,
> alone, unjustifiable, and without excuse.[10]

This is the cause of my "ethical anxiety."

Sartre teaches that man is the being through whom values
come into being, and as soon as man realizes that it is he who
posits all values, he will not want anything but freedom as the
basis of all values. In this sense Existentialism is a *humanism*,
because it makes man the only legislator in the realm of values.
It is a humanism, also, in that it considers this world a *human*
world and man as its "revealer," insofar as man is the means by
which things are manifested. For it is man who sets up the relationships among things.

Further, Existentialism is a humanism insofar as it teaches
that, having reached his age of reason, man has to recognize that
he stands alone in the world and can rely only on himself. As
Simone de Beauvoir says, the human individual is an "absolute
value," and he alone has to lay the foundations of his own
existence. "Every man needs the freedom of other men," she
writes.[11] In its atheistic version, Existentialism is an attempt to
redefine existence, not in subhuman, materialistic terms, not in
suprahuman, theological terms, but in human terms, which are
those of subjectivity.

From all these points of view Existentialism is a humanism.
It is a humanism, however, only in the sense of the Sophists
and their principle, "man is the measure of all things," but no
longer in the sense of the Stoics. For the Stoic idea of the
universal man, or human nature, independent of space and time,
subject to the same moral requirements—which forms the basis

---

10 *Ibid.*, p. 77.
11 *Pour une Morale de l'Ambiguité,* Paris, 1947, pp. 100, 218; American
edition, *The Ethics of Ambiguity,* New York, Philosophical Library, 1948.

of traditional humanism—has been replaced in Existentialism by the idea of the man here and now, the man of a specific historical epoch and a specific geographical environment.

While Sartre insists that Existentialism is a humanism, Heidegger has always rejected humanism. But after Germany's defeat in World War II, Heidegger rationalized his attitude by writing: "I think against humanism, because it does not place man's humanity high enough." [12] Was this the reason that he joined the Nazi Party?

Sartre's axiological humanism—the idea that man is the only legislator in the realm of values—rests on his Existentialist thesis that our knowing mind is only secondary to our existence, a mode of our existence, and that reason comes into being only through freedom. Consequently, this freedom or this existence cannot be limited by any product of reason or knowledge, such as truth or significance, or by values and things recognized.

Things are determined by things. But being himself action, man is anything but a thing and can therefore not be determined by things. There are some people who realize this, who recognize their freedom and consider themselves as free creators and the unfounded foundation of all values. They assume responsibility for their value-founding choice and the anxiety arising from it. According to Sartre, they exist "authentically" and in "good faith."

The great majority of people, however, deny their freedom, hiding it from themselves with all kinds of deterministic excuses. They exist "unauthentically." They are "cowards" or, as far as they try to prove the necessity of their existence, they are "stinkers." By denying their freedom, they try to flee from anxiety by grasping themselves from outside, as things. But we cannot overcome our anxiety, because, according to Sartre, "we are anxiety." I cannot flee from what I am. I can flee in order not to know, but I must know that I am fleeing. Consequently, the flight from anxiety is only a way of becoming conscious of our anxiety. But that means apprehending anxiety "in bad faith."

Those who, in order to evade their freedom, responsibility,

---

[12] "Über den Humanismus," *Platons Lehre von der Wahrheit*, Bern, 1947, p. 75.

and anxiety, choose to consider themselves as things, determined by other things, will also consider values as given things by which they are being determined. They are possessed by what Sartre calls the "spirit of seriousness" (*esprit de sérieux*), designating the tendency to "consider values as transcendent data, independent of human subjectivity." [13] Dominated by this spirit, a person renounces his human condition by renouncing his freedom to choose the values in which he will believe, the significance he will ascribe to things, because he is afraid of responsibility, afraid of anxiety. Heidegger says that most people have no "courage for anxiety" (*Mut zur Angst*).[14] But that is exactly what Existentialism requires of us: courage for anxiety. Those who do not have it, those who are dominated by the "spirit of seriousness," submit themselves to the hierarchy of values, standards, and significances set up in a given society and transmitted by education and convention. He who accepts these ready-made, thinglike values gives up his human personality. For, as Nietzsche has said, the word "man" means "valuator." [15] But at the same time the spirit of seriousness will deliver man from the responsibility of a value-choosing freedom and help him to hide his anxiety from himself.

The man dominated by the spirit of seriousness is merely an overgrown child, because for the child every new thing "has already been seen, named, and classified by other people. Each object presents itself to him with a label; it is extremely reassuring and even sacred, because the look of adult persons still clings to it. Far from exploring unknown regions, the child skims through an album; he takes the census of a herbarium." [16]

As already mentioned, many persons remain all their lives in this axiological condition of children, accepting ready-made values and becoming something like value-registering automatons. This is their "spirit of seriousness," which Existentialism fights.

---

13 *L'Etre et le Néant*, p. 721.
14 *Sein und Zeit*, p. 254.
15 *Also sprach Zarathustra*, Leipzig, 1899, p. 86; American edition, *Thus Spoke Zarathustra*, Chicago, Henry Regnery & Co., 1957, Gateway ed., p. 64.
16 Sartre, *Baudelaire*, Paris, 1947, p. 60. American edition, *Baudelaire*, Norfolk, Conn., New Directions, 1950.

The people of Argos in Sartre's tragedy *Les Mouches* (*The Flies*) are in this axiological condition of children, for they accept the values ready-made for them by their king and queen and are remorseful even of the crimes not committed by themselves but by their princes. The rulers like such immature people because they can govern them easily. Zeus, representing all rulers, delights in such people.

Only now are we able to understand why Sartre declares in *Nausea* that "nobody has rights," and calls those who believe in them "stinkers." It is because rights are also given, thinglike, and ready-made; they are substantialized, guaranteed values which precede us and determine us as things determine things, hiding from us our freedom to set up new aims. In his essay *"Matérialisme et Révolution"* Sartre says that idealism mystifies the revolutionary worker "by binding him with already given rights and values and masking from him his power of inventing his own paths." And he adds that "materialism, too, mystifies him by robbing him of his freedom." [17]

This latter remark indicates the crux of Sartre's conflict with the Communists, whose philosophy is based on Marx's deterministic dialectical materialism. On the one hand, Sartre, who, too, affirms to be a revolutionary, argues that Communism involves the contradiction of seeking human freedom through its materialistic denial; on the other hand, the Communists argue that by teaching that man is free, Sartre betrays the revolutionary worker, since if he were free he would no longer need to liberate himself by revolutionary action. Besides, they insist that dialectical materialism, too, admits human freedom, in the form defined by Friedrich Engels as the recognition of necessity. As a Hegelian, Engels thought that "freedom does not consist in an imaginary independence of natural laws but in a knowledge of these laws and in the possibility thence derived of applying them intelligently to given ends."[18] These ends include a *change* of reality by the action of the masses.

But we will not go into the details of this controversy between two political philosophies which has no bearing on the universal

[17] "Matérialisme et Révolution," *Les Temps Modernes*, II, 10 (July 1946), pp. 13–14.
[18] *Landmarks of Scientific Socialism*, Chicago, C. H. Kerr, 1907, p. 147.

questions we are examining here.[19] Let us say only that according to Sartre, only those possessed by the "spirit of seriousness" believe in ready-made, constituted values and rights, which they can find in society as they find things in nature. He who is aware of his freedom has to invent new values, new rights.

There is still another reason why Sartre rejects constituted values: He does not believe that in any concrete situation they would help to guide our action or to determine our conduct.

Sartre describes the case of a young Frenchman who, during the German occupation, had to choose between staying with his mother, who needed his help, and going to England with the Free French forces. Thus he had to choose between two values, his duty as a son and his duty as a patriot. Which one should he choose? Constituted ethics could not help him, for it prescribes duties toward our parents and duties toward our country, without telling us which of these duties should have precedence over the others in a concrete, conflicting case. Thus the young Frenchman had to choose on his own responsibility, without the backing of constituted ethics.

From cases like this Sartre infers that there is no general ethics. But in this I think he goes too far. In the case mentioned a choice had to be made between two *positive* values, filial love and patriotic duty; and in such cases we have really to invent a solution on our own responsibility, unsupported by a given ethics.

However, if a decision must be made between a positive and a negative value, I think that traditional ethics would guide us with perfect security. If our neighbor's house has burned down, traditional ethics commands us, with perfect clarity, to give him

[19] The American reader can find a more thorough analysis of the political aspects of Existentialism in George Novack's book *Existentialism versus Marxism*, New York, Dell Publ. Co. Inc., 1966; furthermore in Wilfrid Desan's *The Marxism of Jean-Paul Sartre*, Garden City, N.Y., Doubleday, 1965; in Marjorie Grene's *Dreadful Freedom*, Chicago, Univ. of Chicago Press, 1948; H. Marcuse's valuable review, "Remarks on J.-P. Sartre's *L'Etre et le Néant*," in *Philosophy and Phenomenological Research*, VIII, 3 (March 1948); Auguste Cornu's essay, "Bergsonianism and Existentialism," *Philosophic Thought in France and the United States*, ed. by Marvin Farber, Buffalo, Univ. of Buffalo Press, 1950, pp. 151–168. See also our own Ch. 27, "Postscript on Existentialism and Marxism."

shelter. And if, when confronted with the choice between the positive value of assisting a person who suffers and the negative value of abandoning him, we choose the negative one, our bad conscience indicates to us which of these values was the positive one and which the negative. In my opinion, in the case of choice between a positive and a negative value we need not invent our own solution but merely follow the imperatives of the constituted moral values.

So we would not say, like Sartre, that there is no general ethics, but simply that there are cases in which general ethics is insufficient to guide us and where we have to invent our own paths, on our own personal responsibility.

Sartre described the case of one of his comrades in a German prison camp, who told him that after having had many failures in his life he had chosen to become a Jesuit priest, because in these failures he saw a sign from heaven that he should give up secular life and take holy orders. But, as Sartre says, it was this man who chose that kind of interpretation of his failures, and, without knowing it, invented his own path, on his own responsibility.

I think a similar situation can be found in Maxwell Anderson's beautiful play, *Joan of Lorraine*, where the heroine, desperate because she cannot prove the authenticity of her visions and voices, is told by St. Michael that the bishops, who demand such proof, are equally unable to prove the authenticity of their views:

> The Church itself is built on revelations and these reve-
> lations came out of darkness and went back into darkness
> like your own. . . . In all the articles of belief and creed
> not one is capable of proof.[20]

Consequently, everybody has to choose his interpretation of facts and bear the responsibility for his choice, with all the anxiety arising from the fact of his not being backed up by anything. Thus we can understand Sartre's affirmation that "even if God existed, this would not change anything. . . . It

[20] *Joan of Lorraine*, New York, William Sloane Associates, 1946, p. 128.

is necessary that man find himself and convince himself that nothing can save him from himself." [21]

If Sartre wished to teach that action is a response to a unique situation and is a unique creative response, he could have referred to Aristotle's *Nicomachean Ethics*, in which we are told that in the matter of action the general concepts are empty, since every action is related to a special situation and requires special concepts.[22] A similar stand was taken by John Dewey who insisted that "every moral situation is a unique situation having its own irreplaceable good." [23]

It must also be shown how much Sartre owes to Nietzsche, to whom he refers very seldom and never in any essential matter. Yet, it is the essential which Sartre's philosophy shares with Nietzsche's.

Let us begin with individualism of values and of ethics based on atheism. Here Sartre writes:

> Since I have abolished God, the father, there must be somebody to invent values. . . . Life has no significance a priori. Before you were alive, life was nothing; it is up to you to give it a significance, and value is nothing but that significance you are choosing.[24]

And Nietzsche, after having proclaimed that "God is dead," [25] declares of values:

> Truly, men gave themselves all their good and evil. Truly, they took it not, they found it not, it did not fall on them as a voice from heaven.
>
> Man merely assigned values to things in order to maintain himself; he created the significance of things, a human significance! Therefore, he calls himself "man," that is, the valuator.
>
> Valuing is creating: hear it, you creators! Valuation itself is the treasure and jewel of valuated things.

21 *L'Existentialisme*, p. 95.
22 Book II, Ch. 6, 1107 a.
23 J. Dewey, *Reconstruction in Philosophy*, New York, Henry Holt & Co., 1950, Mentor edition, Ch. 7, p. 132.
24 *L'Existentialisme est un Humanisme*, pp. 89–90.
25 *Also sprach Zarathustra*, Vorrede, p. 12; American edition, *Thus Spoke Zarathustra*, p. 4.

Through valuation only is there value; and without valuation would the nut of existence be hollow. . . .[26]

Comparing these two enunciations, one finds they say exactly the same thing; only Nietzsche made his statement sixty years before Sartre and did so with more distinction and poetic ardor.

The "spirit of seriousness" (*esprit de sérieux*) also had been discovered by Nietzsche sixty years before it was found by Sartre. The name Nietzsche chose for it is very similar to the one chosen by Sartre, that is to say, "the spirit of gravity" (*Geist der Schwere*). And Nietzsche opposed it as vigorously as Sartre. Here is how Nietzsche characterized the spirit of gravity:

Almost from the cradle do they give us heavy words and worths on the way; "good" and "evil" does this dowry call itself. For their sake are we forgiven that we live. . . . Thus the spirit of gravity demands.

And we bear loyally what is imparted to us, on hard shoulders over rugged mountains! And when we sweat, they tell us: "Yes, life is hard to bear."

But only man finds himself hard to bear! It is because he carries too many extraneous things on his shoulders. Like the camel kneels he down and has himself well loaded.[27]

And in another paragraph, Nietzsche says:

. . . I also found again my old devil and arch-enemy, the spirit of gravity, and all he has created: coercion, law, need and consequence, and purpose and will, and good and evil.[28]

This is exactly the "spirit of seriousness" by which Sartre characterizes a man who passively accepts values invented by others, kneeling down like an animal to be loaded with them, like Nietzsche's camel, renouncing his freedom to invent his own values, his own standards of good and evil.

Nietzsche resembles Sartre in his opposition to those who believe in already given rights in order to avoid the necessity

26 *Ibid.*, "Von tausend und einem Ziele," pp. 85–86; American edition, p. 64.
27 *Ibid.*, "Vom Geist der Schwere," III, p. 283; American edition, p. 228.
28 *Ibid.*, "Von alten und neuen Tafeln," III, p. 289; American edition, p. 233.

of creating new ones. In *Will to Power* Nietzsche wrote: "The belief that the world as it should be really exists, is the belief of unproductive men who do not want to create a world as it should be." [29]

We have seen the intimate link between freedom and responsibility in Sartre's philosophy. However, sixty years earlier, Nietzsche had already asked: "What is freedom? That one has the will to self-responsibility." [30]

In her novel *The Blood of Others*, Simone de Beauvoir resumes the problem of values as it had been posed—or reiterated —by Sartre. She writes: "I believe that your error is to imagine that your reasons for being should fall to you ready-made from heaven: it is up to you to create them." [31]

We already know that Nietzsche taught the same thing sixty years before Madame de Beauvoir when he wrote that "man merely assigned values to things . . . he created the significance of things. . . ." He was even prepared for the objection made by Madame de Beauvoir's heroine, who says: "But if we know that we ourselves create these reasons for being we can no longer believe in them! That is nothing but a way of duping ourselves." [32]

To this Nietzsche might have replied, with his declaration, in *Will to Power*: "Reject the humble expression, 'Everything is subjective!' Say rather, 'It is our work! Let us be proud of it!' " [33]

Thus Nietzsche's theory of the subjectivity and individuality of all values, his thesis that they are not given to but created by man, and his affirmation that there is no universally binding ethics are integral parts of Sartre's Existentialism.

But we must emphasize an important distinction between Nietzsche's and Sartre's theories of values: While Nietzsche requires that the individual remain faithful to the values freely created and the norms freely set up by himself, Sartre teaches

[29] *Der Wille zur Macht*, Buch 3–4, *Gesammelte Werke*, XIX, 585A, p. 78.
[30] *Götzendämmerung*, in *Gesammelte Werke*, Munich, 1926, XVII, 38, p. 137; English edition, *The Twilight of Idols*.
[31] *Le Sang des Autres*, Paris, 1945, pp. 67–68; American edition, *The Blood of Others*, New York, Alfred A. Knopf, 1948.
[32] *Ibid.*, p. 68.
[33] *Wille zur Macht*, IV, 1059, in *Gesammelte Werke*, XIX, p. 368.

that everybody can posit his values and norms differently on different occasions.

Boris, an important figure in those novels of Sartre which have been integrated in *Les Chemins de la Liberté* (*The Ways of Freedom*), gives the following definition of freedom:

> The individual's duty is to do what he wants to do, to think whatever he likes, to be accountable to no one but himself, to challenge, again and again, every idea and every person.[34]

We would be inclined to consider this a caricature of Existentialism, as an idiot's concept of freedom. For in spite of his being described as a student of philosophy at the Sorbonne and as a former pupil—a favored one—of Professor Mathieu Delarue (for which read, "Professor Jean-Paul Sartre"), Boris is not very bright, and his moral and spiritual horizon (*sit venia verbo*) is no broader than that of the average Parisian gigolo.

However, in Sartre's main theoretical work we find some passages which seem to justify Boris, for instance:

> Since freedom is being-without-any-support, without any springboard, the project must be renewed permanently, in order to be. I am choosing myself perpetually . . . otherwise I should fall back into the mere existence of a thing-in-itself.[35]

But if I have to choose myself perpetually to avoid being debased to thinghood, what guarantees that I will always choose myself in the same way? Sartre recognizes this danger and says:

> We are perpetually threatened by the naughtization of our present choice, perpetually threatened by choosing ourselves, and, consequently, becoming other than we are.[36]

Thus our choice and valuation of the whole world would be different, since by choosing himself man chooses the world.

We know Sartre's thesis—in conformity with Nietzsche's—that value does not reveal itself to a contemplative intuition which would grasp it as being a value, for this would restrict human

---

[34] *L'Age de Raison*, p. 143.
[35] *L'Etre et le Néant*, p. 560.
[36] *Ibid.*, p. 543.

freedom. Value is only revealed to an active freedom which makes it exist by the mere fact of recognizing it as such. It seems that Sartre is afraid that even the values which we set up by a free creative choice would, in the long run, hamper our freedom because they are ready-made things—ready-made by ourselves, to be sure, but nevertheless ready-made with respect to a present or future moment of our existence. Freedom, according to Sartre, is the possibility of "naughting" the past, my own past and all the values created by myself in that past.

In its radicalism this philosophy of freedom tries to avoid our becoming slaves not only of values set up by other people, but also of values set up by ourselves. In Sartre's philosophy Bergson's idea of life as an eternal renewal finds its most perfect expression.

On the other hand, Existentialism dissolves the classical unitary universe of values not only into a multiplicity of axiological microcosms, into millions of creative egos, each of which has its own world of values; it goes so far as to dissolve each ego into thousands of momentary egos, each of which has its own world of values and its own ethics. While for Nietzsche the value-creating moral individualism is only the privilege of certain exceptional beings (*he who cannot command himself has to obey*), for Sartre all men can attain freedom if they make the necessary effort. In the latter's system moral pluralism has reached its utmost extreme.

It is true that in Simone de Beauvoir's *Ethics of Ambiguity* we find something of Nietzsche's postulate to remain faithful to one's creative choice of values. "To will," she says, "means to commit myself to persevere in my will." [37] And in Sartre's more recent writings on literary and political subjects we find a tendency toward fidelity to one's original choice. The tendency, however, is not substantiated by his theoretical philosophy as expounded in *Being and Nothingness*. In dealing with the concrete problems which he encounters as an editor of a monthly magazine, Sartre puts more and more water in his wine. But at this point we wish to examine the pure essence of his philosophy.

[37] *Pour une Morale de l'Ambiguité*, p. 39.

xi

Second Critical Intermezzo

THE DISSOLUTION of the ethical universe in Sartre's philosophy means an extreme axiological atomism, not only in space but also in time. In Sartre's world everyone should invent his own values and norms, and is free to invent them differently on different occasions. However, I do not see how in such a world any community would be possible, not even a community of two persons, for even this would presuppose a certain continuity of evaluation.[1]

The strangest thing in Sartre's philosophy of values is the fact that a constituted value or right, by the mere fact of its being constituted, is an antivalue, or a "stinker's" right. But cannot a constituted value be a positive value, a constituted right be a valuable right? One would think so, since, after all, this seems to depend only on the contents of the value or right. No, says Sartre, a constituted value or right cannot have any positive character because a value or right, by the basic fact that it is constituted, limits our freedom and conceals from ourselves our power of inventing our own paths.

We have here another proof of Sartre's uncompromising absolutism, which is so typical of the Existentialist temperament. It compels him to place the criterion of values in their state of aggregation rather than in their contents, so that only a value *in statu nascendi* would be a positive one, no matter what it expresses.

[1] John Dewey was right in insisting that to form a community "there must be values prized in common." *Freedom and Culture*, New York, Putnam's Sons, 1939, p. 12.

We have our doubts whether this radical axiological individualism of Sartre's is truly sincere. For if, in addition to the values we set up by our individual choices, there are no other values, why should we then suffer from that "ethical anxiety" which pervades the whole of Sartre's work? In our opinion "ethical anxiety" presupposes the belief in absolute standards, independent of our choices—standards which we are afraid of violating by our individual choices of values. Is it not that Existentialists believe in such absolute standards emotionally, while denying them intellectually? Only under this assumption does the concept of "ethical anxiety" appear meaningful.

Stating that "the revolutionary philosophy must always be a philosophy of transcendence," going beyond any state it has reached, Sartre's philosophy implies the idea of a permanent revolution against all constituted values and rights, even those constituted by one's own revolution. Thus the revolutionary would never be able to enjoy the values and rights he has fought for, and we may ask ourselves why he should fight for them? Marjorie Grene is right when she says, "Here revolution for freedom implies revolution against freedom";[2] and she sees in this a hint of a much more profound difficulty in Existential theory: that freedom as such does not appear to be an adequate replacement for more substantive conceptions of values. John Dewey had already insisted on the merely negative character of freedom.

Maintaining that by accepting constituted values and rights man loses his freedom and is debased to thinghood, Sartre's philosophy seems to be inconsistent with any society; for every society, including a socialist one, is built on certain constituted values and rights.

In his attempt to rehabilitate subjectivity, Sartre took into consideration only the subjective side of values. But in addition to expressing the appreciation of some subject and thus a subjective feeling, most values have objective validity and transcend the subject.

How can these two characteristics be reconciled? How can a sentiment be independent of the subject who feels it?

These questions have been answered by Emile Durkheim, the

brilliant French sociologist, who says that our appreciation is objective by the reason of its being collective. There are social judgments which in comparison with individual judgments are objective. The hierarchy of values is thus found to be removed from the subjective and variable sensibilities of individuals.

> The latter find outside themselves a pre-established classi-
> fication which is not their work, which expresses something
> completely different from their personal feelings, and to
> which they are forced to conform.[3]

This fact is explained by Durkheim's whole conception of society as something other than a simple collection of individuals; the system formed by the association of individuals represents a definite specific reality that has its own traits. Naturally nothing can come from the collectivity if individual minds do not exist. But, according to Durkheim, this necessary condition is not sufficient. These minds must be associated and combined in a certain manner for a society to exist. From this combination social life follows; and it is this combination which explains it. In aggregating, interpenetrating, and fusing, the individual souls give birth to a being that constitutes a psychic entity of a new kind. Durkheim calls it "collective consciousness" and considers it as distinct from the individual minds which constitute it.[4]

Of course, this collective consciousness, resulting from the fusion of individual consciousnesses, must also have values which are different from those of the individual components. This explains why the individuals find a pre-established hierarchy of values outside themselves, one which is not theirs, as individuals, which represents something other than their personal feelings, and to which they are forced to conform.

Durkheim has shown that this pressure to conform, which is exerted on each individual by the collective, is the criterion of any social phenomenon, of any society. In rejecting this

---

[3] "Jugements de Valeur et Jugements de Réalité," *Sociologie et Philosophie* (Paris, 1929), pp. 122–123.
[4] *Les Règles de la Methode sociologique*, Paris, 1895; American edition, *The Rules of Sociological Method*, Chicago, Univ. of Chicago Press, 1938, trans. by S. A. Solovay and J. H. Mueller, ed. G. E. G. Catlin.

pressure as an attack on individual freedom, Sartre in effect—and despite his denials—rejects society as a whole. His philosophy of values seems to me much closer to anarchy than to the socialism he says he fights for.

Since social life transcends infinitely the life of the individual in time and in space, it seems to me that its values cannot simply be rejected in the name of a strangely conceived rehabilitation of subjectivity.

In fighting all established values and rights, Sartre uses also the Marxian argument that "the system of values current in a society reflects the structure of that society and tends to preserve it." [5] However, even this argument would not refer to all values without any distinction. The fact that every value is a relation between an object and an appreciating subject permits the designation of all values as "subjective"; and this seems to confirm Sartre's doctrine. However, in my opinion, subjectivity of values does not necessarily mean individuality of values, because, in spite of their being relations of objects to appreciating subjects, values can be independent of the individual peculiarities of the appreciating subjects.

In one of my books I have made the following distinctions: *individual values* are those which depend on the individual peculiarities of the appreciating subjects, while objective values are those which, in spite of their being relations between objects and appreciating subjects, are independent of the individual peculiarities of the appreciating subjects. These objective values can be divided into collective and universal values. Collective values I define as those which depend on the collective peculiarities of the social group that affirms them, and universal values as those which, in spite of their being relations between objects and appreciating subjects, are independent of both the individual and the collective peculiarities of those who affirm them.[6]

If we apply this distinction to Sartre's argument, it seems that only the system of *collective* values current in a society reflects the structure of that society and tends to preserve it; while this

[5] "Matérialisme et Révolution," *Les Temps Modernes*, I (1946), p. 12.
[6] See A. Stern, *Philosophie du Rire et des Pleurs* (Paris, 1949), pp. 207–31; and "Society and Values," *The Personalist* (Los Angeles), XXIX, 3 (Summer 1948), pp. 242–51.

can be affirmed of neither the individual nor the universal values, such as, for instance, those of logical and mathematical truth.

But Sartre makes no distinction among individual, collective and universal values. Thus his struggle against constituted values refers to all of them indiscriminately, and his philosophy of values is a theory that lumps all values together.

On closer analysis, Sartre's postulate that each person has to invent his own system of values, is quite inconsistent, since it arises from a disregard of history. The average individual born into this world has to accept an enormous body of empirical and scientific truths, which have been developed over a period of time and which form the patrimony of human civilization. Of course, everybody has the right to question these truths if he has serious reasons for believing that they are not truth but error. The great reformers of science have done so, to the everlasting benefit of mankind. But it would be foolish to ask—not in the name of truth but in the name of freedom—that each individual perform again all scientific experiments and re-invent all scientific theories, disregarding completely the achievements of four thousand years of civilization—*not* because these achievements are considered *erroneous*, but only because they are *constituted*. It seems to me equally foolish to ask, in the name of freedom, that each individual re-invent all his moral and aesthetic values and disregard those evolved during civilization's four thousand years, not because they are unreasonable but, again, only because they are constituted. When Nietzsche tried to "transvaluate" our moral values, he did so not because they were constituted but because he believed that they were wrong, that they were based on false principle.

On one hand, the re-invention of all moral and aesthetic values by each individual would be practically impossible; on the other hand, it would be extremely unjust toward the history of civilization, that is to say, toward the work of the hundreds of generations that have lived and striven before us. Sartre may easily say, "We do not believe in progress";[7] but this does not sweep away the tremendous body of moral values and orders

[7] *L'Existentialisme*, p. 79.

of moral values established by the instructions of Ptah-Hotep (4000 B.C.), Moses' Ten Commandments, the teachings of Buddha, Confucius, the Stoics, Christ, Spinoza, Kant, and the modern social moralists. The same objection to Sartre's dictum holds true for the body of aesthetic values and standards set up since Myron, Polycletus, and Praxiteles through Michelangelo, Delacroix, and French Impressionism up to Surrealism; or from Homer to Shakespeare, Goethe, and Verlaine; or from Palestrina to Debussy. To disregard these bodies of constituted moral and aesthetic values, *only because they are constituted,* would mean to disregard four thousand years of civilization, of human history; it would mean that each man must begin civilization *ab ovo* and become an artificial primitive.

"I am of bad faith," Sartre says, "if I choose to declare that certain values existed before me." [8] But I think Sartre is of bad faith in denying them, and thus denying history, civilization, and our spiritual heritage, which he actually uses so extensively.

Of course, the individual should not accept all constituted values *blindly,* as if they were things found in nature. For value is a correlative concept which always presupposes subjective valuation. As soon as subjective valuation disappears and is replaced with values which impose themselves not by their merit but by the mere fact of their being constituted, the concept of value itself will disappear, and axiology will turn into ontology. I think I have shown elsewhere that this is one of the consequences of the phenomenology of values of Max Scheler and Nikolai Hartmann.[9] In this respect Sartre's struggle against the "spirit of seriousness" is justified to a certain extent, just as was Nietzsche's war on the "spirit of gravity."

If, following Aristotle's maxim, we try to find the middle road between the extremes of Sartre's Existentialist and Scheler-Hartmann's essentialistic conceptions of values, we should say:

---

[8] *Ibid.,* p. 81.

[9] See A. Stern, *La Filosofía de los Valores,* Segunda edición, revisada y ampliada, Buenos Aires, 1960, esp. pp. 39–84; "Le Problème de l'Absolutisme et du Relativisme axiologiques," *Revue Internationale de Philosophie* (Brussels), (July 1939) and "The Current Crisis in the Realm of Values," *The Personalist,* Univ. of Southern California, School of Philosophy, Los Angeles, XXXI (Summer 1950), pp. 245–259.

Values should be neither *rejected* nor *accepted* for the mere reason of their being constituted. What we should do is to re-evaluate the constituted values, accepting those which we find compatible with our moral and aesthetic conscience, rejecting those which are not, and inventing new values where we find it necessary. Elsewhere I have tried to show on what principles our moral, aesthetic, or, in short, our axiological conscience is built; but the arguments need not be repeated here.[10]

By the proposed re-evaluating of constituted values we would still have enough freedom left to invent new axiological paths, especially in those cases where these values turn out to be insufficient to guide our conduct. In such cases, where action becomes a unique creative response to a unique situation, our value-inventing freedom can manifest itself in full.

However, in those cases where there are systems of constituted values to guide us, we should re-evaluate them and try to understand why they were precious to our fathers and forefathers. Then we may accept or reject them according to their merits. It is in this sense that we should understand Goethe's admonition: "What thou hast inherited from thy fathers, acquire it to make it thine."

[10] See A. Stern, *Die philosophischen Grundlagen von Wahrheit, Wirklichkeit, Wert*, Munich, 1932, esp. pp. 322–430; *La Filosofía de los Valores*, Buenos Aires, 1960, esp. pp. 151–175; *Philosophy of History and the Problem of Values*, The Hague, Mouton & Co., 1962; and "The Current Crisis in the Realm of Values," *The Personalist* (Summer 1950).

FREEDOM IS the all-powerful, triumphant idea in Existentialism. We have already seen how this idea shaped Sartre's ontology, his axiology, and his ethics. Now we shall see that the idea of freedom also dominates Sartre's concept of literature and politics.

Many people have wondered about the intimate link between Existentialism and literature. It cannot be just an historical accident that so many Existentialist philosophers are at the same time playwrights, novelists and—in some cases—poets. To be sure, one reason is that they are gifted for both kinds of expression, the philosophical and the literary one. However, this cannot be the only reason, for it does not explain why this phenomenon occurs so often with Existentialists and so seldom with traditional philosophers. My explanation is the following:

While *science* examines the mutual relationships among empirical objects without any regard for the subject, both *philosophy* and *literature* concentrate on the relationships between man as a subject and the objective world.

In *traditional philosophy*, however, this subject is abstract, it is any *possible* subject in relation to the objective world, it is the subject *as such*, timeless and spaceless. In *literature*, on the contrary, the subject which experiences the objective world is *individualized*, it is a concrete subject of a specific historical time and a specific geographical, cultural, and social environment, with particular psychological, physiological, intellectual, and moral dispositions. In short the subject of literature is a person, an individual, a character, for example, Achilles or Hamlet, while the subject of philosophy is impersonal and disembodied. It is the abstract representative of subjectivity, like Kant's *Bewusztsein überhaupt*, i.e., consciousness in general.

Now, we have seen earlier that Existentialism tries to substitute a concrete, individualized subject, a "man of flesh and blood" here and now, for the abstract, disindividualized subject of traditional philosophy, and with this it tends to eliminate the main difference between philosophy and literature. Therefore, so many Existentialist philosophers—Kierkegaard, Nietzsche, Unamuno, Sartre, Camus, Gabriel Marcel, Simone de Beauvoir, Jean Wahl, etc.—found in the poem, the novel, the drama, perfectly adequate means for the expression of their philosophical ideas.

In his essay, *What Is Literature?*[1] Sartre propounded the theory that literature and any other kind of art is a social phenomenon. It is not just a way of individualistic self-liberation of the writer, and Sartre denies that the author writes for himself. He writes for the reader and needs the reader for the complete peformance of his work, just as the painter needs the spectator and the composer the listener. All the words of a book could be read one by one and still the meaning of the work would not emerge, were it not that the reader's mind gives it meaning. In other words, the meaning of a novel or a poem must be a meaning to the reader; the image suggested by the writer must be formed by the reader's mind; the thought that the author wants to convey must be the reader's thought, the result of the reader's intellectual and emotional activity. Without it, there would not be any literature, any art. Sartre calls this mental and emotional activity of the reader or spectator a "re-invention" and says: "It is the conjoint effort of author and reader which brings upon the scene that concrete and imaginary object which is the work of the mind. There is no art except for and by others."[2]

Sartre recognizes that the author guides the reader's and spectator's mental activity, "but all he does is guide him. The land-

---

[1] *What Is Literature?* New York, Philosophical Library, 1949, trans. of "Qu'est-ce que la littérature?" in *Situations* II, Paris, 1948. See also *Literature and Existentialism*, New York, Citadel Press, 1962.

[2] *Ibid.*, p. 43.

marks he set up are separated. . . . The reader must unite them. . . . In short, reading is directed creation." [3]

It is astonishing that Sartre presents this doctrine as if it were his own, although it had been propounded several decades before him by Benedetto Croce. Sartre, however, never mentioned Croce as the real inventor of the aesthetic doctrine of collaboration of the artist and his public.

Croce had pointed out that in order to have aesthetic experience, the spectator or reader must be actively creating.

> Everyone of us is something of a painter, something of a sculptor, something of a musician, something of a poet: but how little in comparison with those who are so called just because of the higher degree in which they possess the most common dispositions and energy of human nature.[4]

Furthermore, he says, "the little dose of inventive imagination I possess requires the aid of Shakespeare to intensify it to the point of forming within itself the whole tragedy of Othello's passion." [5]

There are different possible explanations of Sartre's adoption of Croce's aesthetic theory without mentioning its author: Without a knowledge of Croce's aesthetics, he may have arrived independently at the same conclusions. Or he might have read

---

[3] *Ibid.*, p. 45.

[4] B. Croce, *Estetica*, Bari, 1928, p. 14; American edition, *Aesthetic as Science of Expression*, New York, Noonday Press, 1953.

[5] *Problem di Estetica*, Bari, 1923, p. 471. Croce's aesthetic doctrine has been widely criticized. In his excellent *Introduction to Aesthetics*, New York, Ronald Press Co., 1952, esp. pp. 145–147, Hunter Mead insisted on the reciprocal influence between the artist's idea and the material in which it is expressed. In the process of artistic expression, which requires the solution of many technical problems, the artist is often forced to modify his original idea. Professor Mead denies that any appreciating layman can possibly reproduce these creative experiences of the artist, so that appreciation cannot be considered a subform of creation. Mead's objection mainly refers to painting, sculpture, and music, but—though to a lesser extent—also holds good for literature; language too has its material and formal problems, unknown to the reader, which the writer has to solve. While the spectator, listener, and reader cannot truly reproduce the artist's creative experience, I think that they must at least perform those mental and emotional processes which the painter, musician, or writer suggests by his work.

Croce's aesthetic theories a long time ago and have assimilated them so fully that he finally believed they were his own. The analysis of his relation to Nietzsche has already shown that Sartre has a tremendous power of assimilation of other people's thoughts. This gift has also its positive aspects, for it leads Sartre sometimes to an interesting development of the foreign ideas he has adopted. This is especially true of Croce's aesthetic doctrine.

Since the creation of the writer can find its fulfillment only in the reader's intellectual and emotional activity, Sartre concludes that the writer appeals to the reader's freedom to collaborate in the production of the work. With this conclusion Sartre goes beyond Croce. If the reader believes in the writer's story, it is because of his free choice to believe in it, because of a kind of "will to believe," to use a term from William James, but without its theological implications. In developing his doctrine Sartre tries to show that the reader's feelings have their source in freedom and are, therefore, generous. "The author writes in order to address himself to the freedom of readers, and he requires it in order to make his work exist." [6]

On the other hand, the writer requires that the reader recognize his creative freedom, and thus reading becomes a pact of generosity between the author and the reader. They must trust each other, and this confidence springs from generosity. All apparent causality in a work of art is based on finality. Sartre gives the example of a certain tree on the first plane of a painting of Cezanne's, which is in its place not because of natural causes, but because of a plan of the whole or a finality, the source of which is the artist's creative freedom.

With the concept of finality Sartre takes up a basic idea of Kant's aesthetics, in spite of criticizing it, and in many respects Sartre's aesthetics is a synthesis of Kant's and Croce's theories. Art, Kant says, should look "as if" it were nature; it must be the result of finality and thus of freedom, but this finality should not be noticeable; the work of art should be intentional, without appearing so. And Sartre says that the final goal of art is to recover the totality of the world "as if" it had its source in

[6] *What Is Literature?*, p. 51.

human freedom, which is about the same. Croce, on the other hand, defined beauty as the successful expression of the artist's intuition and insisted on the necessity that this intuition be re-expressed by the spectator, reader, or listener. Sartre defines aesthetic joy as the feeling "that the work is achieved," and also insists on the joint effort of the author and the reader or spectator in the final production of the work of art. What Sartre adds is the idea that the work of art is an appeal of the creator's freedom to the freedom of the reader or spectator, so that the latter may become a re-creator.[7]

Existentialist humanism insists very strongly on the role of man as a "revealer" of reality, since it is man who sets up the relationships between the parts of reality. Art is a way of revealing and condensing these relationships, and Sartre thinks that one of the chief motives of artistic creation is to make us feel that, as revealers of its relationships, we are essential to the world.

From his thesis that writing is an appeal of the writer's to the reader's freedom and that reading is a pact of confidence and, consequently, of generosity between the two, Sartre draws important political conclusions. The author requires of the reader a free cooperation with his whole person, his thoughts and feelings, his passions and his scale of values. Now Sartre concludes that "the unique point of view from which the author can present the world to those freedoms whose concurrence he wishes to bring about is that of a world to be impregnated always with more freedom." [8] That means that it would be an abuse of the reader's confidence and generosity if the writer should try in his book to justify human injustice. It is impossible, Sartre thinks, that the reader could enjoy his freedom while reading a book "which approves or accepts or simply abstains from condemning the subjection of man by man." [9]

We find here one of the most interesting sociological aspects of Sartre's theory of literature. Literature has been defined by him as an appeal to pure freedom, and he infers that the reader cannot feel in himself a pure freedom when the writer invites him to identify himself with a group of oppressors. "Nobody

[7] *Ibid.*, pp. 48, 57–58, *passim.*
[8] *Ibid.*, p. 63.
[9] *Ibid.*

can suppose for a moment that it is possible to write a good novel in praise of anti-Semitism." [10] Sartre thinks that the same would be true of a novel advocating the oppression of the Negro or of the working class.

From this Sartre draws a very high moral imperative for the writer: that of winning an inner victory over his race, his class, his nation, and his passions in a perpetual effort to liberate himself and other people.

But Existentialism, like phenomenology, is a philosophy of the concrete. It rejects the idea of abstract, "eternal" freedom. Freedom *is* not, but wins itself in a victory over a concrete situation. According to Sartre, there is no freedom except in a given situation, for nobody can shake off fetters by which he has not been chained. These fetters are the given facts and external situations which man, this free project, encounters in his world. Freedom consists in overcoming any given situation.

In this sense also writing, like other human projects, should try to overcome a given situation, and the most powerful situations are those collective ones we call historical. Sartre thinks that literature has to overcome the historical situations given at a definite period and that each book has to propose a concrete liberation, conditioned by a concrete situation.

We see that this leads from the ancient concept of a literature of description and narration to a literature of action, a literature of praxis, engaged in definite projects of liberation. Sartre's exciting drama, *The Respectful Prostitute*, is a perfect expression of his concept of a *littérature engagée*, or committed literature, each manifestation of which is a definite project of liberation. What the writer should do, according to Sartre, is reveal to the reader his power of acting, of creating and destroying in each historical situation. But to be able to fulfill this mission, the novelist must write for a public which has the freedom of changing everything, including the abolition of classes and the realization of the final goal of which Sartre dreams and which he calls a "socialist democracy." [11] Thus the ideal public which Sartre wishes is, according to his confession,

---

[10] *Ibid.*, p. 64.
[11] *Ibid.*, pp. 159, 290.

not the bourgeoisie but the revolutionary working class. Up to now, however, the latter has been very reluctant to accept Sartre as a literary leader.

To Sartre, literature is "the subjectivity of a society in permanent revolution," in constant renewal of its institutions and orders whenever they show a tendency to petrify. This conception corresponds to that ideal of fluidity and creative evolution which, according to Bergson, is one of the features of life, and which Existentialism tries to stimulate in everything touching human existence.

In the eleventh of his famous theses against Feuerbach, Karl Marx had declared that up to now, "the philosophers have only interpreted the world, in various ways; the point, however, is to change it." [12] Sartre, obviously, adopted this battle cry when he wrote: "We are no longer with those who want to possess the world, but with those who want to change it," [13] summoning the writers to engage themselves in the task of disclosing the world in the perspectives of a possible change. He also adopts Marx's ideal of a future "classless society" which would liberate literature.[14]

All this leads certain people to think of Sartre as very close to Communism, but they overlook the deep-seated differences between the philosophy of Communism and the philosophy of Existentialism. Sartre rejects the materialistic ontology of Marxism and its determinism based on Hegel's dialectical logic, which would deprive man of his freedom of choice and suppress his subjectivity.[15] He reproaches Marxism for having become a kind of "Church"[16] by not allowing the development of different shades of opinion within itself.

The Communists, on the other hand, accuse Sartre of egocentrism, nihilism, anti-humanism, idealism, lack of integration

[12] K. Marx, "Thesen über Feuerbach," in Marx-Engels, *Die deutsche Ideologie*, Berlin, 1953, p. 595; English edition, "Theses on Feuerbach," Appendix of *The German Ideology*, ed. by R. Pascal, London, 1928.

[13] *What Is Literature?*, p. 238.

[14] *Ibid.*, cf. pp. 158, 263–64, et al.

[15] "Matérialisme et Révolution," *Les Temps Modernes*, I (June 1946), pp. 14, 22, 25, etc., and especially, *Critique de la raison dialectique*, Paris, Gallimard, 1960, I, pp. 108–110, etc.

[16] *What Is Literature?* pp. 149–150.

of man in society, etc. One of Sartre's Communist critics, the Frenchman Auguste Cornu, now a professor of comparative literature at the University of Leipzig (in East Germany), summarizes these objectives:

> Sartre's Existentialism . . . appears, in sum, as the ideological expression of the decadent bourgeoisie at the period when capitalism is breaking down. It translates this decadence into an escape from reality, the isolation of the individual, and the affirmation of the ego's absolute autonomy and superiority to the world . . .[17]

George Lukacs, Hungary's leading Communist philosopher, recognizes Sartre as an "authentic thinker of high class," but reproaches him for "sketching a caricature of Marxism and winning an easy victory over it." [18]

Existentialist anxiety is described by the Communists as an historical and class phenomenon, a symptom of the decomposition of the bourgeoisie, and Sartre does not deny it. Moreover, he insists that this decomposition can disclose certain aspects of the human condition.

In July 1952, an essay of Sartre's in *Les Temps Modernes*, entitled "The Communists and Peace" (No. 81, pp. 1–50), stirred up much controversy. Its thesis is: "The USSR wants peace and proves it every day." In this essay Sartre considers the Communist Party as the "only political organization" which represents the proletariat in the French parliament, and affirms that it is the right of the workers of his country to demonstrate for peace. There is no doubt that in recent years Sartre's ideas have moved toward the left. While in his novel, *La Mort dans l'Ame* (Death in the Soul), published in 1949,[19] he had accused the USSR of having "thrown death into the soul" of the French proletariat by concluding a pact with Nazi Germany, his article of 1952 criticizes this pact only mildly by saying that it "lacks delicacy." Some American correspondents interpreted Sartre's

---

[17] "Bergsonianism and Existentialism," *Philosophic Thought in France and the United States*, ed. by Marvin Farber, Buffalo, Univ. of Buffalo Press, 1950, p. 166.

[18] *Existentialisme ou Marxisme?* Paris, 1948, pp. 144–148.

[19] American edition, *Troubled Sleep* (New York, 1951).

essay "The Communists and Peace" as proof that its author had "virtually come into the Stalinist camp." They overlooked, however, the deep philosophical abyss which, despite Sartre's admiration for Marx and Lenin, separated him from dialectical materialism.

In his most recent theoretical work, the gigantic *Critique de la Raison dialectique* (Paris, 1960), Sartre tries to justify theoretically his juxtaposition of Existentialism and Marxism, taking issue with the latter's recent direction and even with some of Marx's, Engel's, and Lenin's theses, while recognizing the intrinsic value of Marxist philosophy. We shall speak about this most recent turn in Sartre's thought in our last chapter.

Politically Sartre sides now (1965) with the Communists. In the late forties he had written that the politics of Stalinist Communism was incompatible with the honest exercise of the writer's profession, and had founded a political movement with the neutralist slogan, "neither America nor the USSR, but the intermediary!" At that time a leading Soviet Russian writer called Sartre publicly "a jackal with a ball pen," while several Communist publications referred to him as "enemy of mankind," "poet of slush," and "grave digger of literature." However, in 1963, Simone de Beauvoir wrote the following about Sartre and herself: "Since the beginning of the Cold War we have chosen the USSR. Since she has been devoted to a policy of peace and has destalinized, we do not limit ourselves to preferring her: her cause, her chances, are ours." [20]

Yet Sartre is not, was not, and probably never will be a member of the Communist Party.

[20] S. de Beauvoir, *La Force des Choses*, Paris, 1963, p. 667; American edition, *Force of Circumstance*, New York, Putnam, 1965.

xiii
Existentialism and Resistance

AFTER VICTORY IN EUROPE, when the steel curtain which the Germans had lowered around France had disappeared, the world discovered in that country an intellectual and literary landscape quite different from what it had been before the ordeal. The most striking of the new features of postwar France was Existentialism. And since this philosophy and its literature reflect many problems created by the experiences of the Resistance movement against the German invader, many people considered, and still consider, Existentialism as a philosophy and literature of the French Resistance. This point of view is surely too narrow, even though it contains some truth.

On the one hand, we have to realize that Existentialism was created in the middle of the nineteenth century by the Danish Protestant theologian Søren Kierkegaard and that it later developed in twentieth-century Germany during the period between the two world wars, in the books of Jaspers, Heidegger, and others. Also in France, Existentialism appeared some years before World War II, especially in the writings of Gabriel Marcel. And Sartre himself published his Existentialist novel *La Nausée* in 1938, one year before the outbreak of the war.

On the other hand, we must also realize that up to that time interest in Existentialism was restricted to a few specialists. When, on the eve of World War II, I devoted some of the lectures in one of my philosophy courses at the Sorbonne to an analysis of Heidegger's Existentialism, the majority of my students manifested no more interest in this theory than in the other movements I discussed in that series of lectures. Sartre's novel *La Nausée*, which at this time was already published, did not stir up much philosophical attention; and in comparing it with Sartre's later works we see that, although it posed some Existentialist problems, it offered no definite solutions. Most readers did not even understand the position of the problem of existence in *La Nausée*, because it was posed outside any definite historical situation which they could have shared.

All this changed radically when France, later than other European countries, realized fully that the period since the victory of 1918 had not been one of peace but only of "reprieve" between one world war and another, more terrifying one. Sartre, very ably, compares this discovery to that of Charles Bovary in Flaubert's famous novel, who, finding after his wife's death the letters she had received from her lovers, suddenly saw slipping away twenty years of conjugal happiness he had already lived. "Frenchmen were stupefied on discovering their historicity," Sartre writes.[1] Suddenly they found themselves geographically and historically "situated" as neighbors of a country where an extreme situation had developed which, sooner or later, would engulf them.

In order to understand the relations between Existentialism and the Resistance, we have to realize that the former is a *philosophy of extreme situations*, flourishes in extreme situations, and produces a literature of *these extreme situations*. In average situations man takes existence for granted. He does not question it, because it is as unproblematic and tasteless as the ever-present saliva in our mouths. As Paul Valéry once said, it is only by chance that we think of the permanent conditions of our lives.

In extreme situations, however, the whole trend of our consciousness is changed. In those extreme situations that we call *crises*, man asks himself anew the ultimate questions of the meaning, the essence, and the value of human existence. This questioning and the answers it produces are Existentialism, which thus can be defined as a *philosophy of crisis*.

The crisis which brings about the philosophical meditation on existence can be individual, as in the case of Kierkegaard's

---

[1] *What Is Literature?*, pp. 211–212.

personal drama, or collective, as in the tragedy lived by Sartre and his comrades in the French Resistance movement. When provoked by a collective crisis, the Existentialist movement has much more social dynamism, as a comparison between Sartre's and Kierkegaard's philosophies easily shows. While the latter needed almost three-quarters of a century to be taken into consideration, the former became known throughout the world within two or three years.

There are different kinds of extreme situations which may bring about a crisis of existence in an individual or in a collective group. In his novel *The Plague*, Albert Camus showed how a terrifying epidemic brings people to new reflections on, and new insights into, the essence, meaning, and value of human existence. But among the crises of collectives, the historical kind has a privileged philosophical character, for these crises are produced by man and yet find him hopelessly subjected to their destructive forces.

In Germany the extreme situation bringing about a crisis of existence began in 1933, when Hitler rose to power. There followed a revival of Kierkegaard's Existentialism, which started the opposition against Nazism in that sector of the German Protestant Church close to Karl Barth.

In France the extreme situation provoking a crisis of existence arose in 1940, with the invasion of the country by Hitler's soldiers, the breakdown of the Third Republic and the system of values attached to it, and the enslavement of the whole nation. In this extreme situation Existentialism, as a philosophy calling into question the whole of human existence and its values, received its strongest impetus in France. It ripened into a philosophy which was everybody's concern, and it found its answers in an effort to overcome this crisis of existence.

But does this not mean that philosophy, by its very nature a quest of eternal, timeless truth, becomes subjected to historical relativity? Does it not constitute a new kind of historicism based on the principle of *veritas filia temporis* (truth is a daughter of time)?

We have already seen how Existentialism rejects the concept of eternal truth and resists any kind of flight from existence here and now into timeless entities. To Existentialists, the contemplation of eternal Platonic ideas is a kind of escapism, a running away from the problems of concrete existence, which is always imprisoned in a definite time and a definite space. Existentialism is indeed, in many respects, a historicism.[2] In an earlier discussion of Sartre's axiology we found an astonishing disregard for *past* history and the values it produced during its evolution. It is history already made and no longer interesting to Existentialists, because it no longer "exists." What Sartre calls historicity is *present* history, the history we have to live, into which we are forced by circumstances, a history whose meaning we have to choose, and which we have to overcome, to surpass, and to transcend in a supreme effort toward freedom.

Furthermore, the historicity of Existentialist philosophy and literature does not mean a total subjection of the philosophical quest of the absolute to historical relativity. Sartre clarifies this point in *What Is Literature?* when he says that "the war and the occupation, by precipitating us into a world in a state of fusion, perforce made us rediscover the absolute at the heart of relativity itself."[3] And in another passage of this same book he speaks of the task "to create a literature which unites and reconciles the metaphysical absolute and the relativity of the historical fact."[4] With the term "metaphysical" Sartre designates an effort to embrace human existence and human condition in its totality. That is what French Existentialism tried to do during the crisis created by the extreme historical situation of the German occupation and, especially, of the resistance against it.

Developed during that period of dreadful oppression, Existentialism in its French version is basically a philosophy of freedom, the most radical ever conceived since Fichte, who—and not by pure chance—wrote his philosophy of freedom during the occupation of Prussia by the French troops of Napoleon I.

But the Existentialist concept of freedom is intimately linked to that of situations, as we have seen in the preceding chapter, and as we shall see later in a more detailed way.[5]

We said previously that for Existentialists freedom *is* not, but wins itself in a victory over a concrete situation, which, in many cases, is an historical one. We saw that, according to Sartre, there is no freedom except in a given context, and we tried to clarify this thesis by using the metaphor that nobody can shake off fetters by which he has not been chained. These fetters are all the facts and external situations man encounters in the world, in the being-in-itself. Freedom, as we saw, consists in surpassing and transcending these given situations, or the whole of given facts and obstacles which Sartre calls "facticity." We have to surpass it, projecting ourselves toward goals we have chosen. As Simone de Beauvoir defines ethics, it is "the triumph of freedom over facticity." [6]

In Chapter Nine we referred to Kierkegaard's principle "man chooses himself." This choice of one's self is the fresh decision which enables a man to cut the shackles of the past and to stand free. To make such a new choice of oneself in a free decision is to take one's life in one's own hands, to be the master of oneself, refusing any longer to allow circumstances to play that part. This doctrine of Kierkegaard's has a strong appeal to twentieth-century Existentialists. The tearing away of the self from the past and from other circumstances by a new choice of his being became an integral part of Sartre's Existentialism, when, after its temporary defeat in June 1940, France needed a new beginning. In teaching that such a new beginning was *possible*, through a new choice of one's self, Sartre's doctrine stimulated the fighters of the French underground. He insisted that man is not a thing, determined by other things, either natural or historical, but is free. Yet he has to *use* this freedom to overcome defeat.

All of this helps us to understand why the extreme historical situation of 1940–1945 had so strong an influence on the development of Existentialist ethics and the theory of freedom in

---

[5] Ch. 19, "How Free Is Our Project?"
[6] *Pour une Morale de l'Ambiguité*, p. 64.

France. It was the "test case" of Existentialist freedom, so that Sartre could make the following statement, which only appears paradoxical:

> We were never more free than during the German occupation. We had lost all our rights, beginning with the right to talk. Every day we were insulted to our faces and had to take it in silence. Under one pretext or another, as workers, Jews, or political prisoners, we were deported en masse. . . . And because of all this we were free. Because the Nazi venom seeped even into our thoughts, every accurate thought was a conquest. . . . At every instant we lived up to the full sense of this commonplace little phrase: "Man is mortal." And the choice that each of us made of his life and his being was an authentic choice because it was made face to face with death, because it could always have been expressed in these terms: "Rather death than. . . ." All those among us who knew any details concerning the Resistance asked themselves anxiously, "If they torture me, shall I be able to keep silent?" Thus the basic question of liberty itself was posed, and we were brought to the verge of the deepest knowledge that man can have of himself. For the secret of man is not his Oedipus complex or his inferiority complex: it is this limit of his own liberty, his capacity for resisting torture and death.[7]

What Sartre says here in dry words is exemplified in pathetic action and sacrifice in his tragedy *Morts sans Sépulture*.

Telling us that "even the pincers of the executioner do not deliver us from being free,"[8] the philosopher seems to justify those who see in Existentialist freedom an inner freedom, similar to the Stoic freedom to say "yea" and "nay," when we are confronted with the overwhelming determining power of the external world. The rapid spread of Existentialism in a France occupied by the Germans is often explained, especially in America, by the hypothesis that under the brutal totalitarian oppres-

[7] *The Republic of Silence*, ed. A. J. Liebling, New York, Harcourt, Brace, 1947, pp. 498–499.
[8] *L'Etre et le Néant*, p. 587.

sion free human action toward the world had become impossible, so that the frustrated freedom had to flee into the interior of the human soul. Professor Larrabee, for instance, sees in Existentialism a kind of cult of inner freedom.[9]

Sartre, however, would not accept this interpretation. In his essay *Materialism and Revolution* he opposes vigorously the concept of inner freedom, designating it as an idealistic mystification. "Freedom," he says, "reveals itself only in action, is identical with action." According to him there is no interior or exterior of man, and freedom is engagement in action in order to change the present and to create a future.

Consequently, under the occupation, Existentialism was not a cult of inner, subjective freedom, but a philosophy of action, encouraging action by showing that there is no freedom except through action and that through action there is always another chance left, as long as we exist and are in the making. "We exist only when we are acting," says Jean Blomaert, the underground leader in Simone de Beauvoir's novel *The Blood of Others*.[10]

Thus we realize to what extent the French version of Existentialism is linked to the moral situation of the Frenchman of 1940, who, as the title of one of Sartre's novels hints, had "death in his soul" and needed a doctrine which would help him to overcome this moral death.[11]

Sartre described the "literature of resistance" which this period produced as an example of a literature the purpose of which was not the enjoyment of the reader, but his torment. What it presented was not a world to be contemplated, but to be changed. In the previous chapter we could see Sartre's tendency to generalize this concept of the literature of resistance into that of a literature of historicity and action, which rejects *l'art pour l'art*. It seems doubtful, however, whether that type of literature can be maintained outside extreme situations.

In the novels and dramas which the Resistance produced, we

[9] H. A. Larrabee, "Existentialism Is Not Humanism," *The Humanist*, Vol. 8, No. 1 (Summer 1948) , p. 10.
[10] P. 177.
[11] *La Mort dans L'Ame*, Paris, 1949; American edition, *Troubled Sleep*, New York, Alfred A. Knopf, 1951.

do not find characterization. Existentialism rejects the concept of character, as we shall see in studying its psychoanalysis. The heroes we find in the dramas and novels of the Resistance are free human projects, trapped in certain situations, in extreme situations, which they have to overcome by action, thus winning genuine freedom in the midst of the most terrifying oppression. We see this in Sartre's tragedies, *The Victors* and *The Flies*, and especially in the three novels already published of the tetralogy *The Ways of Freedom*. In the first two of these novels, the action of which takes place before the outbreak of World War II, there are no critical situations, and so we find its hero Mathieu Delarue unable to commit himself. But in the third novel, *Death in the Soul*, France's defeat has occurred. And, for the first time, we see Delarue commit himself in an action of military resistance against the invader in the summer days of 1940, when on the rest of the front the resistance of the French army had ended. Militarily, this solitary action of a handful of French soldiers who volunteered under the command of a lieutenant is meaningless. Morally, however, it is extremely meaningful; for by his decision, engagement, and action the hero wins his liberty, affirming himself as a free human project—a being-for-himself— denying that man is a thing—a being-in-itself, entirely subject to the facticity of a situation. He wins a victory of existence over being.

We find a similar evolution in Jean Blomaert and Hélène, the heroes of Simone de Beauvoir's novel of the Resistance, *The Blood of Others*.

All of this shows that the purpose of the French Resistance movement was not only military and political—although it wanted to harm the enemy's military operations and create a spirit which would make political collaboration impossible. The Existentialists insist, indeed, that the main purpose of the Resistance was philosophical and moral. Simone de Beauvoir, for instance, writes: "The Resistance did not pretend to have a positive efficiency; it was negation, revolt, martyrdom, and in this negative movement freedom was positively and absolutely confirmed." [12]

[12] *Pour une Morale de l'Ambiguité*, p. 184.

In addition to this philosophy of freedom, the French Resistance also needed a new, subjectivistic philosophy of values. This, too, was offered by Existentialism. To understand the necessity of such a philosophy at that time, we have to realize that during the four years of German occupation the young Frenchmen lived in a "vacuum of values." They could no longer believe in the hierarchy of values in which they had been educated—that of the Third Republic; for these values had proved too weak to impede their country's catastrophe. But they were also unable to believe in the new values proclaimed by the German invader and his French lackeys, led by the collaborator Pétain. Could they believe in the values propagated through the London radio by the exiled General de Gaulle? But he had been condemned to death as a traitor to his country by France's official courts, and every "patriot" was forbidden to listen to his speeches as though they were the devil's gospel.

The transvaluation of all values in which the young Frenchmen had been educated, created total bewilderment. From one day to the next they heard the negative value of freedom and the positive value of servitude proclaimed, along with the negative value of equality and the positive value of a hierarchy of superior and inferior races, of masters and slaves; as well as the negative value of the idea of a brotherhood of nations and the positive value of treason to an allied nation and one's own nation; the negative value of intelligence and the positive value of instinct; the negative value of law and the positive of violence; the negative value of democracy and the positive of dictatorship; all presented with the quavering voice of a kind old grandfather who wanted to protect his poor immature grandchildren. Those who, on the eve of invasion, had been stigmatized as traitors, were now praised as heroes, while the heroes of yesterday were stigmatized as traitors. The "good" of yesterday became the "evil" of today; the "evil" of yesterday, the "good" of today.

I lived this period in France as a soldier in the French army, and I was a witness to the total axiological bewilderment of my younger comrades, who no longer knew what to believe. In this tragic situation only one alternative was left to these young Frenchmen: either to believe no longer in any value and to become nihilists; or to choose a system of values of their own, using their liberty of choice, in complete isolation, without backing by any recognized, official ethics, and to assume total responsibility for their choice.

The nihilists became epicures, purveyors of the black market, and agents of the enemy. Those who used their axiological freedom to set up new values and norms in which they could believe joined the underground and became soldiers of the Resistance. Their lot was "total responsibility in total solitude," one of Sartre's definitions of freedom.

It *was* a total solitude; for the society surrounding them— a nation officially collaborating with the enemy—refused to support them either because of fear or because of compliance. And it *was* a total responsibility; for when they chose to go to the *maquis* and to fight the government of their own country, the lives of these men and of their comrades were at stake—perhaps, also, their honor as Frenchmen. For who guaranteed them that *they* were right and Pétain, the revered hero of Verdun, who once had saved the country, was wrong? What if they had been mistaken in their choice of democratic values and this choice would now cause imprisonment and torture to members of their family, torture and death for the comrades under their orders or for themselves? We understand easily the terrifying anxiety arising from this responsibility, which few were ready to share with them. Not only did the official moral code *not* back up their lonely choice of values, it condemned it vigorously. Only through total engagement in action could these young men overcome their feeling of being forsaken.

Thus, life in France from 1940 to 1944 turned out to be a practical school of Existentialism for the best elements of the nation. Through a terrifying experience the fighters of the French Resistance learned that man "is condemned to be free" in his evaluations and decisions, that he has to act to be free, and that it is through anxiety that he becomes conscious of his freedom. It was the life of the *maquis* that taught them the basic principles of Sartre's ethics: There is only one *good* for the individual—to recognize his freedom and act while recognizing it; there is only one *evil*—to deny one's freedom in order to evade the responsibility it implies; and, finally, that in choosing freedom for himself every *maquisard* chose the freedom of all.

But if, during the occupation, the men of the Resistance formed a community, which Sartre calls the "republic of silence," it was only because they remained faithful to the values they had chosen in their aloneness. And thus they were, perhaps, more Nietzscheites than Sartreites.

Psychologically speaking, the German occupation of France was divided into two phases. In the first, the invader tried to use the velvet touch in a vain effort to win over the French people and to make them accept slavery under the euphemism of collaboration. In the second phase, when this hope had faded, in the middle of 1942, and the Resistance had grown stronger, the monster used its claws in the bloodiest tortures man can imagine. To these two periods correspond two different kinds of literature of the Resistance, and, to a certain extent, even two different philosophies. Typical of the first period was Vercors' novel *Le Silence de la Mer* (The Silence of the Sea); typical of the second, Sartre's tragedies *The Flies* and *The Victors*.

In the philosophical interpretation of the two phases of French history from 1940 to 1945 we may distinguish two different points of view. In 1943, Sartre published his main philosophical work, *Being and Nothingness*, which was conceived partly before the war, partly on the Alsatian front, and partly during the first period of the occupation. In this work we find the relativistic theory of values, which we discussed in a previous chapter,[13] and which was applied by many members of the Resistance. This relativism Sartre never revoked. However, in a retrospective appraisal of the second period of the German occupation, he developed certain ideas which are entirely incompatible with that theory. This was done in his book *Situations II*, published in France in 1947, two years after the liberation. Describing the devilish tortures suffered by the members of the Resistance who were captured by the Nazis, Sartre writes: "We heard whole blocks screaming, and we understood that 'evil,' fruit of a free and sovereign will, is like 'good,' absolute."[14]

Now if good and evil are absolute values, then we have returned to Platonism and Sartre's relativism is void. I would,

13 Ch. 10, "Freedom and Values."
14 *Situations II*, p. 248.

however, not draw this conclusion; for axiological relativism is an inescapable consequence of atheistic Existentialism, and the latter was never revoked by Sartre. There has been no change in his theoretical philosophy, and I am inclined to consider this contradiction as one of those inconsistencies in his work which show that emotionally Sartre is an axiological absolutist. Let us not forget Pascal's dictum: *"Le coeur a ses raisons que la raison ne connaît point"* [15]—The heart has its reasons which reason does not know.

[15] *Pensées,* IV, 277, p. 458.

xiv
Our "Being-for-Others" and Their "Gaze"

Agnes was a pretty girl living in a small American town. Her father put her on a train, gave her fifty dollars and promised to send her the same amount monthly for a time. She was supposed to go to Birmingham, Alabama, to study shorthand at a business college. But she never took the courses; instead, she became a manicurist in a cheap barbershop. Men came to the shop, put their hands down the neck of her dress and squeezed her. Soon she was "making more money on the outside after hours" than at the table. All of her family—Papa, Mama, and the others—knew that she lived in a cheap hotel in New Orleans and that she was not a stenographer. But when she went home, once a year, at Christmas, they did not say anything. They just sat and looked at her all the time.

Agnes became desperate, almost hysterical: "Once a year, at Christmas, they sit and look at me, but none of them ever says anything about it. They all sit in the parlor saying to themselves, 'We are looking at you, Agnes.'"

The story, "We Are Looking at You, Agnes," is told by Erskine Caldwell [1] with masterly simplicity and gives an impressive idea of the inexorable feeling of guilt and shame the "gaze" of other people can arouse in us. Did Erskine Caldwell realize that the basic thesis of his story had been expressed at the beginning of the nineteenth century by Hegel in the *Phenom-*

---

[1] "We Are Looking at You, Agnes," *We Are the Living*, New York, Viking Press, 1933, pp. 17–25.

enology of the Spirit? There Hegel says: *"Das Selbstbe-wusstsein ist an und für sich, indem und dadurch, dass es für ein Anderes an und für sich ist: das heisst, es ist nur ein Aner-kanntes."* [2] In other words our self-consciousness exists only because it exists for another person. Thus self-consciousness is basically "acknowledgment" by another person; and our being-for-others is a necessary condition for the development of our self-consciousness, our being-for-ourselves. Or, as Sartre puts it, "the way to interiority passes through the other person." [3] The other person is interesting to me only to the extent that he reflects myself, that is to say, to the extent to which I am an object to him. Since I am an object only in so far as I exist for the other person, I have to obtain from that other person the acknowledgment of my being. The other person is the mediator between me and myself. Thus my being-for-myself depends on my being-for-others. "By its very nature shame is acknowledg-ment; I acknowledge that I am as the other one sees me." [4]

We see that Hegel's theory of the lack of independence of our self-consciousness has become an important part of Sartre's Existentialism, in spite of the fact that, historically, with Kierke-gaard, Existentialism sprang from an opposition to Hegel's philosophy.

Hegel's thesis that self-consciousness is real only as long as it knows its echo in another person has been developed and com-pleted by Sartre's theory of the "gaze." If I exist for the other person, I do so through his gaze (*le regard*). Consequently my fundamental relation to the other person is determined by the permanent possibility of being seen by him. The gaze of the other self reveals to me not only that I am an object to him, but also that the other self is a subject. "It is my shame or my pride which reveals to me the gaze of the other self. . . . Shame is . . . shame of oneself; it is the acknowledgment that I am that object which another self looks at and judges." [5]

---

[2] "Herrschaft und Knechtschaft," *Phänomenologie des Geistes,* ed. G. Lasson, Leipzig, 1907, p. 123; American edition, *Phenomenology of Mind,* New York, Macmillan, 1931.

[3] *L'Etre et le Néant,* p. 292.

[4] *Ibid.,* p. 276.

[5] *Ibid.,* p. 319.

Thus we see that in his short story "We Are Looking at You, Agnes," Erskine Caldwell expressed a fundamental Existentialist thesis—and this in 1933, years before Sartre started with Existentialism.

William Faulkner also gives an impressive example of the gaze of other people as revealers of our moral being, and Sartre expressly referred to this brilliant American writer in his principal philosophical treatise. The French Existentialist cited a scene in the novel *Light in August*, in which Faulkner describes the stabbing to death of the alleged Negro Christmas by Percy Grimm, the fighter for white supremacy. The victim does not resist, but before dying he "looks at" his murderer and his helpers.

> He just lay there, with his eyes open and empty of everything save consciousness. . . . For a long moment he looked up at them with peaceful and unfathomable and unbearable eyes. . . . Upon that black blast the man seemed to rise soaring into their memories forever and ever. They are not to lose it, in whatever peaceful valleys, beside whatever placid and reassuring streams of old age, in the mirroring faces of whatever children they will contemplate old disasters and newer hopes. It will be there, musing, quiet, steadfast, not fading and not particularly threatful, but of itself alone serene, of itself triumphant.[6]

In France's own literature of the nineteenth century, namely in Zola's powerful novel *Thérèse Raquin*, we find another excellent example of the Hegelian and Sartrean ideas of the other person serving, through a gaze, as a mediator between us and ourselves. There it is the judging and crushingly condemning gaze of a mute and lame old woman which drives the heroine, Thérèse Raquin, and her former lover, Laurent, to the realization of their guilt as murderers and to suicide.

Sartre's heroes sometimes express feelings similar to those of Zola's and Faulkner's murderers or of Caldwell's Agnes, whose shame and guilt, aroused by the mere gaze of the members of her family, like the gaze of Gorgon Medusa, petrify her into

[6] *Light in August*, New York, Random House, 1950, p. 407.

the being she really is. Everybody's gaze can become the petrifying gaze of Medusa, changing the other for-itself into an in-itself and depriving it of its freedom. The most interesting human document of this kind is the letter that Mathieu receives from his false friend Daniel, in Sartre's novel *The Reprieve*. It reads, in part, as follows:

> You must have experienced, in the subway, in the foyer of a theater, or in a train, the sudden and irksome sense that you were being looked at from behind. . . . Well, that is what I felt for the first time, on September 26, at three o'clock in the afternoon, in the hotel garden. . . . I became more compact and concentrated, I was both transparent and opaque, I existed in the presence of a look. . . . Ah, Mathieu, what a discovery! I *was seen*, I struggled to know myself . . . and all the time I was seen, the inexorable look, an invisible steel blade, was on me. . . . Believe me, I first loathed this incessant violation of myself. . . . What anguish to discover that look as a universal medium from which I can't escape! But what a relief as well! I know at last that I am. I adapt for my own use, and to your disgust, your prophet's foolish, wicked words: "I think, therefore I am." . . . I say: "*I am seen, therefore I am.*" I need no longer bear the responsibility of my turbid and disintegrating self: he who sees me, causes me to be; I am as he sees me. . . .

Then, although he is a businessman who says he has never read Hegel, Daniel comes to the following Hegelian conclusions:

> For one instant you were the heaven-sent mediator between me and myself, you perceived that compact and solid entity which I was and wanted to be in just as simple and ordinary a way as I perceived you. . . . I then understood that one could not reach oneself except through another's judgment. . . . Without me you would be that same unsubstantial entity that I am for myself. It is by my agency that you can at times get an occasional and doubtless rather exasperating glimpse of yourself—as you really are. . . .[7]

---

[7] *The Reprieve*, pp. 405–407.

This letter may seem psychologically improbable, when we realize that it comes from a greedy businessman without philosophical education, a low character and a pederast. However, philosophically, it is a very important document, and the readers of Sartre's novels who are not familiar with his ontology may be puzzled by it. But once seen within the system of this ontology, everything becomes clear. Let us sum up some of the basic philosophical implications of this letter.

In our previous chapters we have seen that Sartre distinguishes two modalities of being: "being-in-itself" and "being-for-itself." To this, now, a third modality is added: that which Sartre designates with Hegel's term "being-for-others" (*être-pour-autrui*).

The being-in-itself, which is that of inanimate objects, was characterized as being what it is, as coinciding with itself, as being subjected to the principle of identity, as including no negation, as "as full as an egg."

The being-for-itself, or human consciousness, was characterized as being what it is not and not being what it is. It *is* not at all, but is always creating itself; consequently, it never coincides with itself, thus falling outside the principle of identity. It is through the being-for-itself that nothingness comes into the world. Being never what it is, being always separated by a region of nothingness from what it has to be, the being-for-itself, or human consciousness, is "full" of nothingness, of negation; it is an ever-questioning hollow projected toward the future, toward its possibilities, *"un creux toujours futur,"* as Paul Valéry says in *Le Cimetière marin.* The being-for-itself is nothing but the pure "naughtization" of the being-in-itself; it is like a "hole in the womb of being." [8]

But we have seen that man's freedom, also, coincides with this hole, this nothingness which is in his heart and which compels him to make himself into something instead of being something. Thus being-for-itself is basically freedom, which also means that it is "transcendence"; for by its freedom the being-for-itself is able to transcend or to surpass itself, to go beyond itself, and also to surpass or transcend the being-in-itself, the brute inani-

[8] *L'Etre et le Néant*, p. 711.

mate things, by projecting itself toward its possiblities. Sartre speaks of a "transcendence which surpasses and naughts the given data toward an end." [9] The being-for-itself is always consciousness *of* something and through it only consciousness of itself, so that it is always outside itself, transcending itself. It is a free projection toward its possibilities, it "naughts" any given datum, and it is defined by its ends. Sartre compares being-for-itself, or human consciousness, to a "gliding slope," on which we cannot sit down without being thrown outside, toward the being-in-itself. This, too, is a picture of transcendence, which, according to Heidegger, coincides with consciousness and existence, or *Dasein.* "Holding itself into nothingness existence (*Da-sein*) is already beyond the real in totality. This 'being beyond' (*Hinaussein*) the real, we call transcendence." [10] Thus, as Heidegger explains in *Vom Wesen des Grundes*, it is almost tautological to say "the human being transcends itself." To "exist" means, etymologically, *ex-sistere*, to stand out or to step out.

Now comes the third modality of being, the "being-for-others." At first the other person I see appears as a mere being-in-itself, a phenomenon of nature, no different from all the inanimate bodies I perceive around myself. It is through his gaze that the other person reveals himself to me as a being-for-itself, a subject, a consciousness, a free project of itself, able to transcend itself and to transcend all given data toward its own possibilities, its own ends. But this means also that by his gaze this other person can transcend me and change me from a being-for-itself into a being-in-itself, from a free project into a determined thing, into a solidified object—as I can change him by my gaze. "The people I see are congealed by me into objects, I am in relation to them what they are in relation to me." [11] By looking at other people, I measure my power, and by looking at me, they measure theirs. Thus being-for-others is, basically, *conflict*, a struggle of two transcendences, each of which tries to "out-transcend" the other.

Of course, it is not precisely the eyes, as physiological organs, which look at me: it is the other person as a subject, a con-

9 *Ibid.,* p. 597.

10 *Was ist Metaphysik?* Frankfurt, Klostermann, 1960, p. 35; American edition, *Existence and Being,* Chicago, Henry Regnery & Co., 1949, 1951.

11 *L'Etre et le Néant,* p. 324.

sciousness. Thus the gaze of the other person includes all kinds
of judgments and evaluations. Being seen by the other person
means to grasp oneself as an unknown object of uncognizable
judgments. A judgment, according to Sartre, is the transcendental
act of a free person. The fact of being seen changes me into a
being without defense against a freedom which is not my freedom. Being seen by the other person makes us slaves; looking
at the other person, we are masters. I am a slave as long as I
depend in my being on the freedom of another self, which is
not mine but which is the condition of my being. And I am
master when I make the other self depend for its being on my
freedom. It was Hegel who introduced this distinction between
"slave" and "master" (*Herr und Knecht*) in the theory of
knowledge. For him, there are two forms of our consciousness:
"*die eine das selbständige, welchem das Fürsichsein, die andere
das unselbständige, dem das Leben oder das Sein für ein anderes
das Wesen ist: jenes ist der Herr, dies der Knecht*"[12]—the one
is the independent [consciousness], to which the being-for-itself
is the essence, the other is the dependent one, to which the life or
the being-for-others is the essence: the former is the master,
the latter the slave.

Sartre applies this distinction of Hegel's and thinks that it is
my gaze which would change the other person into a slave and
the other person's gaze which would change me into a slave and
make him the master of the situation. As a slave a person loses
all his possibilities and becomes a "transcended transcendence."

Thus by the appearance of the other person, the other self,
a new aspect comes into my situation, an aspect which I cannot
master, which escapes me on principle, since it is that of the
other person. This unforeseeable reverse side of reality is that
which André Gide calls "*la part du diable*" ("the devil's share"),
an aspect of existence which Sartre sees expressed especially in
the work of Franz Kafka.

Of course, I can regain my own freedom and transcendence,
using my gaze to transcend the other person's freedom and transcendence, changing his subjectivity into a petrified object, alie-
nating his possibilities. But then the other self can look again

---

[12] *Phänomenologie des Geistes*, p. 127.

at me and again transcend and enslave my freedom and transcendence. And so on.

One remembers a scene in Chaplin's remarkable picture, *The Dictator*, where Hitler and Mussolini, each sitting in a kind of dentist's chair, are lifting their seats by means of cranks, so that each in turn would rise above the level of the other and surpass him. Robert Campbell sees in this scene a witty symbol of the struggle between two transcendences.[13] And we agree with him. However, the matter itself is far from being funny. Sartre realizes this. It would be a vain effort, he says, for man to try to escape the dilemma, "to transcend the other one or to allow one's self to be transcended by the other one." And he concludes that the essence of human relations is not Heidegger's *Mitsein* ("being-with"), *but conflict*.

And now Sartre tries to show that all possible relations be-tween one's own and any other self—even love—are only differ-ent forms of conflict. "Conflict is the original sense of the being-for-others." [14] All relations between persons are attempts by each of them to subjugate or to possess the other's freedom. No ill will is the cause of this situation, but the mere fact of existence. As soon as I exist, I establish a factual limit to the freedom of the other person. I *am* that limit, and each of my projects draws that limit around the other self. Sartre concludes that *"respect for the other person's freedom is a vain word."* [15]

This is a rather sad confession from so passionate a fighter for human freedom as Sartre. Besides, his emphasis on conflict is too strong. Hayakawa tried to show—not without success—that cooperation, rather than conflict, is the great governing principle of society. Even organized competition among men would be impossible without a tremendous amount of cooperation taken for granted. We see this, for instance, in the case of a strike, which is a withdrawal of cooperation.[16] Emile Durkheim and John Dewey also insisted strongly on social solidarity and joint intercourse as governing principles in society.

---

[13] *Jean-Paul Sartre ou une Littérature philosophique*, Paris, 1947, p. 120.
[14] *L'Etre et le Néant*, p. 431.
[15] *Ibid.*, p. 480.
[16] S. Hayakawa, *Language in Thought and Action*, New York, Harcourt, Brace & World, 1949, pp. 117–18.

While Sartre thinks that, owing to the inevitable conflict among men, the respect of other persons' freedom is a vain word, Simone de Beauvoir seems less pessimistic than her master, for she requires that we "must always respect the freedom of other people and help them to liberate themselves." [17]

Before closing the first part of this book, there is still more to be said about the petrification of the other subject by means of the gaze. Why is it that the gaze petrifies the other subject and changes it into an object? Well, we know that, according to Sartre's Existentialism, the being-for-itself, or subject, *is* not, but is always in the making, always becoming. But when I am looking at the other person, that is, when I am judging him, I do not judge him as far as he is becoming—because I cannot know his possibilities—but as far as he *is*, at the very moment of my judgment. Thus, I am perpetuating this moment of his evolution. It is just as though I should see the projection of motion pictures showing a person walking toward a certain goal, and, suddenly, I should stop unrolling the film, before the man has reached his goal. He would then be perpetuated, or petrified, in the momentary position of having, for instance, one foot raised to take the next step, which he would never make. He would no longer give the impression of a subject projected toward its possibilities, but would appear as an inanimate object. Expressed in Sartre's terminology, this means that by the gaze of the other one, the being-for-itself is changed into a being-in-itself, into a thing. It is nailed down as it is in the moment of the judgment, as if it were what it is and were no longer in the making. But the being-for-itself can never coincide with itself. It is always in the making and, therefore, always "on reprieve," since its future is its free project. Only at the moment of the self's death, when the being-for-itself has changed completely into a being-in-itself and has lost all its possibilities, only then "the chips are down"—only then does this person coincide with himself.

Thus all our judgments on a living person are provisional; for by looking at him—with our physical or our mental eye—we change him into a being-in-itself and disregard his potential

[17] *Pour une Morale*, p. 85.

freedom, his future possibilities, which we cannot know and by which he may refute our present judgment. The gaze of Medusa, petrifying a person and obliging him to be forever what he is at a given moment, may thus be an injustice toward him. But this gaze will be a relief to those persons who want to be delivered from their freedom and their responsibility for continuously creating themselves.

It is this kind of relief which was expressed in Daniel's letter, when he wrote: "What a relief. . . . I need no longer bear the responsibility of my turbid and disintegrating self: he who sees me causes me to be; I am as he sees me. . . ." [18]

By gladly accepting the calm and permanent being of an inanimate thing, delivered of freedom, responsibility, and anxiety, Daniel renounces his human condition and flees into "bad faith." We will meet more men of this type in our discussion of Sartre's Existential psychoanalysis.

[18] *The Reprieve*, p. 407.

PART TWO

SARTRE'S EXISTENTIAL PSYCHOANALYSIS

Choice and Complex

"EMPIRICAL PSYCHOANALYSIS tries to determine the *complex*.
. . . Existential psychoanalysis tries to determine the *original*
choice." [1]

With these words Sartre defines the basic difference between
Freud's psychoanalysis, which he calls "empirical," and his own.
Does this mean that Sartre rejects the concept of complex? Not
at all. We shall see later that he himself uses the concept of complex and even introduces two new complexes, which he calls
Acteon complex and Jonah complex. He does not even deny
the existence of Freud's Oedipus complex or Adler's inferiority
complex, but does deny that they are irreducible, ultimate data.
Sartre believes these complexes can be traced back to something
more fundamental, namely, man's original choice. As we consider
the assumptions of his Existential philosophy, we shall understand easily the goal of his type of psychoanalysis.

We have only to remember the fundamental thesis of Sartre's
Existentialism: existence precedes essence. According to this
assumption man exists first; he springs up in the world and is
defined afterward. At the beginning he *is* not anything. He will
become what he has projected to become, but there is nothing
previous to his project of himself. And his project expresses his
original choice. Since, according to Sartre's Existentialism, man *is*
his choice, we understand why this philosopher had to establish
a new discipline, Existential psychoanalysis, which was to attempt to determine man's original choice, and his fundamental
project with the individual varieties that constitute each person
in his uniqueness.

[1] *L'Etre et le Néant*, p. 657.

The first principle of Existential psychoanalysis is that man is a unified whole and not an arithmetical sum. In this respect Sartre's new discipline is in accord with Freud's psychoanalysis, with Adler's individual psychology and with other trends in modern psychology. Now if man is a whole, he must express himself entirely in even his most insignificant and most superficial conduct. There is no individual taste or relationship that would not be revealing. Thus the aim of Existential psychoanalysis is to decipher the empirical behavior of man and to interpret it. Sartre wishes to reveal the apparently differing significances implied in each human act and then to trace all of them back to successively fewer and more inclusive significances, up to an ultimate significance. He recognizes that he has this starting point in common with Freud. "For Freud as for ourselves, an act is not limited to itself; it refers immediately to deeper structures." [2]

Like Freud, Sartre considers the human act as "symbolic," as translating a deeper desire which has to be interpreted with reference to an initial determination. However, this determination is not a "complex" nor a "libido," nor a Nietzschean "will to power," nor an Adlerian "superiority goal." It is an original choice and a fundamental project, whereas all the terms of Sartre's predecessors include secondary conditioning. The choice is a choice of one's position in the world and therefore involves the person as a whole, just as the complex does. Furthermore, choice and complex are both previous to logic. It is the fundamental project that determines a person's attitude toward logic.

We know that Alfred Adler deduces the inferiority complex from the inferiority of the child's organs, even the organs of the healthy child, as compared with the organs of an adult. For Sartre the inferiority complex is a free project of a person's own being-for-himself in the world, confronted with the other person. If I am that person, I myself have *chosen* that inferiority, which I recognize and against which I struggle. My inferiority complex is nothing but the projection of my initial plan of failure organized into a system of individual failures. One who suffers from inferiority has chosen to be the executioner of himself.

[2] *Ibid.*, p. 535.

He makes of himself the means to attain certain ends. A chosen humiliation, like masochism, for instance, can be used as a tool for delivering him from the existence as a being-for-itself; it can be an initially chosen project for getting rid of his own anxiety-inspiring freedom for the benefit of other people. In choosing inferiority our fundamental project may be to have our being-for-itself entirely absorbed by our being-for-others. For Sartre, the inferiority complex can arise in us only if it is founded on a free apprehension of our being-for-others. The inferiority we feel may be the chosen tool to make us similiar to a thing, a being-in-itself, free from responsibility.

> Thus inferiority is a free and total project of myself as inferior to others; it is the manner in which I choose to accept my being-for-others, the free solution I give to the existence of the other person, that insuperable scandal.[3]

However, the fact that someone chooses inferiority does not mean that he is content with an *aurea mediocritas,* for in so choosing he creates the revolt and despair which reveal that inferiority. I may, for instance, persist in doing a certain type of work because I am inferior to the task, while in another domain, I would be able to do a satisfactory job. A man may choose a fruitless endeavor *because* it is fruitless, perhaps because he prefers to be the last one rather than to disappear in the crowd. "But it is clear that I can choose as my field of action the domain in which I am *inferior* only if that choice implies the deliberate *will* to be *superior*."[4] The man who chooses to be an inferior artist, Sartre says, necessarily chooses to want to be a great artist; otherwise the inferiority would not be felt or recognized. The choice of inferiority implies, according to Sartre, the permanent realization of the "distance" between the goal and the actual result.

All these Sartrean ideas sound strangely familiar to any student of Adler's individual psychology. But Sartre insists that man "chooses" inferiority, and in so doing, and maintaining it, he is of "bad faith"; for he is fleeing from the acknowledgment of the

---

[3] *Ibid.*, p. 537.
[4] *Ibid.*, p. 551.

true aims he has chosen, and which he tries to hide from himself in order to escape the responsibility for his choice. Later, we shall examine this concept of bad faith, especially in relation to the "unconscious," as that term is used by Freud and rejected by Sartre.

This short analysis of Sartre's interpretation of the inferiority complex shows that the French Existentialist is much closer to Adler than he may know or want to admit. Adler too had recognized that inferiority was, in a way, our free choice:

> In psychology we cannot speak of causality or determinism. . . . Man makes one thing the cause and another thing the effect, and then joins the two. Much appears as causally determined, although causality was only attributed to it. This goes so far that even *organ inferiorities* are effective only to the extent that we *wish*. Man can raise these inferiorities to rank and dignity; he can make them a cause.[5]

Furthermore, when Sartre maintains that the choice of inferiority implies the deliberate will to superiority, he also is in accord with Adler, who said:

> A thoroughgoing study has taught us that we can best understand the manifold and diverse movements of the psyche as soon as our most general presupposition, that the psyche has as its objective the *goal* of superiority, is recognized.[6]

It is well known that Adler interprets man's superiority goal as a compensation and overcompensation of an inferiority complex. Sartre's affirmation that the choice of inferiority implies the deliberate will to be superior is very close to Adler's conception. And if the Viennese psychiatrist insisted that the patient "is intensifying his feeling of inferiority and *yet freeing himself from responsibility* by attributing this inferiority to heredity, the fault of his parents, or other factors,"[7] he expressed an idea

[5] *The Individual Psychology of Alfred Adler*, ed. by H. L. and R. Ansbacher, New York, Basic Books, 1956, p. 91.
[6] *The Practice and Theory of Individual Psychology*, p. 7.
[7] *Ibid.*, p. 104.

which, thirty years later, was developed by Sartre in his famous doctrine of "bad faith." Sartre says: "The artist who wants to be great and chooses for himself inferiority, intentionally maintains that *distance*; like Penelope, he destroys during the night what he has done during the day."[8] This is a bright observation, but we have to remind Sartre that Alfred Adler devoted a whole study to "the Problem of Distance," insisting that a person suffering from an inferiority complex "attempts unerringly to interpose a 'distance' between himself and the anticipated act or decision. . . ."[9] Adler even used the example of Penelope;[10] but Adler did this in 1914, and Sartre enunciated his approach in 1943. Sartre recognized that a part of his Existential psychoanalysis had been influenced by Adler:

> Thus, as one sees, our analysis allows us to accept the two levels where Adler locates the complex of inferiority: like he does, we admit a fundamental recognition of this inferiority, and like he does, we admit a vague, ill-balanced development of acts, works and affirmations destined to compensate or to mask this deep feeling.[11]

Yet, as we saw and shall see to a larger extent, Sartre's indebtedness to the creator of Individual Psychology goes far beyond the two theses mentioned.

Sartre's Existential psychoanalysis starts from the premise that neither Freud's nor Adler's complexes, nor their instincts (*Triebe*), are really fundamental projects, original choices. In Sartre's eyes, Freud's libido and Oedipus complex and Adler's goal of superiority and inferiority complex are only "psycho-biological residues" lacking self-evidence; they cannot constitute the ultimate term of our analysis. One may easily conceive a man whose libido would not be his original and undifferentiated choice and who would not express himself by a will to superiority. Sartre claims these instincts and complexes are not general character traits of all men and are not irreducible. They can be traced

---

[8] *L'Etre et le Néant*, pp. 551–552.
[9] Adler, *op. cit.*, p. 104.
[10] *Ibid.*, p. 105.
[11] *L'Etre et le Néant*, p. 552.

back to the "fundamental project," expressing our original choice which is the *being* of man, because, for Existentialism, there is no difference between existing and choosing oneself.

What is the difference between Sartre's "fundamental project" and any other project, such as those expressed in complexes and instincts or in other, less basic choices? The answer is that Sartre's "fundamental project" is a project which does not concern a man's relation to this or that particular object in the world. The fundamental project, which is what a man *is,* expresses his being-in-the-world as a whole; and since the world itself is revealed only in the light of a goal, the fundamental project posits as its goal a certain relationship to being in general which a man chooses to maintain. Existential psychoanalysis is a specific phenomenological method which aims at explaining a man's fundamental project.

THERE ARE MANY POINTS on which Sartre's Existential psychoanalysis is in accord with the empirical psychoanalysis of Freud and his followers. For instance, both of them take into consideration the *situation* of the person to be analyzed, since both deal with man as he lives in the world. Both try to reconstitute the life of the individual from birth to the beginning of the analysis, using any kind of objective material, such as letters, witnesses, etc. Each "historical" fact in the life of the individual is considered as a factor and a symbol of his psychic evolution.

On the other hand, there are many basic problems on which the Viennese classical psychoanalysis and its Parisian existentialist counterpart are in complete disagreement. One of them is Freud's determinism. To be sure, it is not a "horizontal" determinism, which would explain an action merely by its temporal antecedents; it is a "vertical" determinism, explaining an act by its simultaneously existing, underlying desire, which, itself, rests on a still deeper complex. However, since, for Freud, complexes are acquired in early childhood and determine the child's subsequent life, this vertical determinism is actually based on a horizontal one. In empirical psychoanalysis the complex exists before its symbolic manifestations, so that it is constituted by the *past*. "Consequently," Sartre concludes, "the dimension of the future does not exist for [Freudian] psychoanalysis."[1]

Sartre is ready to adopt the method of Freud's empirical psychoanalysis when it tries to reveal the significance of an act by

[1] *L'Etre et le Néant*, p. 536.

assuming that every action, even the most unimportant, is not the simple effect of the previous psychic condition, but is integrated as a secondary structure in the wholeness of the individual. "But if we adopt the method of [Freud's] psychoanalysis . . . we must apply it in a reverse way. . . . Instead of understanding the considered phenomenon by its past, we conceive the understanding act as a return of the *future* toward the present."[2]

We must agree with Sartre that the dimension of the future does not exist for Freud's psychoanalysis. But how does this criticism apply to Alfred Adler's Individual Psychology? Was it not Adler who wrote, for example:

> Let me observe that if I know the *goal* of a person I know in a general way what will happen. . . . If I am acquainted only with the *causes,* know only the reflexes, the reaction-times, the ability to repeat such facts, I am aware of nothing that actually takes place in the soul of a man.[3]

This was written in 1914, when Sartre was nine years old. Adler's whole life work was dedicated to the search for man's "goal" or "life-plan." Adler continues:

> Every phenomenon, if it is to give us any understanding of a person, can only be grasped and understood if regarded as preparation to some goal. . . . As soon as the goal of a psychic movement or its *life-plan* has been recognized, then we are to assume that all the movements of its constituent parts will coincide both with the goal and the life-plan. . . . The properly understood part-movements must, when combined, give the integrated life-plan and final goal. Consequently, we insist that, without worrying about the tendencies, milieu, and experiences, all psychical powers are under the control of a directive idea and all expressions of emotion, feeling, thinking, willing, acting, and dreaming, as well as psycho-pathological phenomena, are permeated by one unified life-plan.[4]

Now, is not Sartre's *original choice* the counterpart of Adler's *goal,* and Sartre's *fundamental project* the replica of Adler's *life-*

[2] *Ibid.*

[3] *The Practice and Theory of Individual Psychology*, p. 3.

[4] *Ibid.*, pp. 4–6.

plan? And goal and life-plan, unlike Freudian psychoanalysis, do imply the dimension of the future. Adler was little interested in the causes of certain illnesses, but very much interested in the *purposes* which the patient wished to achieve in "arranging" his symptoms. And it was from the angle of the *future,* anticipated by the patient in his goal, that Adler explained the patient's present. This is exactly the "return of the future toward the present," which Sartre claims to be one of the original features of his Existential psychoanalysis.

If Sartre insists that man's choice may be changed, Adler affirmed the same, with regard to the life-plan when he wrote: "The psychotherapeutic treatment has for its object to show the patient . . . that he can change his life-plan. . . ."[5]

Sartre may reply that his *original choice* and *fundamental project* have a more basic philosophical meaning with ontological implications which cannot be found in Adler's goal and life-plan. We do not deny it, and shall later explain the deeper ontological significance of those Sartrean concepts. But being a psychiatrist and not a philosopher, Adler was not interested in giving an ontological foundation to his goal and life-plan concepts. In practice, however, these Adlerian conceptions have the same explanatory functions as Sartre's, and they were propounded thirty years before Sartre published his *Being and Nothingness.*

When Sartre wrote so many pages to explain in just which respects he disagrees with Adler, why did he not put more emphasis on the basic ideas they had in common, the ideas he borrowed from Adler? Should this not be considered an example of that "bad faith" Sartre so violently denounces, and which he defines as lying to oneself and masking from oneself an unpleasant truth?[6]

---

[5] "Individual-Psychological Treatment of Neurosis" (1913) , *Theory and Praxis of Individual Psychology,* p. 50.

[6] For a more thorough discussion of the relations between Sartre's and Adler's theories, see my articles "Existential Psychoanalysis and Individual Psychology" in *Journal of Individual Psychology,* Vol. 14, pp. 38–50 (May 1958) , and "La Psychologie Individuelle d'Alfred Adler et la Philosophie," *Revue Philosophique de la France et de l'Etranger* (Juillet-Septembre 1960) , pp. 313–326.

AMONG THE TEACHERS who left their imprint on Sartre's mind was Emile Chartier, better known under his pseudonym Alain. Alain was a strong believer in personal freedom. It was he who taught Sartre that what we call "character" is not an unchangeable stamp impressed upon an individual, but a kind of oath (*serment*), freely taken by the individual. He who says, "I am an irascible person," has neither inherited nor acquired this temperament, but has committed himself freely to anger. That is to say, anger is the free project of his being-for-others.

From this premise Sartre draws the very radical conclusion: "There are no characters, there is only a project of oneself."[1] Only for the other person do I appear as a character. For the other person who grasps me as an object, I am noble or vile, an irascible coward or a courageous character; and by the other person's gaze this aspect is reflected on me. That means that, as a being-for-myself, I do not have a character but am only my free project. As a being-for-others, that is to say, as an object, I appear to have a character. As long as I allow myself to be fascinated by the other person's gaze, I will grasp myself not as a subject but as an ego-object, just as he grasps me with his gaze. And I will see myself as endowed with a definite, invariable character, which is, in reality, nothing but a psychic substance. He who says, "I am now fifty years old, and it is too late for me to

[1] *L'Etre et le Néant*, p. 637.

change," considers himself under the image of an invariable substance, a thing-in-itself.

To a philosopher of freedom and action—and in this respect Sartre is the most radical, not only since Bergson but also since Fichte—substance must appear as an inhuman, subhuman concept. Therefore Sartre rejects substance in any form, be it called character, temperament, human nature, or what you will. Principles like heredity, education, environment, and psychological constitution are in his eyes nothing but "the big explanatory idols of our epoch," because they correspond to a substantialist interpretation of man.

On the other hand, Sartre does not want to grind down the individual into a kind of psychic dust. What we call an individual *is* a unity in his eyes also, but it is "a unity of responsibility." This unity may be "lovable or hateful, blamable or praisable, in a word *personal.*"[2]

Thus we may classify Existentialism as a *personalism.*

This personal unit, of which substance is only a "caricature," is considered by Existentialism as a free unification. And this unification comes before the diversity which it unifies. It is what Scholasticism called *unitas ante rem.* It is unification in the world, the unification of an original project, and this unification is a "non-substantial absolute."

It is from this viewpoint that Sartre tried to write Baudelaire's biography, which, as he told me in a letter from Algiers, he considers a practical application of his Existential psychoanalysis.

The term "character" comes from the Greek word χαρακτήρ which means "coinage" or "stamp." We are accustomed to use this term in the sense of the stamped peculiarities a person possesses as a result of his heredity and environment. Geneticists and sociologists will not easily accept Sartre's thesis of the nonexistence of characters, for their experimental research has taught them a quite different lesson. Yet, certain psychologists may agree with Sartre. Referring to the variety of personalities, Alfred Adler wrote: "Not their origin but their end, their ultimate goal, constitutes their individual character. . . . The individual . . . wears the character traits demanded by his fictional goal, just as the

---

[2] *Ibid.*, p. 648.

character mask (*persona*) of the ancient actor had to fit the *finale* of the tragedy."[3] Here, too, character in the traditional sense has disappeared.

One wonders how Sartre could become such a powerful dramatic author without using characters. His Goetz von Berlichingen, in *Le Diable et le bon Dieu* (*The Devil and the Good Lord*), no longer shows any of the features of a character. He has no definite coinage, but is a sequence of three different beings, each of which has a different project. In the first part of the drama, his fundamental project is to do evil for evil's sake, as a refusal of a world which rejects him. In the second part, his basic project is to do good, because it seems to be impossible and because it is "the best way of being alone."[4] In the last part, after having liberated himself from the belief in God, Goetz's project becomes one of fighting in a revolutionary war for the liberation of the mutinous German peasants, that is, to do good by using evil in the form of violence. Each of these projects changes him into another type of person, and yet we feel that these types are united by a bond, for which Sartre's concept of "unity of responsibility" seems indeed to be an adequate expression.

The great tragic authors of France's classical age, especially Corneille and Racine, were eager to observe the rules of tragedy established by Aristotle, and the French Academy watched closely to see that these rules were not violated. Nothing is farther from Sartre's mind than preoccupations of this kind, and yet—ironically enough—his conception of a characterless drama is in agreement with Aristotle's classical teachings. "In a play," the great Greek philosopher wrote, "they do not act in order to portray characters. It is the action, i.e., its fable or plot, that is the end and purpose of tragedy. . . . A tragedy is impossible without action, but there may be one without characters."[5]

Sartre's theatre is a late and forceful confirmation of this ancient doctrine.

---

[3] *The Individual Psychology of Alfred Adler*, p. 94.

[4] *Le Diable et le bon Dieu*, Paris, 1951, p. 103; American edition, *The Devil and The Good Lord and Two Other Plays*, New York, Alfred A. Knopf, 1960.

[5] Aristotle, *De Poetica*, 1450A.

xviii
Thε Unconscious ANd
Bad FAitH

"Existential psychoanalysis rejects the postulate of the unconscious."[1] With this categorical statement Sartre draws a clear line between his type of psychoanalysis and that propounded by Freud, Jung, and most of their followers.

It is the concept of "bad faith" (*mauvaise foi*) which, in Existential psychoanalysis, replaces the notions of the unconscious and repression.

Sartre establishes a basic relation between bad faith and the lie; bad faith is a lie of a specific type, a lie to oneself. A man is of bad faith when he knows the truth and tries to hide it from himself. A person of bad faith is conscious of his bad faith. Acting in bad faith, a person is the deceiver and the deceived at the same time. As far as I am the deceiver, I must know that I am deceiving myself; and as far as I am deceived, I believe in the lie I have manufactured, hiding from myself that I am the manufacturer. In bad faith I am running away from the truth, but I cannot really be ignorant of the fact that I am running away.

Now, according to Sartre, Freud replaces bad faith by a lie without a liar. In empirical psychoanalysis the liar, who is I myself, is replaced with the concepts of the unconscious, the *id*, repression, etc., which are different from me. I am an ego, but I am not the *id*, that unconscious drive which compels me to steal. Freud's ideas of the *id* and of a censorship acting without our knowledge allow us to consider ourselves not as liars but as

[1] *L'Etre et le Néant*, p. 658.

deceived persons of good faith. And for this reason Sartre rejects the Freudian concepts of the unconscious, the *id*, censorship, repression, etc., because they are nothing but vehicles of bad faith, means of practicing our bad faith in good faith.

Condemning the "mythological," personifying, metaphorical language of Freud, Sartre affirms that in order to do its job the "censor" in our soul must know the truth it is repressing into the unconscious. The censorship operates a selective principle, allowing decent impulses to pass and repressing only indecent, illicit sexual and aggressive impulses. How can the censor select and separate one from another without being conscious of them? How can censorship distinguish between repressible and nonrepressible impulses without being conscious of distinguishing them? Is it possible, Sartre asks, to conceive a knowledge which would be ignorant of itself? And here again he refers to Alain, who said, "To know is to know that one knows," although this thesis had been refuted by Piaget's child tests, and perhaps by Plato's dialogue *Meno*.

Sartre concludes that censorship is conscious of itself. It is conscious of being conscious of the tendency to repress in order not to be conscious of it. Thus censorship is action in bad faith. In the eyes of our Existential psychoanalyst, Freud's empirical discipline does not help us to fight bad faith, because it introduces between the unconscious and the conscious an autonomous consciousness of bad faith which it calls "censorship." Sartre insists that Freud's distinction between the *ego*, the *id*, and the *super-ego*[2] is nothing but a "verbal terminology."

Existential psychoanalysis holds that the very idea of "dissimulating" something implies the unity of one and the same psyche and, within this unity, a double activity aimed equally at locating the hidden something and hiding it. These two activities are complementary. In separating conscious and unconscious events by means of censorship, Freud has not succeeded, says Sartre, in dissociating those two activities. How can the repressed tendency "disguise" itself without the consciousness of being repressed or disguised and without a project of disguise? Further-

[2] See, e.g., Freud, *An Outline of Psychoanalysis*, New York, W. W. Norton, 1948.

more, Sartre asks, how can one explain the pleasure or anxiety accompanying the symbolic achievement of the tendency unless consciousness does have, in spite of censorship, an obscure comprehension of the aim to be reached, as simultaneously desired and forbidden? Having split the conscious unity of the psyche, Freud, according to Sartre, has always to suppose a kind of "magic unity," which binds together all psychic phenomena. What empirical psychoanalysis has done is to change bad faith into a fictitious intrusive person called "the censor," but this does not mean that bad faith has been eliminated.

But did not Sartre himself prove that the contrary of bad faith, sincerity, is merely a self-contradictory ideal which man cannot reach? He himself has shown that constitutionally man is not what he is, and is what he is not. Consequently, man can never coincide with himself, and only complete coincidence with himself would be sincerity. Being split into a subject and an object, man cannot coincide with himself and is therefore necessarily incapable of complete sincerity. Only things coincide with themselves, but things cannot be sincere because they have no consciousness. The only being capable of sincerity would be God, for he would be at the same time a being-for-himself (consciousness) and a being-in-itself (objective world). But Sartre does not believe in God.

The champion of sincerity requires that a lazy man be sincere in recognizing that he is lazy. But in achieving this sincerity and recognizing that he is lazy, the lazy individual admits that he is a thing which cannot change; he denies the very freedom which would allow him to change and to project himself toward becoming an industrious person. But denying one's freedom means to be of bad faith. Thus, in his very act of sincerity, an act of good faith, man is of bad faith. And in refusing to recognize his laziness as a definite thinglike constitution, in recognizing his freedom and its possibilities, the lazy man refuses to be sincere; but, at the same time, he avoids bad faith which would be the denial of his freedom. Admitting that "this contradiction is constitutive of the requirement of sincerity," Sartre was not entitled to reproach Freud, who, in introducing the concepts of unconsciousness, censorship, and repression, did not eliminate bad faith. Was Sartre really sincere when he required from empirical psychoanalysis the achievement of the ideal of sincerity which he himself had found incompatible with the very nature of human consciousness?

However this may be, in opposing Freud's hypothesis of the unconscious, Sartre sides with one of Freud's pupils, the Viennese psychiatrist Wilhelm Stekel, who had broken with his master. Stekel, in his study on frigid women, says: "Every time I was able to push my investigation far enough, I ascertained that the nucleus of the psychosis was conscious." He mentions, for instance, that many women whom matrimonial deception has made "frigid," only mask from themselves and from their partners the pleasure they actually find in the sexual act. Following Stekel, Sartre speaks of a "pathological bad faith" in these women, which Freud's empirical psychoanalysis would be unable to explain.

Existential psychoanalysis draws the conclusion that there is no such thing as an "unconscious," that everything psychic is conscious. But if this is so, it is hard to understand why Sartre needs to establish a new type of psychoanalysis. If nothing is hidden in the unconscious, why is it then necessary to analyze an individual? What other function can psychoanalysis have than to bring to consciousness certain tendencies which had been repressed into the unconscious, and thus to relieve an individual of this repressed material and its neurotic manifestations?

To this Sartre answers with the very subtle distinction between "consciousness" and "cognition," which is the basis of that compromise he tried to achieve between Descartes and Heidegger; it is expressed in his *cogito préréflexif.* Sartre's prereflective *cogito* differs from Descartes' *cogito* in that it is conscious, without having cognition. This assumption helped him to avoid Descartes' primacy of cognition and to affirm Heidegger's primacy of existence, without giving up the Cartesian subjectivity.

Applied to Existential psychoanalysis, this distinction signifies that "if the fundamental project is *lived* by the subject completely consciously, it does not at all mean that it must also be *known* by it; rather the contrary is true."[3] Our consciousness lacks the means which would permit both analysis and conceptualization.

---

[3] *L'Etre et le Néant*, p. 658.

"It is penetrated with a great light, without being able to express what this light enlightens."[4] It is a "mystery in full light." Sartre's distinction between "consciousness" and "cognition" seems to coincide with Emil Froeschel's distinction between "not-expression-ripe" and "expression-ripe" psychic events, which is likewise supposed to replace Freud's correlation between "unconscious" and "conscious" factors.[5]

Sartre thinks that the individual, led by the psychoanalyst, would not be able to recognize the complex, if it had been unconscious. But the individual does not only *accept* a hypothesis offered by the psychoanalyst, he sees what it is. This is only possible if he has never ceased to be conscious of the profound tendencies of the complex, which is not different from its consciousness itself. Sartre concludes that the psychoanalytic interpretation only allows man to "take cognition" (*prendre connaissance*) of what he is, and not to "take consciousness" (*prendre conscience*) of that fact; because man never loses consciousness of what he is. For Sartre's Existential psychoanalysis, no pyschic reality is unconscious, and it could not logically be otherwise, since his Existentialism identifies consciousness with existence.

With his war against the concept of the "unconscious," Sartre wishes to refute not only Freud, but also Adler. "It seems to us," Sartre writes, "that the concept of bad faith . . . should replace those of censorship, repression, and the unconscious, which Adler uses."[6]

To this we have to answer that Adler's Individual Psychology does not use the concept of censorship, which is a Freudian concept.

As for the idea of repression, Adler practically discarded it. As early as 1911 Adler criticized Freud for using such unclarified constructs as repression and for considering it as the essential and preliminary condition for the development of symptoms. In fact, Adler replaced repression almost entirely by the "safeguarding tendencies" of the self. According to Professor Ansbacher,

4 *Ibid.*
5 E. Froeschel, *Philosophy in Wit* (New York, Philosophical Library, 1948) , pp. 13–30.
6 *L'Etre et le Néant*, p. 552.

"Adler accepted repression, if at all, only as one of the many safeguarding devices."[7]

As for the unconscious, Sartre is closer to Adler than he realizes. Sartre writes: "We do not establish between the two levels considered, the difference between the unconscious and the conscious, but the one which separates the non-reflective fundamental consciousness from reflective consciousness."[8] This means that while being conscious of his fundamental project, man does not always understand it; his nonreflective consciousness is unable to fix its objects "by concepts." And we remember Sartre's metaphor that this nonreflective consciousness is penetrated by a great light, without being able to express what that light enlightens. Now Adler meant almost the same when he wrote:

> Man knows more than he understands. . . . Man understands nothing about his goal but still he pursues it. . . . The unconscious is nothing other than that which we have been unable to formulate in clear concepts. . . . It is not a matter of concepts hiding away in some unconscious or subconscious recesses of our minds, but of parts of our consciousness, the significance of which we have not fully understood. We cannot oppose "consciousness" to "unconsciousness" as if they were two antagonistic halves of an individual's existence.[9]

This is certainly not the language of the radical advocate of the unconscious, which was the picture of Adler given by Sartre when he insisted, supposedly in opposition to the psychologist, on a unity of consciousness that does not admit a split into a conscious and unconscious part. A deeper study of Adler's work might convince Sartre that the thinker he had been fighting as an adversary might be better used as an ally.

[7] *The Individual Psychology of Alfred Adler*, p. 264.
[8] *L'Etre et le Néant*, p. 552.
[9] *The Individual Psychology of Alfred Adler*, pp. 232–233.

How Free Is Our Project?

We have seen that Existential psychoanalysis is a discipline aimed at uncovering a man's original choice, a man's fundamental project. Now we have to ask ourselves to what extent this project is free. In this respect Sartre admits very narrow limits of our freedom, which he designates by the words "situation" and "facticity." We choose the world, however, not in its context, but only in its significance, by choosing ourselves. We choose ourselves only in our *way* of being and not in our being *itself* and are thus responsible only for our *way* of being.

My factual "situation," for example, is characterized by my position in the world, by all the obstacles I meet and all the help I receive, all the resistance I have to overcome in order to reach my aim. However, this situation exists only in correlation with my project, my attempt to transcend the actual facts in my journey toward a goal. For reality is revealed to me as a resistance or an aid only in the light of my free project. A big mountain, for instance, offers tremendous resistance if my free project is to build a railroad, for then I have to dig a tunnel through it. On the other hand, it is a big help if my free project is to see the surrounding landscape. Only in the light of my free project is this mountain either an obstacle or a help; in itself, it is neutral.

Here again Sartre had important predecessors, for twenty-three years before him John Dewey wrote: "Conditions and events . . . are either obstacles to our ends or else means for their accomplishment."[1] And eight years before Sartre, Ortega y Gasset

[1] J. Dewey, *Reconstruction in Philosophy*, New York, Henry Holt & Co., 1950, Mentor edition, Ch. 5, pp. 102–103.

wrote: *"El hombre no encuentra cosas . . . lo que encuentra son puras dificultades y puras facilidades para existir;"*[2] that is, man does not meet things . . . what he meets are mere difficulties and mere facilities for existing.

Yet Sartre drew some original conclusions from these premises by affirming that man meets obstacles only in the field of his freedom, and there is no freedom except "in situation." Thus facticity, or situation, becomes a condition of freedom and not, as determinism affirms, an obstacle to it. Nobody can escape from a jail in which he has not been imprisoned. Man encounters everywhere obstacles and resistances which he has not created. This encountering is what Sartre calls "facticity" or "situation." However, the obstacles and resistances become obstacles and resistances only by virtue of and through man's free project.

We are free only with respect to, and *in spite of*, a given situation. "Without obstacle, no freedom!" Sartre says; and freedom becomes for him tantamount to escaping from being-in-itself. Our free action supposes a "naughtization" of an actuality. Taking into account situation, actuality, facticity, Sartre concludes that our freedom is freedom of choice and not freedom of obtaining.

To act freely does not mean for Sartre to act without a motive. However, the motive does not determine the action, and appears only by virtue of and within a chosen project. And the project is free. Only by virtue of and within his free project to become the ruler of all Gaul, did the power of the Occidental Church appear to Clovis as a motive for conversion. The motive owes its entire meaning to the project the person adopts; and that project is free.

Also my choice of myself meets with great opposition from facticity. "Can I choose to be tall if I am short?" asks Sartre, who is far from being a giant. He answers that in a comparative sense he himself chooses his body to be weak only if his project is to become a boxer or a baseball star. However, if he remains in the city—for Sartre that means in the café—and chooses nothing but discussions and literary work, his body will not be weak. It is

[2] J. Ortega y Gasset, "Historia como Sistema," *Obras Completas,* tomo 6, p. 32.

weak only in the light of a certain free project, which he has not chosen, that of becoming an athlete. Thus freedom creates its own obstacles and is limited only by itself.

We have here an example of that sophisticated skill with which Sartre changes compulsion into freedom and freedom into compulsion, necessity into choice and choice into necessity; and we understand a caustic remark on Existentialism in the satirical Parisian magazine *Le Canard Enchaîné*: "I say *my freedom* as I say *my wife*. This does not prevent me from being a cuckold."

The only true limit to our freedom Sartre admits, is that arising from the existence of some other person. "I am a Jew, an Aryan, handsome or ugly. . . . I am all this for another person . . . without any hope of modifying it. . . . I am something which I have not chosen to be."[3]

Theoretically, Sartre is not much worried about this situation. For since this limit of his freedom is the freedom of another person, he can maintain his thesis that freedom meets no limit but in freedom. However, practically, the fact that the one freedom is mine and the other is not mine makes a great deal of difference. Sartre does not deny it. We are "cast" into the world, face to face with the other person, and thus our existence is a limit to his freedom and his freedom is a limit to ours. It is in this that Sartre sees the origin of the concepts of guilt and sin in a world where there is no God. It is *vis-à-vis* the other person that man is guilty. And in his impressive play *Huis Clos* (*No Exit*), Sartre showed that the other person's "gaze," impeding our escape into behavior of bad faith, is the real meaning of the idea of hell.

Now, through the glance of the other I am, for instance, a Jew. He determines me as such; I am it for-the-other, without having chosen it. What attitude have I to take in order to recover my freedom in this situation? Here is Sartre's answer:

A Jew is not first a Jew and afterward ashamed or proud; but it is his pride in being a Jew, his shame, or his indifference which will reveal to him his being-a-Jew. And this being-a-Jew is nothing besides his free manner of accepting

3 *L'Etre et le Néant*, pp. 606–607.

it. . . . In fury or in hate, in pride or shame, in disgusted refusal or in joyful claim, I have to choose to be what I am.[4]

It is remarkable that Sartre published this courageous statement in 1943, in Paris, under the Nazi occupation!

If his doctrine that freedom creates its own obstacles in the inanimate world reminds us of the theories of Fichte, his thesis of free acceptance of what we are reminds us of the ethics of the Stoics. Nevertheless, Sartre's doctrine hás its personal note. He thinks that race, ugliness, and so on, can appear only within the limits of one's own choice of inferiority or of pride; that is to say, these features can appear only with the significance which my freedom ascribes to them. I do not choose to be to the other person what I am to him, but if I am to myself what I am to him, it is only because I choose to be as I appear to him. But I am free not to choose to be as I appear to the other person. Only my own recognition of the freedom of the anti-semites, that is to say, only my own acceptance of my being-a-Jew for them, can constitute a true limit of my freedom. "If it pleases me, however, to consider them as *mere objects,* my being-a-Jew disappears immediately and yields to the simple consciousness of being a free and unqualifiable transcendence," for the being-for-itself cannot *be* anything. Paul Valéry put it another way: *"L'esprit est le refus indéfini d'être quoi que ce soit. Ce qui n'est pas fixé n'est rien, ce qui est fixé est mort"*[5]—the spirit is the indefinite refusal to be anything whatsoever. That which is not fixed is nothing; that which is fixed is dead.

The ability of freedom and of its most powerful weapon, the gaze, to change another subject into an object has been exemplified in Sartre's most moving tragedy, *The Victors.* In the play, Lucie, a young woman who had joined the French underground, has been tortured and raped by the fascists, who wanted to make her betray her comrades. She suffered every humiliation and did not speak; but she looked at her torturers and her gaze changed them into objects. They could violate her body, but not her freedom. "They have not touched me," she says, "nobody has touched me. I was of stone and I did not feel their hands. I

---

[4] *Ibid.,* p. 612.
[5] *Tel Quel,* Paris, 1943, II, p. 193.

looked at them and I thought: Nothing is happening. Nothing has happened."[6]

We are inclined to call this behavior "stoic." It is also Existentialist. In both teachings the ultimate freedom left to us toward a world which we cannot change is our freedom to have our "Yea" or "Nay," to accept or to refuse.

[6] *Morts san Sépulture*, Lausanne, 1946, p. 128; English edition, London, Hamilton, 1952.

Sex and Love in Existential Psychoanalysis

Trying to determine a man's original project, his fundamental choice, Existential psychoanalysis rejects Freud's libido theory, because Sartre does not consider sexuality a fundamental relation. A fundamental relation must be a project of *being*, must be more basic than sex.

In spite of rejecting Freud's pan-sexualism, Sartre's Existential psychoanalysis, nevertheless, assigns an important role to sex, and most of his novels and short stories are almost pornographic. Should this be considered a typical feature of Existentialism? Apparently many Frenchmen feel that way. Sartre himself recounts that a French lady, who had used a lascivious expression, excused herself afterward, saying: "My goodness, I am becoming Existentialist!" But as a matter of fact, Existentialism in itself had no specific relation to sex until Sartre made it "sexy." Perhaps this is also one reason for the tremendous success of Sartre's version of Existentialism. In Heidegger's work there is no reference to sex, for he thinks that existence is the same for men and women. And interest in his type of Existentialism is restricted to professional philosophers.

But Sartre's Existentialism has aroused the interest of many persons who are not in any sense specialists in philosophy. Sartre does not believe that we are sexual beings because we have sexual organs. He thinks that, inversely, we have sexual organs because we are sexual beings. Infantile sexuality precedes the physiological maturity of sexual organs, and neither eunuchs nor women after the menopause cease to have sexual desires. Goethe was seventy-four when he fell in love with the nineteen-year-old Ulrike von Levetzow. When she refused his offer of marriage, he sublimated his disappointment into the heartrending "Marien-bader Elegie."

For Sartre sexuality is not a contingent accident linked to our physiological nature; it is a *necessary ontological structure of our being-for-others.*

It is *desire* which reveals to us our own sexuality and that of the other person. But what is desire?

Trying to answer this question Sartre says that we have to give up the idea that our desire is lust, for this would not explain the fact that our desire always goes toward an object, that it leaves the limits of our subjectivity. Any subjectivistic theory is unable to explain the fact that man desires a woman or woman a man and that neither of them simply desires lust, a merely subjective condition. Thus, it is necessary to define desire by its transcendental object. Desire is consent to desire; it engages the whole personality. "I am an accomplice to my desire."[1] But if that is so, we have to understand *love* as the basis of desire. Love is one of the typical attitudes of the being-for-itself in its being-for-others. We have already seen that, according to Sartre, the original sense of our being-for-others is *conflict,* and this holds even for love.

While I am trying to enslave another person, that other person tries to enslave me; and while I try to deliver myself from the enslavement of that other person, that other person tries to deliver himself of my hold. While the relations between the being-for-itself and the being-in-itself (the inanimate world) are unilateral, the relations involved in the being-for-others are reciprocal. Love shows it in the clearest form.

We have seen that it is by his gaze that the other person is revealed to us as a self: under the other self's gaze we feel our own being-for-others as a kind of being possessed. I am possessed by another self, whose gaze shapes my body and sees it as I will never see it. The one who looks at me possesses my secret, the secret that I am as an object. Shame is the feeling of being an object, of recognizing myself in that dependent and congealed

[1] *L'Etre et le Néant,* p. 457.

object which I am for some other person. The fear of being surprised in the state of nudity is explained by the fact that our body symbolizes our objectivity without defense. To dress oneself means to dissimulate our object-character, to claim the right to see without being seen, the right to be a mere subject. When Adam and Eve recognized that they were naked, they were ashamed, feeling their degradation into mere objects to be looked at, each by the other.

Being "possessed" by the gaze of another self, I try to regain my being for myself. One way in which I can regain it is by absorbing the other person's freedom, which possessed mine, that is to say, by *uniting* myself with the other person *as* a self. But this project is difficult to achieve. For Sartre calls our attention to the fact that it would not do for me to efface my object character by objectivizing the other person. This would only mean to get rid of my being-for-the-other-person, a project I can reach through indifference. What is required in love is that I get possession of the other person in so far as he or she is a self, a subject, a freedom endowed with a gaze, for only as such he or she possessed my being.

If love were nothing but the desire of physical possession of the other person, it would be easily satisfied. But we know that it is much more than this. Love wants to possess the other self's freedom *as* a freedom. For if through my gaze I change my love partner into an object, I have not reached my aim, and I stay alone. The lover does not want to possess the beloved as one possesses an object. He wants to possess her as a subject, a living freedom.

Now sexual desire must express this aspiration of love. Therefore the desire does not aim at possessing the beloved person's body in its physiological reality, but as the incarnation of the other person's freedom. Thus it is necessary that the other person's freedom, his being-for-himself, pervade his whole body, even up to its surface, "so that in touching this body I am finally touching the other self's free subjectivity. This is the true sense of the word possession."[2] A caress is the expression of touching the other self's free subjectivity, as far as it is embodied.

[2] *Ibid.*, p. 463.

Sartre does not deny that in sexual desire we try to possess another person's body, but we want to possess it as far as this body itself is possessed by the partner's freedom, that is to say, in so far as the other person's consciousness identifies itself with his body.

However, this project of desire, Sartre says, is condemned to failure, not only because the pleasure which characterizes the climax of sexual possession kills the desire, but because when this ecstasy of lust arrives, the consciousness of each partner is only consciousness of his own body; it is a reflective consciousness, in which the transcendental character of desire has disappeared. In the climax of sexual possession, pleasure itself becomes the unique object of a person's consciousness; the whole of his attention is directed reflexively toward the embodiment of his own freedom, and that of the love partner is forgotten. Basically, desire is the wish to possess the other person and his self, his consciousness, incarnated in his body. But what desire finally achieves is only possession of ourselves. Sartre probably agrees with the French writer François Mauriac, who says: "We never find the body we have been seeking. . . . Voluptuousness is a battle without a victor."[3]

But though the project of desire is condemned to failure, how about love? In Existential psychoanalysis this human passion has to fulfill a great mission. We know already that, to Sartre, man's existence is completely contingent, without any foundation. In love we try to discover a foundation of our being. By our partner's love, we try to become justified. Each of the love partners wishes to be the absolute choice of the other, not a relative, contingent one. The lover feels himself offended, degraded, when the partner says that she has chosen him "among others." Only if both of them can say, "We were created for each other," does the choice appear as an absolute one. Then the being-in-the-world of the beloved one is justified, and the one love partner becomes the real foundation of the other's existence. He becomes the absolute source of all values and is protected against any devaluation. He becomes the absolute center of reference for the

[3] F. Mauriac, *Fleuve de Feu*, Paris, 1923, pp. 124–125; English edition, *The River of Fire*, London, Eyre & Spottiswoode, 1954.

partner and her absolute value. How often do we hear that a woman in love says of her beloved: "I would steal for him, kill for him!" This means that she has sacrificed traditional ethics to her partner and considers him as the absolute source of all values.

Before being loved, Sartre says, our existence was that of a "protuberance," completely unjustified and unjustifiable. But being the "absolute" choice of our love partner, having been "created" for him or for her, we feel that our existence is wanted in every detail by an absolute freedom—that of our partner. Thus we no longer feel ourselves to be supernumerary (*de trop*). "That is the basis of the joy of love: to feel our existence justified."[4]

Thus love would be the appropriate means to overcome our nausea, the feeling of the contingency and gratuitousness of our existence. In Sartre's Existentialism love has, as we see, a real metaphysical meaning. However, love is likewise a project which is condemned to failure. In his first Existentialist film, *Les Jeux sont faits* (*The Chips Are Down*), a work of high artistic value, Sartre shows the destiny of a man and a woman who, having met after death in a fantastic world of shadows, discover that they have been "created for each other." They are allowed to return to earth and to live their lives again. But only if their project of absolute love and mutual justification succeeds will they be allowed to stay on earth. Otherwise they will die again after twenty-four hours. And they die; because the project of love is condemned to failure. Why? Here are Sartre's reasons:

We have seen that love is the project of recovering oneself from another self, of becoming the other person's absolute choice and thus of being justified by the other person's choice. This project can be realized only if the lover succeeds in being loved; for only then will he have conquered the other person as a self, as a freedom, as a subject, as a transcendence looking at him as he wishes to be looked at. "Thus it seems that love, in its essence, is the project to be loved."[5]

However, Sartre thinks that this project is a contradictory ideal. For each of the lovers wants the other to love him, without realizing that love is the wish to be loved; so that, for instance, in

[4] *L'Etre et le Néant*, p. 439.
[5] *Ibid.*, p. 443.

wanting my beloved to love me, I really only want her to want me to love her. Sartre concludes that the amorous relation is a system of infinite reflections, a deceiving mirror game which carries within itself its own frustration. Love is a kind of "dupery."

If our project were to abolish the other person's freedom and subjectivity, it would be hatred; love does not require the abolition of the other person's freedom, but only its enslavement by himself. But there remains always the possibility that my love partner may awaken from the self-enslavement of her liberty which is her love, and then use her newly conquered liberty to enslave mine, to change me into an object. And vice versa. From this springs the perpetual insecurity of lovers. Finally, Sartre thinks that love is always made relative by the presence of other people. In love each consciousness tries to shelter its being-for-others in the enslaved, and therefore benevolent, freedom of the love partner. However, as soon as the two lovers are seen together by other people, each of them not only feels his own objectification, but also that of the partner. Immediately the one partner is no longer the absolute transcendence which is the foundation and justification of the other partner's being, but a transcended transcendence, transcended not by the love partner but by other people. The coward deserter Garcin, in Sartre's dismal *No Exit*, wants to shelter his being-for-others and, through it, his being-for-himself, in possessing and enslaving the consciousness of Estelle. If she loves him, his own repugnant picture will be reflected to him in entire purity. And if he loves Estelle, she will see her own picture in his enslaved consciousness no longer as that of the infanticide that she is, but wonderfully transfigured.

Thus we see that love as an attempt to possess another person's freedom *as* a freedom, but as a self-enslaved freedom, is also one of those "avenues of flight" that man finds in order to escape into bad faith and an unauthentic existence.

In *No Exit*, the scene of which is hell, these attempts of Garcin and Estelle are frustrated by the permanent presence of a third person, Inez, representing other people. By her gaze both lovers are petrified into objects and compelled to be what they are in the eyes of other people, and, through them, in their own eyes. This gaze is petrifying only if it is a free gaze, the judgment of a master and not an enslaved gaze, enslaved by the one who wishes to be seen as he sees himself when he looks in the mirror of his self-indulgence, his vanity, his bad faith. But—as the three main characters of *No Exit* find out—there is no mirror in hell. It would not be hell if people were free to look in the mirror of their self-righteousness and to see themselves as they want to be seen. It *is* hell also because the electric light cannot be switched off and the eyes of people have no lids, so that each character of the play must "live," day and night, under the gazes of its roommates. The scene of *No Exit* is hell, because each of its characters depends in its being-for-itself on its being-for-others and is thus forced to be for itself what the others judge it to be and what it really is.

Thus we understand why, at the end of this grim drama, Garcin exclaims: "There is no need for grills. Hell is other people!"[6]

But if love is a project condemned to failure, are we better off with hatred? Not at all. Hatred is resignation, for in it the individual abandons the attempt, made in love, to regain its being-for-itself by a union with another person. A man who hates tries to cease being an object for another person by destroying that other person. Hatred aims at the death of the hated subject. But what man wants to attain by the death of the other subject is, symbolically, the destruction of all other people. "The person I hate represents, in fact, all other persons."[7] By destroying all other consciousnesses I would be free from the possibility of being enslaved by others and would recover my absolute non-substantialized freedom as a being-for-myself.

But, like love, hatred also is condemned to failure. The man who hates cannot kill all people. And even if he kills one person he hates, he will not be able to eliminate the fact that the other person has existed. But in dying the other person has become a part of the world-in-itself. As long as the other person is alive, I can always try to buy back myself in his consciousness, to change the image which I am in his consciousness. But when his consciousness has disappeared, that which I have been for him is

---

[6] J.-P. Sartre, "Huis Clos," *Théâtre*, Paris, 1947, p. 167; American edition, *No Exit and Three Other Plays*, New York, Vintage Books, 1960, p. 47.
[7] *L'Etre et le Néant*, p. 483.

petrified by his death and will be that image irremediably in itself, in the past, without any possibility of ever reconquering my picture and changing it. The other one has taken the "key" of my alienation with him into the tomb. We know that, according to Existentialism, as long as a man lives he *is* not but only makes himself. Only at the moment of his death has his essence become completely crystallized, and only then he *is*, only then does he coincide with himself and become a being-in-itself. Thus by killing the man who despises me, I would change his contempt for me into a part of his eternal essence and thus perpetuate it. This makes it clear why Sartre also considers hate as a project condemned by its very nature to failure.

We understand now why everything we have done to other people is perpetuated forever by their death. In Sartre's profound tragedy, *The Flies*, Egistus says:

> Do you not know that the dead are pitiless? Their grievances are indelible because their account has been closed forever. Is it by good deeds, Nicias, that you will erase the evil you did to your mother? But what good deed can ever reach her? Her soul is a torrid noon, without a breath of wind; nothing moves there, nothing changes, nothing lives, a big fleshless sun, a motionless sun, consumes her eternally. The dead are no longer . . . and therefore they have become the incorruptible guardians of our crimes.[8]

Among the basic possible projects of our being-for-others Sartre also counts masochism and sadism, and he shows that they too are condemned to failure. But since no normal person would have any doubt about this, we need not go into it here.

As far as other possible relations with another self are concerned—collaboration, struggle, rivalry, emulation, engagement, obedience—Sartre does not examine them in detail but only says that "they all include sexual relations as their skeleton."[9] Thus we see that in spite of repudiating Freud's libido theory, Sartre gives quite an important place to sexuality. We already know that to him sexuality is a necessary ontological structure of our being-

[8] "Les Mouches," *Théâtre*, pp. 47–48.
[9] *L'Etre et le Néant*, p. 477.

for-others. He even designates it as a "fundamental structure," but only of our being-for-others and not of our being-in-the-world, which is our very existence. It is in this respect that he seems not to go as far as Freud.

Sartre shares Freud's view that there are no "innocent" children. He recognizes, with Freud, the sexual significance of certain objects surrounding the child. But he does not believe that an already constituted sexual instinct has given these objects and forms their sexual significance.

> It rather seems to us that these matters and forms are grasped for their own sake and that they reveal to the child different *modes of being* and relations to being of the being-for-itself which will clarify and shape his sexuality.[10]

Some Freudian psychoanalysts have noticed that most small children are attracted by all kinds of holes: holes in the sand, in a wall, holes in their own bodies or in the bodies of other persons. Many babies try to push their little hands into their mother's mouth or the mouths of other people. Freud insisted on the fact that the first phase of infantile sexuality is an oral one.

> The baby's obstinate persistence in sucking gives evidence at an early stage of a need for satisfaction which, although it originates from and is stimulated by the taking of nourishment, nevertheless seeks to obtain pleasure independently of nourishment and for that reason, may and should be described as "sexual."[11]

We also know that the second phase in infantile sexuality, according to Freud, is called "sadistic-anal." In both the first and the second phase a hole in its own body is the center of the infant's sexuality.

Sartre denies that the child's attraction to these holes can be interpreted as a presentiment of the female sexual organs and the sexual act, for this would presuppose an experience the child cannot have. And, obviously, he does not believe in Freud's "archaic heritage" which a child brings with him into the world,

10 *Ibid.*, p. 704.
11 *An Outline of Psychoanalysis*, p. 28.

"before any experience of his own, as a result of the experiences of his ancestors."[12] Sartre, on the contrary, thinks that it is the objective nature of the hole the child perceives in the world which will enlighten for him the objective structure of the anal zone and will give a "transcendent significance" to the erogenous zones which the child had only felt existentially.

For Existential psychoanalysis the hole is the symbol of a *mode of being*. It is the symbol of *nothingness* which we have to fill with our flesh. Therefore the child cannot help putting his fingers in the holes of his body. According to Sartre, the hole represents to us the image of emptiness in man.

> To stop the hole means originally to sacrifice one's body so that fullness of being may exist, that is to say, to yield to the passion of the being-for-itself to shape, to complete, and to save the wholeness of the being-in-itself.[13]

Also the opposite activity, that of boring holes, appears to Sartre as requiring Existential analysis which, however, he has not yet attempted.

But if the hole is the Existential symbol of nothingness, we understand why we spend a good deal of our lives in stopping up holes: to achieve symbolically the wholeness of being. Putting his finger in his mouth the child tries to stop up a hole, to fill an emptiness; "he seeks the density, the uniform spheric fullness of the Parmenidean being." Thus, for Sartre, a baby sucking his finger is a kind of instinctive metaphysician. However, he still thinks that Freud supposes in the child an experience it cannot have. But does not Sartre himself presuppose more than experience in the baby, that is, an instinctive philosophical knowledge?

Furthermore, when an adult is eating he stops up a hole, fights nothingness and makes fullness exist—not only the fullness of his belly but the fullness of being.

Only after establishing this basic ontological symbolism of the hole does Sartre's psychoanalysis pass to sexuality. He thinks of the female sex as basically obscene, like every gaping thing. For Sartre the vagina is a "call for being" like all other holes. "The

[12] *Ibid.,* pp. 49–50.
[13] *L'Etre et le Néant,* p. 705.

woman calls for a foreign flesh which should transform her into a fullness of being by penetration and dilution."[14]

The woman feels her condition as a challenge, because she is "pierced." It is in this fact that Sartre sees the very origin of that inferiority complex which Adler finds in many women, accompanied by a "masculine protest" against their feminine condition. Adler tells of a young woman who stood in front of the mirror one day and asked her mother: "Did you too always want to be a man?" But according to Adler, the "masculine protest" of certain women against feminine strivings and sensations has its origin in certain infantile situations, such as, for instance, the uncertainty of her future sex role. Sartre sees the origin of that complex in the fact that the woman is "pierced."

To him the vagina is a mouth, a voracious mouth, which "swallows" the penis and symbolizes castration. In the sexual act the woman tries to castrate the man in order to fill the gap and change nothingness into the fullness of being.

Thus it is a presexual, existential, ontological relation which, in all these cases, is used to explain sexuality. And if I were to sum up the differences between the role of sex in Freud's empirical and in Sartre's Existential psychoanalysis, I should say that in Freud sex is used to enlighten existence, whereas in Sartre existence and its ontological implications are used to enlighten sex.

14 *Ibid.*, p. 706.

The Philosophy and Psychology of Death

WITHOUT DEATH mankind would not have philosophized. This opinion of Schopenhauer's seems to be corroborated by the history of philosophy. While primitive mythology can be interpreted as an obstinate negation of the phenomenon of death as such, the main purpose of philosophy, from Socrates to Epicurus and the Stoics, was to dissipate man's fear of death. The rise of Christianity seems to have changed this tendency, for Saint Paul, Saint Augustine, and later Christian thinkers considered philosophical attempts to appease man's fear of death self-deceit and even sin, since in all these attempts human reason tried to create that which was supposed to result only from divine grace. Nevertheless, death continued to be an inspiring force behind philosophy. There is, however, a great difference between the ancient philosophy of death and the Christian and modern atheistic ways of considering death. As long as we are alive, said Epicurus, death does not exist for us, and when death appears, we no longer exist. In Lucretius' *De rerum natura* we find a similar idea. There was a Roman saying: *Post mortem nihil est, ipsaque mors nihil*—after death there is nothing, not even death. On the contrary, the modern philosophy of death—the Christian as well as the atheistic one—rejects the ancients' attempts to dissipate the fear of death and tries to face death in all its dreadful reality. The whole Christian tradition from the early fifteenth century through at least the first half of the eighteenth century is filled with a strong horror and fear of death, a point of view taken very seriously by leading thinkers like Erasmus. This attitude toward death even affected men's actual dying, whether it was on the scaffold or the sickbed, and it permeated literature.

In the nineteenth century death became a central problem in Schopenhauer's pessimism and in Søren Kierkegaard's Existential philosophy. Finally, in our epoch, Heidegger and Sartre have attracted much interest by their contributions to the philosophy of death, the latter by his psychology of death, as well. Modern philosophers, both atheists and believers, have realistically faced the issue of death and, unlike their Greek forerunners, none has tried to dissipate the fear of it. When Plato said, "those who practise philosophy rightly (ὀρθῶς) learn how to die,"[1] he tried to present death as something desirable, because the true philosopher wishes to free the soul from the "hateful" company of the body. In modern thinkers, we no longer find this tendency. With Existentialism a new approach to death arises. It is characterized by humanization and individualization. Death is no longer considered as something beyond life, but as the last term of life, belonging to that series of events called life. "Man can only meet what is human . . . and death is a human phenomenon. It is the ultimate phenomenon of life, still life. As such it influences the whole life, countercurrentlike."[2]

But even as a human phenomenon, death is usually a general or collective concept. And a philosophy of death may still be a universal, abstract system based on the fact that all human beings have to die. However, Friedrich Schiller has already written: *"Diese Spinnweben von Systemen zerreisst das einzige Wort: 'Du musst sterben!' "*[3] ("These cobwebs of systems are torn to pieces by the single phrase: 'You must die!' ") Therefore, Existentialism not only tries to *humanize* death but also to *individualize* it, replacing the general problem of death with the individual problem, "I must die."

Sartre's philosophy of death is in many respects opposed to that of Heidegger. Since the French Existentialist's ideas were devel-

---

[1] Plato, *Phaidon*, 67 E.
[2] *L'Etre et le Néant*, p. 616.
[3] *Die Räuber*, Act V, Sc. 1.

oped in a polemic against his German mentor, we must first consider the latter's philosophy of death.

Death, as the end of our being-in-the-world, belongs to existence; it "limits and determines the possible wholeness of existence." Consequently, writes Heidegger, our existence is "being toward death" *("Sein zum Tode")*. Since existence is freedom, project, anticipation, it does not suffer anything passively but must be the anticipation and the free project of its own death, as "the possibility of no-longer-being-able-to-exist."[4]

The fact of being "cast into death," Heidegger continues, is revealed by anxiety. From this anxiety most human beings try to escape into the triviality of the anonymous crowd, which says: *"One* has to die some day." But this *Gerede* (idle chatter) that "one has to die" tries to give the impression that death concerns the "one," the anonymous crowd, not the speaker himself. "The one," Heidegger says, "is no one."[5] Thus existence in the anonymous crowd *(das Man)* is a perpetual evasion from the certainty of death as an individual death, a lack of "courage to face the anxiety of death." This evasion Heidegger calls "unauthentic being toward death."[6]

However, our existence becomes "authentic" through the resolute decision to free ourselves from the illusions of the anonymous crowd and to accept our death as our most personal possibility, one which can arrive at any moment and which we have to expect. In accepting freely the anxiety of death as a death which nobody else can die for us, we acquire what Heidegger calls "freedom for death."[7]

In his masterful story, *The Death of Ivan Ilyich,* Leo Tolstoy has shown how difficult it is to change the general problem of death the personal problem of "I must die." The hero of this story, who is about to die, remembers having learned in his logic course the syllogism "All men are mortal, Caius is a man, Caius is mortal." But the *logical* substitution of "I" for "Caius" is to him a *psychological* impossibility, because of the powerful instinct of survival, present in his soul, as in that of most men.

4 Heidegger, *Sein und Zeit,* pp. 234, 250.
5 *Ibid.,* p. 253.
6 *Ibid.,* p. 259.
7 *Ibid.,* p. 266.

Although Heidegger referred to Tolstoy's story only in a footnote of two lines in *Being and Time,* it is evident that his whole philosophy of death is only an abstract formulation of the ideas expressed in *The Death of Ivan Ilyich.*

The matter of having to be prepared to die at any moment is the very theme of the *ars moriendi* books, and it appears in Tudor and Stuart literature in innumerable places. One of the best known examples is the description in Macbeth of Duncan's queen as a good and pious woman who "died every day she lived."[8] Pascal and Nietzsche—who often are called Existentialist philosophers—expressed these ideas long before Heidegger, but in the unpretentious form of aphorisms. Thus we find in Pascal's *Pensées:*

> We like to rest in the society of our fellowman. . . . Being miserable like us, impotent like us, they will not help us. *We shall die alone.* Consequently, we should act as if we were alone. . . . We should seek truth without hesitation.[9]

Heidegger's words "freedom for death" (*Freiheit zum Tode*) were first used by Nietzsche, in the chapter of his *Zarathustra* called "On Free Death":

> My death, praise I to you, the free death, which comes to me because I want it. . . .
> Free for death, and free in death; a holy Nay-sayer, when there is no longer time for Yea: thus understands he about death and life.[10]

And, in his *Götzendämmerung* (*Twilight of the Idols*) Nietzsche says similarly, "Out of love for life should we want death in a different way: free, conscious, without hazard, without sudden attack."[11]

But there is one element, and the most unsound, in Heidegger's

---

8 *Macbeth*, IV, iii.

9 *Pensées*, III, 211, p. 429.

10 "Vom freien Tode," *Also sprach Zarathustra*, I, pp. 106, 108; American edition, "About Freely Chosen Death," *Thus Spake Zarathustra*, Chicago, Gateway Ed., 1957, I. pp. 80, 82.

11 *Götzendämmerung*, p. 144; English edition, *Twilight of the Idols, Complete Works*, Vol. 16, Edinburgh and London, T. N. Foulis, 1909–13.

philosophy of death which cannot be found in Nietzsche: a cult of anxiety of death. Nietzsche preaches philosophical serenity in the face of death: *"Seines Todes ist man gewiss: warum sollte man nicht heiter sein?"*[12]—one is sure of one's death. Why should one not be serene?

Requesting that man live "authentically," by expecting his death at any moment and considering anxiety of death as the criterion of a life's "authenticity" (*Eigentlichkeit*), Heidegger places our whole life under the domination of death. His philosophy is one of *memento mori*. Such a philosophy might be fit for monks who sleep every night in their coffins and who, in life, have nothing to do but to prepare themselves for death. However, applied to a secular life, Heidegger's philosophy of *memento mori* would mean the end of any creative existence. If we want to perform great deeds in life, we must live under the fiction of immortality. When, in 1917, in the most critical moment of World War I, Georges Clemenceau was asked by his nation to lead her to victory, he was seventy-six years old. Had he not lived under the fiction of immortality, had he followed Heidegger's philosophy of intentional and permanent horror and fear of death, that man, who seemed to be so close to the grave, would have been paralyzed, unable to act. But he acted, disregarding the possibility of death at any moment, and led his nation to victory.

The reason was that he probably considered his life only a kind of vessel which had to be filled with values the validity of which went beyond his time. Only by participating in such values can we accept our death as a natural event, which does not affect these values.

Apparently Existentialists do not accept the idea that our existence is only a vessel to be filled with values. For this reason Existentialism gives too much importance to the vessel of existence and is always ready to deny the value of the contents of existence only because its vessel is fragile. However, we have to realize that the contents of that vessel called "existence" are not necessarily linked to any one specific vessel. If the contents are

[12] "Bruchstücke zu den Dionysos-Dithyramben," *Gesammelte Werke*, XX, 60, p. 233.

valuable enough, then they survive their vessel and become part of the objective realm of values belonging to mankind. Homer, Plato, Shakespeare, Kant, and Lavoisier no longer exist. The vessels of their existence broke a long time ago. But the contents of those breakable vessels, the values with which they were filled, survive as part of mankind's objective spirit. Being unable to look beyond the tip of the nose of his own existence, the Existentialist —especially one of Heidegger's type—fails to recognize and appreciate the values of which his own existence is but the perishable vessel. Thus Existentialism easily degenerates into a mean egotism and egoism, tormented by the horror and fear of death.

In addition to this general criticism of Heidegger's philosophy of death there is also a special argument against it. If ever there was a man who had no right to preach a philosophy of individualism, which has to overcome submission to the slogans of the anonymous crowd, it was Heidegger. For when the Nazis became the masters of Germany, Heidegger, without hesitation, adopted all the slogans of the anonymous crowd and became a Nazi. What is Nazism, if not that *"Verfallenheit an das Man,"* that absorption of the individual by an anonymous crowd, which Heidegger had criticized so often?

Sartre quite properly refuses to follow Heidegger's ideas on death. He does not want to place life under the domination of death, because this would mean to meditate on one's subjectivity with the look of another self. For the being-for-itself never meets its own death, which only exists for the other self which survives. "The characteristic of a dead life is that it is a life of which another self has become the guardian."[13] Being dead is being-for-others and no longer being-for-itself; but being dead is also being-in-itself.

This theory of Sartre's needs more explanation. We remember his thesis that man is not what he is, because he is always in the making; he *is* not, but he becomes. However, this refers only to man as long as he is alive. As soon as man is dead, he is what he is, he coincides with himself. And what is man when he is dead? He is his past, and he is in-itself. But to understand this we must take into consideration Sartre's ideas of temporality.

[13] *L'Etre et le Néant*, p. 626.

The present is for-itself; it is the presence of the being-for-itself confronted with the being-in-itself. The present is a perpetual flight from being. "The present is not."[14]

The future is that which I have to be, in so far as it is possible that I may not be it. A being can be for-itself only under the perspective of a "not yet," a being whose complement is at a certain distance, beyond being. Thus everything that the being-for-itself is beyond being is the future. Human consciousness or human existence is lack—lack of coincidence with itself. Those things which each being-for-itself considers as lacking are his possibilities. Every man projects himself toward his possibilities, which are his values. But where are these possibilities? In the future. As long as man is alive he projects himself toward his future in order to unite himself with what he is lacking and thus to become what he is. However, there is always a possibility that he would miss the future toward which he projects himself, and this is another source of anxiety. Man can be his future only in a problematic way, for he is separated from it by the nothingness which he is, by his freedom which always allows him to "naught" his former projects and project himself toward another future.

Finally, we have the dimension of the past, and it is that which explains the "being" of the dead. While the present is for-itself, the past is in-itself, like inanimate things. It is always the past of a definite present. According to Sartre, I do not *have* my past. I *am* my past. The past is the always growing wholeness of the being-in-itself which we are. That is to say, as being-for-myself I am my present and my projection toward the future, while my past has become a part of the world-in-itself, something completely unchangeable, which is my essence and has the solidity of a thing. In this sense, Sartre says that our past is the perpetually growing wholeness of the being-in-itself which we are.

Now, at the moment of my death, I shall be entirely my past and thus a part of the world-in-itself. By death the being-for-itself becomes entirely a being-in-itself, having ceased to be a present and a possible future and become totally past. And the past is the being-in-itself, the essence of a man, which, as we know, becomes crystallized at the moment of his death.

14 *Ibid.*, p. 168.

If as a living being I cannot slip back into my past, it is because this past is in-itself while I am for-myself. The past is that which I am, without being able to live it. If we say of a man that he is a drinker, or a composer, or a good father, we refer, and can refer, only to his past, because only in the past we are what we are in the form of an unchangeable being-in-itself. In the present, as being-for-ourselves, we *are* not but we become, we are projected toward an uncertain future, toward possibilities which can always be "naughted" by our freedom. But in the past, the world of the being-in-itself, there is no freedom. *Facta infecta fieri nequeunt* ("Things done cannot be undone"), as the Romans said; for things belong to the world-in-itself. And our past too belongs to this world, and cannot be changed by our freedom. This is the sense of Sartre's statement, *"Le passé c'est l'en-soi que je suis en tant que dépassé"*[15]—the past is the in-itself which I am as surpassed.

At the moment of death, "the chips are down," no more bets can be made. Death petrifies us forever, from the moment it strikes us. Alive, I am a being-for-myself, as far as I am my present; a being-in-itself as far as I am my past; and a being-for-others, insofar as I am a transcended transcendence, but always able to transcend another self by my gaze and recover my freedom. Dead, I am no longer a being-for-myself, I have become entirely a being-in-itself; because my present has slipped away, my future possibilities have disappeared, and I have become entirely my past. Dead, I am also a being-for-others, but definitely transcended by the gaze of the other, because I am no longer a transcendence, a freedom able to dominate another freedom and to influence my being-for-others. "To be dead means to be the prey of the living ones."[16]

As long as we are alive, we are "on reprieve" (*en sursis*). The man who was a coward in his past, and is still alive, has kept his freedom to "naught" this past, to project himself toward a heroic future and thus give the lie to other people's opinion of him. A living coward is a coward "on reprieve," who can still die a hero. But when he dies a coward, he is a coward forever, his

15 *Ibid.*, p. 162.
16 *Ibid.*, p. 628.

essence has become crystallized as that of a coward. In this sense we say that death petrifies us forever as we are at the moment it strikes us. Our being is left in the hands of other people, like a cloak we abandoned to them at the moment of our disappearance. They can do with it what they wish. Death gives the final victory to the point of view of other people.

The heroes in Sartre's novels and dramas know this. There is, for instance, Sorbier, in the tragedy *The Victors*, a man of the Resistance, who, with his friends, has become a prisoner of the fascists. The friends are waiting for their hearing, that is to say, for their torture and death. Sorbier has a heroic mind, but he knows that he has a sickly body, feeble nerves which may abandon him when they torture him in order to make him reveal the whereabouts of the other men of the underground. He fears not death but physical pain and his own moral weakness under it. He says to his comrade Canoris:

> I tell you that I would betray my own mother. . . . It is unjust that one minute suffices to corrupt a whole life. . . . Oh, there are cowards like me, but they will never know it. They are lucky.[17]

But he is only a coward on reprieve, and by a last free act he dies like a hero. The chips are down, he has become a hero forever, his essence has become entirely crystallized as that of a hero.

On the other hand there is Garcin in *No Exit*, a deserter and coward, who died as a coward and is now in a fictional hell with his essence irretrievably crystallized as that of a coward. "It was only a physical lapse," he says, "that might happen to anyone." Thus he flees into bad faith. But he does not believe his lie to himself, and knows that his surviving comrades consider him the coward he definitely is now, since his whole being has become his past and thus a being-in-itself. Being now the prey of his surviving friends, he exclaims desperately:

"Oh, if only I could be with them again, for just one day; I'd fling their lie in their teeth."[18] But it is too late, the chips are down, his life has become a part of the world-in-itself, it has been

---

[17] *Morts san Sépulture*, pp. 61–63.
[18] *No Exit*, p. 52.

congealed, petrified into the past. *"La mort transforme la vie en destin"* ("Death changes life into destiny"), says André Malraux in his novel *Espoir*. It is in the past that we are what we are. In Hegel's words, "Unser Wesen ist, was gewesen ist." ("Our essence is what has been.")

There is no doubt that Sartre's philosophy of death is extremely interesting. However, it implies the paradox that *alive* man *is not*; and *dead*, he *is*. It is interesting to note that this projection of death into the past can be found as far back as Seneca, who wrote to his friend Lucilius: *"In hoc enim fallimur, quod mortem prospicimus: magna pars eius iam praeterit. Quidquid aetatis retro est, mors tenet."*[19] ("For in this we err that we foresee death in the future. A great part of it lies in the past. Whatever of our age is behind us, belongs to death.")

"One always dies too soon or too late," says Inez in *No Exit*.[20] Very seldom our death comes like the last sound of a melody, making an organic whole of our life. In general, death surprises us in evolution and what it leaves of us is an unfinished project, a sketch, not a detailed painting. Pierre Curie, who with his wife initiated the science of radioactivity, died in a Paris street accident. His existence, which had been projected as a complete and perfect work of art, became a fragment. The perpetual interference of chance with the individual's projects shows that death is not our free possibility but the negation of all our possibilities. Death is the project which destroys all projects, even itself; it is the destruction of all our expectations. Besides, since the dead are the prey of the living, death is the definite triumph of some self other than mine. Sartre summarizes his refutation of Heidegger's philosophy of death in this way:

> We have to conclude, in opposition to Heidegger, that far from being my own possibility death is a *contingent fact,* which, as such, escapes me on principle and springs from my facticity. I can neither discover my death nor wait for it . . . for it is that which disarms all expectations. . . . Death is a mere fact like birth; it comes to us from outside and changes us into something which is outside. . . . There is

[19] *L. Annaei Senecae ad Lucilium Epistulae*, I, 2.
[20] *Op. cit.,* p. 58.

no place for death in the being-for-itself: the latter cannot wait for it . . . nor project himself toward it. . . . Death is only a certain aspect of facticity and of being-for-others. . . . It is absurd that we were born, it is absurd that we die.[21]

This is a clear renunciation of Heidegger's philosophy of "freedom for death" and "being toward death." Consequently, Sartre also refuses to base his distinction between an "authentic" and an "unauthentic" existence on man's attitude toward death. His distinction between the "authenticity" and "unauthenticity" of our existence is based on man's attitude toward his *freedom*. He who recognizes his freedom as the source of all values and accepts the responsibility and anxiety arising from this knowledge exists *authentically*. He who denies freedom and flees from it into bad faith under the pretext of a determinism which compels him, for instance, to be lazy, in the same manner as a stone is heavy—he who accepts ready-made values—exists *unauthentically*. Applying this concept to a definite situation, Sartre says, in his book on the Jewish question:

> If it is agreed that man may be defined as a being having freedom within the limits of a situation, then it is easy to see that the exercise of this freedom may be considered as *authentic* or *unauthentic* according to the choices made in the situation. . . . And the Jew does not escape this rule: authenticity for him is to live to the full his condition as a Jew; unauthenticity is to deny it or to attempt to escape from it.[22]

The anti-Semite always exists unauthentically, for

> he is a man who is afraid. Not of the Jews, to be sure, but of himself, of his own consciousness, of his liberty, of his instincts, of his responsibilities . . . of everything except the Jews. He is a coward who does not want to admit his cowardice to himself.[23]

Thus the difference between authenticity and unauthenticity has a more general meaning in Sartre's philosophy: it is an atti-

---

[21] *L'Etre et le Néant*, pp. 630–631.
[22] *Anti-Semite and Jew*, New York, Schocken Books, 1948, pp. 90–91.
[23] *Ibid.*, p. 53.

tude toward freedom and responsibility, and not just toward death, as it is in Heidegger's philosophy.

To be sure, in *Republic of Silence,* Sartre says that during the German occupation "the choice that each of us made of his life was an authentic choice, because it was made face to face with death,"[24] and thus gives the impression that he uses the term "authenticity" in Heidegger's sense. However, only because death was ever present for the fighters of the maquis, was it the test case of this situation.

In *The Victors* Sartre has, however, shown that there are situations in which even when one is confronted with a choice between life and death, the authentic choice is not necessarily death but can be life. The group of French underground fighters, imprisoned by the fascists, is suddenly told by their hangmen, that if they continue to be silent they will be shot, but if they betray their leader they will be freed. Fortunately, the situation has changed, they can speak without risking the life of their leader, because now they know the latter is in a safe place. They deliberate, and Lucie, the young woman, wants to choose death. She had behaved heroically, had not spoken nor cried under torture. If she accepts death now, her life will end on a heroic note and will enter the past as the life of a heroine. However, if she continues to live, another event may occur which will find her less heroic, and she may spoil her eternal essence as a heroine which she has won so painfully. Thus she chooses death, because she wants to escape from the freedom and responsibility of tomorrow, which would make her a heroine on reprieve.

Another of the underground comrades, Henri, feels as Lucie does. He also wants death rather than life under the responsibilities of a new freedom. He already has to bear the responsibility for the death of Lucie's fifteen-year-old brother François, whom he had to kill because the boy was ready to betray his comrades in order to save his own life.

However, Canoris, a Greek antifascist who has joined the French underground, makes clear to his friends that it needs more courage to accept life and continue to fight the German invader than to die under the bullets of the firing squad; that

24 *Op. cit.,* p. 499.

he who decides to continue life under these circumstances makes an authentic choice, because it is a choice of freedom and responsibility, while he who chooses death, makes an unauthentic choice, because he chooses escape from freedom and responsibility.

We see, then, that while this kind of Sartrean authenticity is contrary to that required by Heidegger, it is ethically far nobler. But there is still another reason why Lucie and Henri prefer death to life. Henri expresses it by saying: "I had already packed up my luggage, I was already on the other side. Now I must return. I shall see all that again. . . . I thought that it was for the last time."[25]

In short, Henri thought he was already in front of the *wall*, where life ends. This symbol of the wall, which is a recurrent theme in Sartre's novels and dramas, characterizes his interesting *psychology of death*.

For Sartre, man is essentially freedom, the anticipation of his own possibilities projected toward his future. But as soon as man knows that he has to die at a definite, very near date, he can no longer "project" himself toward the future; he feels as if a wall had suddenly been erected in front of him, a wall beyond which he cannot go, think, feel, or plan. He is no longer a real man, because being a man means being free to project oneself toward the future, toward one's possibilities; and this is just what he cannot do, because of the wall in front of him. This is the situation of a man condemned to death, or of one so ill that the physicians have told him he will not live to see the next year. Being no longer a man in the sense of a free project toward the future, the individual who stands before the wall has no longer any moral or spiritual community with his former fellow men. His kind now are only those who face the same wall.

That is roughly the idea Sartre expresses not only in his masterful book of short stories published in France under the title *Le Mur* (*The Wall*), but also in many of his other writings, especially in his great tragedy *The Victors*.

In *The Wall* we see, for instance, the Spanish loyalist, Pablo Ibbieta, in his death cell with two other republicans, awaiting

25 *Morts sans Sépulture*, p. 185.

execution by Franco's soldiers. Here are some of his reflections on his fellow prisoner Tom:

> For twenty-four hours I had lived at Tom's side, I had heard him, I had talked to him, and I knew that we had nothing in common. And now we resemble each other like twins, only because we shall die together.[26]

Standing before their wall together, both are unable to project themselves toward their future, both have ceased to be real men; they understand each other, they form a community of situation. But they have nothing in common with the Belgian physician who comes into their cell to see them and who is not condemned. "We looked at the Belgian, we looked at him, all three of us, because he was alive. He had gestures of a living being. . . . He could think of tomorrow."[27]

Thus those who stand before their wall no longer consider themselves living beings; they are virtually dead. Ibbieta continues:

> I tell myself: afterwards, there will be nothing. But I do not understand what this means. . . . I see my corpse: this is not difficult, but it is *I* who see it, with *my* eyes. . . . If I think that I shall no longer see anything, that I shall no longer hear anything, and that the world will continue for others. . . .[28]

Then, reflecting on his previous life, he says to himself:

> I wanted to free Spain, I admired Pi y Margall, I belonged to the anarchistic movement, I had spoken in public meetings, I took everything seriously, as if I were immortal.[29]

The last sentence affirms the idea that in order to accomplish great things in life, we must live under the fiction of immortality. Ibbieta's reflections and his words, "I would not have been able to move my little finger, had I imagined I would die this way,"

[26] *Le Mur*, pp. 22–23.
[27] *Ibid.*, p. 23.
[28] *Ibid.*
[29] *Ibid.*, p. 25.

are the best refutation of Heidegger's idea that in order to exist authentically, we must place our life under the permanent shadow of our personal death, ready to be stricken at any moment.

Ibbieta also thinks of his girl Concha, who will cry when she learns of his death. "However," he adds, "if she looked at me now, her gaze would remain in her eyes, it would not reach me. . . ."[30] Standing in front of his wall, he understands perfectly that he has no longer anything in common with those people who are not prevented by anything from projecting themselves toward their future, even if it is the woman he loves.

This idea is expressed much more powerfully in *The Victors*. We know that Lucie is imprisoned with her underground comrades and that she and all of them have to die under a fascist firing squad, all except John, the man she loved and adored. Now, standing before her wall, she has everything in common with her comrades who are in the same situation, but nothing in common with her beloved who, tomorrow, will leave the jail and can freely project himself toward his future and all its possibilities. And although this is not John's fault, Lucie's love for him has faded away. Listen to a part of their dialogue:

> *John:* Let me stay with you; I shall be silent, if you want, but I shall be here and you will not feel lonely.
>
> *Lucie:* Not lonely? With you? Oh, John, have you not understood yet? We have no longer anything in common.
>
> *John:* Have you forgotten that I love you?
>
> *Lucie:* It was another woman that you loved. . . .
>
> *John:* It is you.
>
> *Lucie:* I am another woman. I no longer recognize myself. . . . Well, you love me. And so what? . . . Our love is so far behind, why do you speak of it? It had really no importance.
>
> *John:* You are lying! . . . It was our life. . . .
>
> *Lucie:* Our life? Yes. Our future. I lived in expectation. I waited for the end of the war. I waited for the day when we could get married. . . . I waited for every evening. . . .

---

30 *Ibid.*, p. 26.

Now I have no longer any future. I expect nothing but my death, and I shall die alone.[31]

These words, "I shall die alone" (*"je mourrai seule"*), are almost exactly the same as Pascal's (*"On mourra seul"*), and express the idea of individualization of death, so dear to Existentialism.

What are love and marriage? A shared human project. But if one of the love partners suddenly stands in front of a wall, the wall of death which stops him from projecting himself toward the future, he has no longer anything in common with the other partner, who still possesses his human condition, his freedom of projecting himself toward his possibilities. This powerful scene shows that, while for idealistic writers love always seemed to be stronger than death, for the realistic Existentialist Sartre death is stronger than love.

This psychology of death, symbolized by the wall, has certainly been developed very brilliantly by Sartre, artistically as well as theoretically. As for its artistic presentation, Sartre had an excellent predecessor, the Viennese writer Arthur Schnitzler, who developed the same psychology of death toward the end of the nineteenth century, of course without using the descriptive symbol of the "wall," an invention of Sartre's. Schnitzler was a physician, who lived in a peaceful world. Consequently his *morituri* had not been condemned to death by the sentence of a war tribunal but by the diagnosis of a doctor. In Schnitzler's master tale *Sterben* (*To Die*), published in 1892, Felix, a young man, is told by his physician that he has but one year more to live, for consumption is slowly killing him. Suddenly placed before his wall, beyond which he cannot see, nor feel, nor think, he loses all moral and spiritual community with his friends, and even with Marie, his sweetheart, who, at first, intends to die with him. But when Felix has to die and will take Marie with him, she escapes in horror from his hands which try to strangle her. To *imagine* one's wall and to *see* it before one's eyes are two different things. For Schnitzler too death is stronger than love.

The basic idea of the wall, that the dying and living do not speak the same language and that there is little they can com-

---

[31] *Morts sans Sépulture*, pp. 146–149.

municate to each other, is even more clearly expressed in Schnitzler's play *Die letzten Masken* ("The Last Masks"), where the dying journalist Rademacher asks the physician at the hospital to call his former friend, the successful writer Weihgast, to his bedside. It is Rademacher's intention to relieve his embittered heart by telling Weihgast, in the most violent words, how deeply he despises him, and that Weihgast's own wife shares his, Rademacher's feelings, and had been his mistress. He even rehearses the tirade before Weihgast's arrival, with his roommate Florian, who also will die soon. But when Weihgast arrives, Rademacher has nothing to tell him but trivialities. And when, afterward, Florian asks him how the conversation went, the dying Rademacher answers:

> What have I in common with him? Are his happiness, his troubles any business of mine? What did we have to talk about together? What have people like you and me in common with persons who will still be in this world tomorrow?[32]

Here we have exactly the same idea which was later developed by Sartre. We also find Sartre's concept of the wall in other connections not related to death; however, it is in his psychology of death that its symbolism is most impressive. And even though we realize that in this field Sartre had a forerunner—Schnitzler—we must recognize that the French philosopher and writer developed that psychology with the penetrating logic and dramatic genius which characterize most of his writings.

As far as Existential psychoanalysis is concerned, Sartre concludes that Heidegger's "fear of death, the resolute decision, or the flight into unauthenticity cannot be considered as fundamental projects of our being." Consequently, it is necessary to "go beyond the results of Heidegger's hermeneutics, toward a more fundamental project."[33] And we know that the search for the fundamental project, this original choice of man, is the very aim of Existential psychoanalysis. The next chapter will try to show what this fundamental project is.

[32] A. Schnitzler, *Die letzten Masken*, in *Gesammelte Werke*, Berlin, 1915, p. 390.
[33] *L'Etre et le Néant*, p. 651.

xxii
Man's Fundamental Project:
To Become God

In the last chapter we saw that man's fundamental project, the ultimate goal sought by Existential psychoanalysis, cannot refer to death. Neither can it be life, nor any particular characteristic of the human condition. "The original project of a being-for-itself *can only aim at its being.*" But what kind of being? This will become clear when we recall some features of the being-for-itself.

Being-for-itself, or human consciousness, has been characterized as a vacuum within the plenitude of being, as negation or "naughtization," as "lack." Being-in-itself, the world of inanimate objects, is fullness, and "lack" springs up only through human consciousness. Sartre thinks that the existence of desire is the best proof that man is basically "lack." If man were what he is, he would not need anything to complete him. But, being not what he is, man is incomplete. It is the full moon which confers upon the crescent its nature as a crescent. Thus we have to determine what it is that man lacks. Sartre answers that this perpetually absent being, which haunts the being-for-itself and which represents value, is the being-in-itself.

We know that human consciousness never coincides with itself; that it never *is*, but is always becoming. Now, Sartre thinks that for this reason man has the desire—or, better, he *is* the desire—to have at the same time the coincidence with itself of the inanimate world, called being-in-itself, and the translucidity of consciousness, called being-for-itself.

We also know that, to Sartre, man's existence is entirely contingent, without foundation or necessity, gratuitous, absurd, and that it was this insight which gave nausea to his character Roquentin. Now the being for which the self is longing is that of a being-in-itself, which is its own foundation, an *ens causa sui*. Such a being would no longer be contingent, gratuitous, absurd. To attain it would mean to overcome the nausea linked to our existence.

According to Sartre's Existential psychoanalysis, this ontological desire of man manifests itself as a nostalgia for the quiet, eternal, peaceful being of the inanimate objects, just as, in Freud's empirical psychoanalysis, man is nostalgic for his prenatal life. And these two desires certainly have something in common. Both can be interpreted as man's desire to escape from his human condition—into the quiet, passive, imperturbable being of a mountain, or, in Freud's case, toward the unconscious, vegetating life of a fetus. Again and again Sartre's characters express this desire in one or another form. Consider, for example, Daniel's confession in *The Reprieve*:

> If I had been an insensible stone figure, incapable of sound and movement, blind and deaf—flies and earwigs and ladybirds would run up and down me, and I should stand, a fantastic, white-eyed statue, devoid of purpose, impervious to pain—I might then have coincided with myself. Not so as to accept myself, heaven forbid! but thus become the pure object of my hatred. . . . Just to be. In the dark, at random. To be a homosexual, just as the oak is an oak. To extinguish the inner eye. . . . Why can't I be what they see?[1]

What Daniel wishes is a flight from the human condition, an evasion from freedom into bad faith and unauthenticity.

Mathieu also has that fundamental desire for the being-in-itself, but as an Existentialist professor of philosophy, he realizes the impossibility of the synthesis aimed at in that fundamental project.

> He reached out his hands and slid slowly over the stone parapet; it was wrinkled and furrowed, like a petrified

[1] *The Reprieve*, pp. 133–134.

sponge, and still warm from the afternoon sun. There it lay, vast and massive, enclosing in itself the crushed silence, the compressed shadows that are inside the objects. There it lay: a plenitude. He longed to clutch to that stone and melt into it, to fill himself with its opaqueness and repose. But it could not help him; it was outside forever.[2]

As a matter of fact, man does not simply desire his return to thinghood, to a simple being-in-itself. His fundamental project is to be at the same time in-itself, like a thing, and for-itself, like a consciousness; determined like a thing, but free like a man; solid and eternal like a rock, but conscious and sensible like a soul.

It is *as* a being which is what it is not, and which is not what it is, that the being-for-itself projects to be what it is. *As* a consciousness it wants to have the impermeability and the indefinite density of the being-in-itself. *As* a naughtization of the being-in-itself and *as* a perpetual evasion from contingency and facticity it wants to be its own foundation.[3]

In short, man's lack, desire, fundamental project, ideal, supreme value is to become an *en-soi-pour-soi*, an "in-itself-for-itself," a self-conscious cosmos which would be the foundation of its own being-in-itself by the mere consciousness it takes of itself.

We realize that this ideal is beyond human possibilities, and as a matter of fact, that *ens causa sui*, or being which is its own cause and foundation, has always been identified with the concept of God. Sartre admits it openly by saying that the fundamental project of man is that of becoming God. "To be a man means to endeavor to be God. . . . Man is, fundamentally, the desire to be God."[4]

Sartre's term *en-soi-pour-soi* is obviously a translation of Hegel's *an-und-für-sich*. In Hegel it is the attribute of the Absolute, returned to itself in highest perfection. Sartre's *en-soi-pour-soi* is

[2] *Ibid.*, p. 362.
[3] *L'Etre et le Néant*, p. 653.
[4] *Ibid.*, pp. 653–654. See the same definition in A. Malraux, *La Condition humaine*, Paris, 1933, p. 271.

an individualization of that universalistic Hegelian concept of the Absolute.

If man's basic desire is to be God, if he cannot choose anything but to be God, is this not the total negation of his freedom of choice? Sartre denies it by saying that if the project of becoming God is the meaning of our fundamental desire, the concrete desire is never constituted by this meaning but is always a particular invention of aims in relation to man's empirical situation. The desire to be realizes itself always as a desire for a certain *way of being.* And this desire for a certain way of being is expressed in those millions of concrete desires which constitute the web of our consciousness.

Now starting from that ontological premise, Existential psychoanalysis sees in a man's empirical desires a *symbolization* of his personal way of achieving that fundamental and general human project. It can be grasped only in and by means of those empirical desires. The way in which a man tries in his concrete, empirical desires to realize the fundamental human project of becoming God characterizes, even creates, his personality. That fundamental desire expresses concretely in the world and in a person's definite situation a general abstract structure, which is the general reality of man in a person. This allows Existential psychoanalysis to state that there is a general human reality, not merely incomparable individualities. And freedom is expressed in the innumerable concrete forms in which humans manifest their choice of being and try to realize their being "in-itself-for-itself." Every concrete desire, that of eating, sleeping, creating a work of art, or helping other people, expresses the personal project of a man to realize his being-in-itself-for itself, and thus characterizes in an individual concretion his whole personality. This is one of the basic ideas of Existential psychoanalysis.

Man's desire is not only defined by the relation "in-itself-for-itself," or the idea of God-man; but it is also relative to that brute and concrete being called object of desire. This can be anything— a piece of bread, an automobile, a woman. Man's desire is one of the aspects of his being-in-the world. If I desire a painting, it means that I want to buy it in order to *have* it. If I desire to write a book, it means that I want to *make* it. If a woman uses rouge and lipstick, it means that she wants to *be* beautiful. Here are the three great categories of human existence: *to have, to make, to be*; and Existential psychoanalysis attempts to study them.

Of these categories, that of *having* seems at first to be the most important in Sartre's Existential psychoanalysis; we have met it already under the name of "possessing." We remember that Sartre defined the essence of human relations, including love, as a mutual attempt of different selves to possess each other's freedom, to appropriate it, to enslave it. And now we shall see that the same frenzy of possession and appropriation also dominates man's relation to things, to the being-in-itself.

Heidegger has said that knowledge in the sense of the discovery of truth is *Raub*, that is, robbery or piracy.[5] Sartre adopted this primitive theory of knowledge of Heidegger's, which the latter had explained also in his booklet, *Vom Wesen der Wahrheit*.[6] For Sartre, scientific research is nothing but an attempt at appropriation. A truth which has been discovered is *my* knowledge. It is a synthesis of the ego and the nonego, expressed by the possessive pronoun "mine." The relation between the discoverer and the object discovered is that of a "rape by looking." This idea leads Sartre to establish the first complex of his Existential psychoanalysis, called the "Acteon complex." In Greek mythology, Acteon was the hunter who peeped through the bushes in order to see the naked beauty of Diana as she was taking her bath. Sartre thinks that the scientist is a hunter who surprises a nude virgin and violates her with his look.

In knowing, consciousness also draws its object toward itself and incorporates it without destroying it, as the whale swallowed Jonah. Therefore, Sartre's Existential psychoanalysis assumes a "Jonah complex," according to which "to know" is to swallow whole without consuming. Sartre supposes here that "the known object is not affected by knowledge," and this idea is the essence of his Jonah complex. But it would seem that the mechanics of quanta, with Heisenberg's uncertainty principle and Bohr's theory of complementarity, form a neat refutation of Sartre's Jonah complex; for these results of modern physics prove that—

[5] *Sein und Zeit*, p. 222.
[6] Frankfurt am Main, V. Klostermann, 1943, 1954.

at least in the microcosmos—observation necessarily modifies the object observed. Sartre recognized this fact later, in his theoretical work, *Critique de la Raison dialectique* (p. 104).

But what is essential for Sartre is the demonstration that knowledge or discovery of truth is a mode of appropriation and ownership. He sees in it an analogy to carnal possession, which offers us the seducing and bewildering image of a body which is "perpetually possessed and perpetually new, and on which possession leaves no trace."[7]

But on this point one may hold a different opinion, as did, for example, the hero of a novel by François Mauriac, who sees "traces of fingers" on a feminine body which "has served already."[8]

According to Sartre's Existential psychoanalysis, not only knowledge and love, but all other human activities, such as art, sport, charity, are nothing but forms of appropriation, and thus modes of the category "to have."

Take sport, for instance. It is a form of play, and in that too Sartre detects an appropriative tendency. To be sure, play is in the first place the opposite of the spirit of seriousness. Seriousness is characterized by an attitude, which ascribes more reality to the world than to the self. Materialism is serious, and for this reason it is the doctrine of the revolutionists. The latter must be serious, since they feel themselves overwhelmed or oppressed by the world they want to change. The serious man is a man of "bad faith," denying his own freedom and considering himself as a consequence of the world. In Sartre's eyes, Marx is the great pontiff of the spirit of seriousness because he is the author of the materialistic principle of the priority of the object; and man is serious when he considers himself as an object and not as a freedom, an initiative.

Now play in itself is subjective. It is an activity in which man makes the rules and where there cannot be any consequences but those following from man's freely posited principles.

Nevertheless, Sartre also states that play is never free of an appropriative tendency. It is, at first, a desire of "being" and

[7] *L'Etre et le Néant*, pp. 668, 678.
[8] *Fleuve de Feu*, p. 23.

then a desire of "having." The category of "making" is always transitory, and, basically, every desire is a desire of being or having. Sport is the free transformation of a milieu of the world into an element which would sustain action. As an example, Sartre takes skiing, a sport he seems to know fairly well. To see a snow-field, he says, means to possess it. The purpose of skiing is not only to allow quick displacements; it is also, and, basically, *to possess* the snowfield. Gliding down a slope assures one of the mastery of matter, of the domination of the snowfield. "Admirable image of power," he adds.[9]

Again we see that Sartre's fundamental project is close to Nietzsche's will to power and Adler's goal of superiority, as man's basic choice. "It is my snowfield, because I have crossed it a hundred times. It is mine." Sartre finds appropriation in climbing mountains, in swimming, in obstacle races, and other activities. A mountain I have climbed for the first time and on which I have raised a flag is "mine."

To this aspect of sportive appropriation Sartre adds that of "the difficulty we have overcome" in the free act of play. This again is one of Nietzsche's ideas. Nietzsche says in *The Twilight of Idols*, "How is freedom measured? By the resistance which has to be overcome, by the endeavor it costs to maintain oneself on top."[10]

In his essays on literature, published in the French original four years after his main treatise, Sartre declared that "*doing* reveals *being*," and, as we know, he demanded a literature of doing, a literature of praxis, of action.[11] In *Being and Nothingness*, however, he puts more emphasis on the concept of *being*, when he writes: "Art, science, play, are activities of appropriation, be it totally, be it partly, and what people want to possess, beyond the concrete object of their quest, is *being* itself, the absolute being-in-itself."[12]

But what is possession? Fichte, under the influence of Rousseau, saw in ownership the result of a social contract, according to which a person renounces the use of the goods of all other people in exchange for the exclusive right to use one thing. "But he who

[9] *L'Etre et le Néant*, p. 673.
[10] *Gesammelte Werke*, VIII, p. 149.
[11] *What Is Literature?* p. 238.
[12] *L'Etre et le Néant*, p. 675.

has not received anything exclusively for himself, has renounced nothing. . . . Not having been included in the compact, he preserves his original right to do in every respect what he wants."[13]

From this Marxism derives the right of the proletariat not to recognize the property relations in the capitalistic world. Sartre, on the contrary, who calls himself a Socialist, refuses to see in property only a conventional social concept. According to him, property is a basic ontological relation between man and the being-in-itself. We assume that this is another reason for the Communists' opposition to Sartre.

For Sartre, ownership is an internal link in being. We recognize the possessor in and by the object he possesses or possessed. This is the significance of relics. We recognize Lincoln in an object which had belonged to him and is now in a museum.

This internal ontological link between the owner and the object owned is explained by a kind of unification. "To possess means to unite oneself with the object possessed under the sign of appropriation."[14] Thus the desire for a particular object is not only a desire for that object, but it is also a desire to unite oneself with the object and to achieve the unity called "possessor-object possessed." Consequently, the desire of *possessing* is reduced to the desire of *being* in relation to a certain object.

The Existentialist Sartre is satisfied with having reduced in this way the desire "to have" to a desire "to be." Nevertheless, the desire "to be" continues to manifest itself in the form of a wild urge "to have," to appropriate, to possess. This longing for possession is the manifestation of the project to be an "in-itself-for-itself," a God-man. In each case the appropriation is characterized by the fact that the object appears to us at the same time as a subjective emanation of ourselves and as a relationship of exteriority, independent of us. For Sartre, the possessive pronoun "mine" expresses an intermediary relationship between the absolute interiority of the ego and the absolute exteriority of the nonego. It is in this syncretism of ownership that the nonego becomes ego and the ego becomes nonego. In this relationship we meet also a "value," or the ideal indication of the total being

[13] J. G. Fichte, *Der geschlossene Handelsstaat* (1800) in *Sämtliche Werke*, Berlin, 1845, III, p. 445.
[14] *L'Etre et le Néant*, p. 678.

which would be achieved by the union of a man and his property. Consequently, appropriation is a relation between the being-for-itself, called man, and the being-in-itself, called thing. It is through ownership that man becomes God in this philosophy of Sartre's, which looks like an ontological foundation of capitalism.

This characteristic of Sartre's philosophy seems to be even more pronounced in his theory of money. Appropriation is to him a kind of creation. In a primitive society I have to create the object which I want to possess. In modern society this creative function is only masked, not abolished: "The object I possess has been bought by me. *Money* represents my power." It is an instrument of possession.

Bacon said knowledge is power. But Sartre says "money is synonymous with power. . . . To have is to create."[15] He thinks the whole of my property reflects the whole of my being. The house, the car I possess, *is* I. Schopenhauer taught that what is important in man is not what he *has* nor what he *represents* in society, but only what he *is*. Sartre, on the contrary, states: *"I am what I have."* Obviously, this union between the for-itself-I-am and the in-itself-I-have seems to attain the ideal of the in-itself-for-itself, man's project to be God. Divinity through ownership— is this not a strange formula for a Socialist?

We must remember, however, that some of Sartre's basic ideas on ownership and money had already been expressed a century earlier by the founder of scientific socialism himself—Karl Marx —although Marx conceived of the ideas as a critique of society. Even Sartre's verbal expressions are similar to those used by Marx in his commentaries on passages from Goethe's *Faust* and Shakespeare's *Timon of Athens*, except that Marx wrote in German and Sartre in French. If we translate the two passages into English, their similarity becomes obvious.

In 1844 Marx wrote: "What I can pay, that is, what money can buy, *is* I myself, the owner of the money. My power is as big as the power of money. . . . If money is the bond which links me with human life, society, nature, and man, is then money not the bond of all bonds?"[16]

---

15 *L'Etre et le Néant*, pp. 679–680.

16 *Geld* ("Oekonomisch-philosophische Manuskripte," 1844) , in *Marx-Engels Gesamtausgabe, Erste Abteilung*, Berlin, 1932, *Band* 3, p. 147.

In 1943 Sartre wrote: "I am what I have. . . . Money represents my power. . . . it represents my magic bond with the object."[17]

It is unnecessary to add that in analyzing the concepts of ownership and money, Sartre, as usual, does not refer to his predecessor.

Sartre comes to the conclusion that appropriation is nothing but the symbol of the self's ideal, or "value." In identifying ownership with value he seems to efface the difference between value and price, which Kant separated so ingeniously.

However, Sartre insists on the *symbolic,* ideal character of all these relations, and not on their utilitarian aspect. No gesture of utilization really achieves the appropriative pleasure, but only refers me to another, as Schopenhauer had already remarked. Sartre thinks that beyond its symbolic value appropriation does not amount to very much. Ownership only indicates one supreme pleasure: that of being the possessor's own foundation, but this is always beyond any appropriative attitude destined to achieve it.

Now Sartre thinks that this insight into the impossibility of really possessing an object explains man's violent desire to destroy. To him, destruction means a kind of resorption of the in-itself by the for-itself, a relationship as profound as that of creation. This approach reminds us of Ernst Jünger's glorification of destruction as a basic human passion.[18]

Man is the foundation of the barn which burns and which he set on fire, Sartre says, hinting at a kind of divinity through destruction. "Destruction achieves appropriation, perhaps finer than creation, for the object destroyed is no longer there to show itself impenetrable."[19]

Albert Camus certainly was inspired by this theory of Sartre's when in his gruesome tragedy *Caligula* he made the Roman tyrant say the following words: "I live, I kill, I practice the frantic power of the destroyer, beside which that of the creator seems to be a grimace."[20]

[17] *L'Etre et le Néant,* pp. 679–680.

[18] *In Stahlgewittern,* Berlin, 1922; American edition, *Storm of Steel,* Garden City, N.Y., Doubleday, 1929.

[19] *L'Etre et le Néant,* p. 683.

[20] *Caligula,* Paris, 1947, p. 209; American edition, *Caligula and Three Other Plays,* New York, Alfred A. Knopf, 1958.

Using something, and thus slowly destroying it, is also an appropriative activity. Besides all utilitarian advantages, usage creates a secret pleasure, because it is a partial destruction caused by us. This is the real reason of our pleasure in *consuming*. Consumption, for Sartre, means at the same time appropriative destruction and alimentary pleasure. Consumption is "destruction by incorporation."[21] Did Sartre not realize that here he was not describing a new feature of his Existential psychoanalysis, but only Freud's *death instinct*? Freud referred to "the act of eating as a destruction of the object with the final aim of incorporating it."[22] Even the wording of Sartre's and Freud's statements is the same.

Sartre's Existential psychoanalysis goes further in applying Freud's death instinct, the aim of which is, according to its author, "to undo connections and so to destroy things."[23] Generosity, for instance, is considered by Sartre not as irreducible, but as a primitive form of destruction. I destroy a thing not only by annihilating it but also by giving it away. While idealism always considered generosity as an unselfish ethical manifestation, Sartre thinks that the rage of destruction, which is at the bottom of generosity, is only a veiled form of the rage to possess. "Donation is a harsh and brief, almost sexual, pleasure: to give is . . . a destructive, appropriative contact." But also the being-for-others interferes with this relationship, for, according to Sartre's Existential psychoanalysis, generosity is an appropriation by destruction, because it uses that destruction "in order to enslave the other person."[24] Sartre concludes by saying that whenever Existential psychoanalysis finds generosity in a person, it has to search for his original project and to try to find out why this person has chosen appropriation by destruction rather than by creation. This will reveal the original relation to being, which constitutes the person in question.

It is a general tendency of any science dealing with human things to reduce values to value-free facts. However, in dealing

[21] *L'Etre et le Néant*, p. 684.
[22] *An Outline of Psychoanalysis*, p. 21.
[23] *Ibid.*, p. 20.
[24] *L'Etre et le Néant*, p. 685.

with generosity, Sartre merely reduces positive values to negative ones. In admitting psychology as such, we should be compelled to accept even this, if only the demonstration were better founded. But I submit that Sartre's reduction of generosity to a desire to possess, to destroy, and to enslave is too farfetched and highly artificial.

We are accustomed to judge the rage to possess as a moral phenomenon. However, Sartre tries to give it a mere ontological meaning. If we want to possess a certain object, it is as a *representative* of the being-in-itself, which we want to appropriate to ourselves in order to be our own foundation and to overcome the nausea of our contingency and gratuitousness.

Every appropriative project aims at changing the ego, or being-for-itself, into the foundation of the world—into the concrete wholeness of the world, the concrete wholeness of the being-in-itself—by means of an ideal identification between the being-for-itself and the being-in-itself.

> To-be-in-the-world means to project to possess the world, that is to say, to grasp the whole world as that which the being-for-itself lacks, in order to become in-itself-for-itself; it means to become engaged in a totality which is the ideal, the value. . . .[25]

This sentence is quoted from the ontological treatise which Sartre published in Paris during the German occupation, and we may be sure that the Nazis liked it. For it could easily be interpreted as a philosophical justification of their dream of possessing the world.

After Hitler's defeat, Sartre may have felt the scandalous implications of this doctrine, for he reversed it completely in his essay on literature, where, as the reader will remember, he affirmed emphatically:

> We are no longer with those who want to possess the world, but with those who want to change it, and it is in the very plan of changing it that the secret of its being is revealed.[26]

[25] *Ibid.*, p. 688.
[26] *What Is Literature?* p. 238.

This Marxian formula fitted very well into the "historical situation" of France in 1947, when it was first published; just as four years earlier, the rather Hitlerite formula, "to be in the world means to project to possess the world," reflected the situation of a Europe dominated by the Nazis. This contradiction may serve as an example of a philosophy "in historical situation," which has abandoned the traditional idea of timeless truth.

Man's desire to possess the whole world is only a logical consequence of Sartre's premise that man's fundamental project is to be God. For God is the being who possesses the world. My freedom, Sartre says, is "a choice of becoming God," and all my projects reflect this choice, in an infinity of ways of being and having. Now Existential psychoanalysis aims at finding in all these empirical and concrete projects, the original manner in which each person has chosen his being. But this means that Existential psychoanalysis must also find out why one person chooses to possess the world by means of certain particular objects, while another person chooses to possess it by means of other objects. For, Sartre insists, the object is not irreducible. We are aiming at the being of the object by means of its manner of being, or its "quality." This leads Sartre to his psychoanalysis of objects and qualities.

xxiii
The Psychoanalysis of Qualities and Foods: Viscosity and Nausea

For sartre's Existential psychoanalysis the material qualities of the objects we want to possess—the fluidity of water, the density of stone, the viscosity of candy—are different symbolic ways of representing being. What we choose in those objects is a certain way in which being reveals itself and can be possessed. Red and blue, the taste of tomatoes or green peas, are not considered by Existential psychoanalysis as irreducible facts, and neither are our preferences for, or dislikes of, these qualities.

Existential psychoanalysis first wants to reveal the "ontological meaning" of these qualities, and only then will it try to explain a person's preference for, or dislike of them. It is only in this way, and not by considerations of sexuality, Sartre says, that his new discipline will be able to explain the tastes of certain persons: for instance, why Peter or Paul like oranges but would vomit if compelled to eat oysters. Thus Existential psychoanalysis no longer maintains the old dictum *de gustibus non est disputandum* ("tastes are beyond discussion"). For tastes, or the preference of certain poets for certain metaphors—Poe's fluidity of water, Rimbaud's geological images—symbolize a certain way of choosing being. Existential psychoanalysis does not consider the preference for sweet, bitter, or viscous things as irreducible, but sees in these qualities certain aspects of being, and in the preference for these qualities certain fundamental choices of being characterizing certain persons. For a man "is" what he prefers.

Schopenhauer says that there are two kinds of thinkers: those who became philosophers by observing the world and those who became philosophers by reading a book. Sartre, certainly, belongs to the latter group. He became a phenomenologist by reading Husserl, an Existentialist by reading Heidegger, and an Existential psychoanalyst by reading Gaston Bachelard—and also Freud and Adler, of course. For the basic idea of Existential psychoanalysis, and even a part of its development, can be found in Bachelard, especially in his *Psychanalyse du Feu* (*Psychoanalysis of Fire*) and in his *L'Eau et les Rêves* (*Water and Dreams*). Bachelard, a professor of philosophy at the Sorbonne, died a few years ago.

But we do not mean to say that Sartre is merely a compiler. He has a remarkable creative talent, but one which always needs to be inseminated and stimulated by other people. Metaphorically speaking, his creative talent is feminine rather than masculine.

In *Water and Dreams*, Bachelard distinguishes between a "formal" and a "material imagination." The latter is a kind of physics and chemistry of our dreams, including the daydreams of the poets, which compel them to borrow their metaphors from certain realms of nature. Bachelard thinks that in all those images it is the matter which commands the form. The material things themselves have a significance, a symbolism, which has to be explained in relation to the personality of the one who chose it. In considering, for instance, the poetry and prose of Edgar Allan Poe, Bachelard thinks that there is a synthesis of beauty, death, and water in the metaphors.

Sartre does not like Bachelard's term "material imagination," because, according to him, Existential psychoanalysis is not interested in *images*, or metaphors, but wants to explain the significance of *things*. However, in spite of his term "material imagination," Bachelard too is interested in the material significance of things. This becomes clear, for instance, when he says:

> . . . that the voices of water are hardly metaphoric, that the language of water is a direct poetical reality, that the brooks and the rivers *sonorize* the mute landscapes with a strange fidelity, that the rustling water teaches birds and men how to sing, to speak, to repeat, and that there is . . . a continuity

between the word of water and the word of man. Conversely, we will insist on the fact . . . that, originally, human language has a *liquidity* . . . a water in the consonants.[1]

Thus, as Sartre himself admits, the difference between him and Bachelard seems to be largely terminological. Sartre insists with vigor on the necessity of applying psychoanalysis not only to persons but also to things, and of creating a "psychoanalysis of things." The latter would have to determine the way in which each quality, each thing, and each matter is an objective symbol of being and in what relation it stands to man. It tries to determine what Sartre calls the "metaphysical contents" of every revelation of being. "What," he asks, "are the metaphysical contents of the qualities red, yellow, polished, rough?"

When we say that a man's shaking hands are "slimy," or when we speak of a "viscous" smile, we believe that we are just using a metaphor. "You are wrong," Sartre says, and he goes on to explain to us that viscosity, like any other quality, is of an objective nature "which is neither material (and physical) nor psychical, but which transcends the opposition of the psychical and the physical by revealing itself to us as an ontological expression of the world as a whole. . . ."[2] For Sartre viscosity symbolizes being in a certain way; and it is not by analogy, nor by a projection of our feelings into that quality that the latter acquires a symbolic character. He thinks that in order to establish a symbolic relation between viscosity and sticky meanness, we must already have felt meanness in viscosity and viscosity in certain forms of meanness. What he seems to have in mind is a kind of a priori link between the *physical* quality of viscosity and the *moral* quality of meanness, a link we may discover, but which we do not create. It is as though we sprang up in a world in which *feelings* and *acts* are endowed with *material qualities* such as viscosity, softness, etc.; and *material substances* endowed with *psychical significances*, which make them repugnant, horrible, attractive, etc.

Sartre believes we are confronted with a boundless universal symbolism, which expresses itself in our likes and dislikes for

[1] *L'Eau et les Rêves*, Paris, 1942, p. 22.
[2] *L'Etre et le Néant*, pp. 698.

these or those objects whose materiality in itself is significant. If we find a feeling viscous or bitter, this is not an image, a metaphor, but *"une connaissance,"* a knowledge.

It seems to me that, in conceiving his psychoanalysis of qualities, Sartre was again strongly influenced by Edmund Husserl, and especially by the latter's idea of "material ontological disciplines" of an a priori character, whose task would be "to analyze the essences of nature eidetically."[3] What these material ontological natural sciences (to which Husserl wanted to subordinate the empirical natural sciences) look like in actual fact we can see from the *Realontologie* of his disciple, Mme Hedwig Conrad-Martius, which Husserl found worthy to be published in his yearbook of phenomenology, although it is composed of "revelations," such as the following:

> Light-giving is a source of light in itself. It spreads light by virtue of being lit inwardly. . . . Pure light is in pure self-glorification. . . . Shining, as such, implies emergence and start, self-transcendence, devotion and revelation, purely and simply.[4]

I think that this phenomenology of light, the merely verbal character of which is obvious, has to be considered as a forerunner of Sartre's psychoanalysis of viscosity and other qualities. The difference is only that Sartre did his analysis with much more intelligence than the German woman philosopher, whose "intuitive revelations" on the "essence" of light are almost ridiculous. Both of them, however, use Husserl's phenomenological method. Sartre thinks that viscosity is discovered by Husserl's phenomenological "intuition" and that it is an "objective" quality, an objective structure of the world. Considering the great importance of the concept of viscosity in Sartre's philosophy and in his novels and dramas, we translate here some characteristic passages about this quality:

[3] *Ideen zu einer reinen Phänomenologie*, Halle, 1922, p. 20; American edition, *Ideas: General Introduction to Pure Phenomenology*, New York, Macmillan, 1952, 1958.
[4] "Realontologie," *Jahrbuch für Philosophie und phänomenologische Forschung*, IX (1929), pp. 339, 341, *passim*.

The viscous reveals itself essentially as suspicious, because in it fluidity slows down; it is the coagulation of liquidity, that is to say, it represents in itself a growing triumph of the solid over the liquid. . . . The viscous is the agony of water. . . . Water is more transient, but one can possess it, even in its flight. . . . A drop of water touching the surface of a sheet of water is immediately changed into a sheet of water . . . it is like a spiritualization and de-individualization of a particular being, which dissolves itself in the great wholeness from which it sprang. . . . This symbol . . . seems to have a great importance in the constitution of pantheistic schemes; it reveals a particular type of relationship between being and being. . . . However, in the viscous (which melts) there is at the same time a visible resistance, like the refusal of an individual who does not want to be annihilated in the whole of being. . . . In the unseizable character of water there is a pitiless hardness which gives it a secret sense of metal: it is like steel finally incompressible. The viscous is compressible, and gives, at first, the impression of a being which can be possessed. . . . The viscous is docile; only at the very moment in which I think I possess it, it possesses me. In this appears its essential character. . . . I open my hands, I want to drop the viscous, but it clings to me, it pumps me, it sucks on me. It is a soft, driveling, feminine activity of aspiration. . . . There is a poisonous possessiveness; there is a possibility that the in-itself absorbs the for-itself . . . and the in-itself draws the for-itself into its contingency, its undifferentiated exteriority, its existence without any foundation. . . . The viscous is the revenge of the being-in-itself. . . . To touch the viscous means to risk being diluted into viscosity. This dilution is dreadful, because it is the absorption of the being-for-itself by the being-in-itself.[5]

We easily recognize in these words the deep symbolism of the viscous and its prominent significance in the whole of Sartre's philosophy. To demonstrate his Existential psychoanalysis of qualities, he could have chosen any quality. If he chose viscosity,

[5] *L'Etre et le Néant*, pp. 699–702.

it was because it is the symbol of nausea and our whole nauseous existence, in which the ego, the free being-for-itself, is again and again threatened with absorption by the being-in-itself, the absurd, contingent, brute thinghood which stagnates and solidifies the liquidity of our freedom. For the liquidity, or fluidity, of water is the symbol of our consciousness, our freedom; and the slackening of this liquidity, its stagnation and growing solidification into the stickiness of the viscous, is the symbol of our collapse into thinghood, the loss of our freedom and our human condition.

However, thinghood would seem to be better symbolized by the solidity and hardness of a stone than by the sticky structure of the viscous. And, as a matter of fact, in expressing their yearning for the quiet, peaceful being of inanimate objects, the characters of Sartre's novels always dream of becoming hard like stone. We saw in *The Reprieve* that Mathieu wanted to melt into the stone of a balustrade of the Seine River, and Daniel wanted to become a stone figure, a white-eyed statue, incapable of sound, blind, and deaf.

But it is impossible for a man to attain this totality of thinghood symbolized by the statue, the brute and mere being-in-itself. As Kant has said, man is a citizen of two worlds (*Bürger zweier Welten*), the moral world of freedom and the physical world of determinism. When Sartre says that man is partly a being-for-itself and partly a being-in-itself, this only translates Kant's dualism into another terminology. For the being-for-itself is freedom, and the being-in-itself is the deterministic world of thinghood. But Sartre added something very important to this Kantian dualism: the insight that man is never entirely the one and never entirely the other; he has never entirely the fluidity of water and never entirely the solidity and impenetrability of a stone. On his way from the fluidity of his consciousness to the hardness of a stone, man is *coagulated* into something intermediate, which is *viscous*. The human body, this soft, gelatinous mass imprisoning freedom by thousands of sucking, clutching, pulpy arms, is basically viscous and the source of a permanent nausea. Only after studying the psychoanalysis of the viscous can we fully understand Sartre's novel *Nausea*, which reflects the lessening of the fluidity of our freedom, the solidification of our consciousness, our slow debasement into the soft, formlessness of chaotic, in-animate nature, the "absorption of the being-for-itself by the being-in-itself," which, for Sartre, characterizes viscosity and in which he sees the symbolization of the "antivalue" (*antivaleur*).

In an earlier chapter we saw that being-in-itself is represented not only by the material world, but also by our own past. And in Sartre's eyes, the predominance of the latter seems to be one of the greatest dangers to freedom. In this connection he speaks of a consciousness which wants to project itself toward its future, its possibilities, but which is suddenly, sneakingly, held back by the invisible suction of its past and slowly diluted into this past. The past is in-itself, while the present of consciousness is for-itself. Thus, the absorption of the present by the past is tantamount to an absorption of the being-for-itself by the being-in-itself, and this again, by Sartre's definition, is viscosity. If the wealthy society woman and the labor leader, who fall in love in Sartre's screen-play *The Chips Are Down*, fail to make a new common start in life, it is also because they cannot free themselves from the octopuslike embrace of the arms of their respective pasts.[6]

When our consciousness becomes "viscous," our ideas become "sticky." The horror in viscosity is that time becomes "viscous," that facticity progresses continuously and sucks up our being-for-itself, our freedom. In that state of viscosity it is no longer the being-for-itself which would absorb the being-in-itself in order to become its own foundation and to achieve the supreme value. It is, on the contrary, the being-in-itself, the brute thinghood, which absorbs the being-for-itself and its freedom, and draws it into complete exteriority and contingency. Consequently, the victory of viscosity is exactly the reverse of man's project to pos-sess the world and thus to become God, for viscosity is man's being possessed by the world. And since the realization of the project of man's possessing the world would mean the realization of the absolute positive value, the victory of viscosity (symbolizing

[6] Gerhart Hauptmann speaks in this respect of the "specters" of our lives of yesterday and compares their function to that of a "backward pulling funnel." See his *Gabriel Schillings Flucht*, in *Gesammelte Werke*, Berlin, 1912, IV, pp. 184, 197.

man's being possessed and absorbed by the world) necessarily symbolizes the absolute negative value, or what Sartre calls the antivalue.

If viscosity is the symbol of the absorption of the being-for-itself by the inanimate being-in-itself of things, what must Existential psychoanalysis think of a person who likes viscous substances in any form, and, especially, in the form of food?

Sartre answers this question only indirectly in his novels and dramas but, nevertheless, with sufficient clarity. A person who likes viscosity would allow his freedom to slow down and finally to stagnate and coagulate into the solidity of things. A person who likes viscosity would give up his human condition in favor of the world, he would give himself the opacity of a thing which is determined by other things. Such a person would ascribe more importance to the world than to his ego and would consider himself as a consequence of the world rather than a free power, transcending the world by his projects. He would accept ready-made values as though they were things and not the result of human freedom. Burying his freedom under the soft, viscous masses of his materiality, in order to avoid the responsibility and anxiety linked to it, he would be a man of bad faith, a slave to the spirit of seriousness, and his existence would be unauthentic.

These are some of the conclusions Sartre's Existential psychoanalysis would draw from the fact that a person likes viscosity. But are not these conclusions too far fetched to be drawn from such simple facts as that a person likes caramels, honey, or cream? These inclinations seem harmless to us, but not to Sartre, who has recognized the devilish character of viscosity and thinks that "taste is assimilation." He insists that "the synthetic intuition of food is . . . an assimilatory destruction. It reveals to me the being with which I am going to make my flesh."[7]

This reminds me of Feuerbach's materialistic principle *"der Mensch ist was er isst"* ("man is what he eats"), which Nietzsche sarcastically applied in his criticism of German cooking, that "degeneration of pastries into paperweights," with the conclusion that the "German intellect is indigestion."[8]

---

[7] *L'Etre et le Néant*, p. 707.
[8] *Ecce Homo*, in *Gesammelte Werke*, Munich, 1928, p. 193.

The materialistic principle that man is what he eats is used by Existential psychoanalysis in a new sense, for here man does not become what he eats, but is already what he wants to eat. "Man is what he prefers," Sartre says. "What I accept and what I reject with disgust is the very being of that existent, or, if one prefers, the totality of the food proposes to me a certain mode of being, which I accept or which I refuse."[9] Consequently, in accepting viscous food with pleasure or in rejecting it with disgust, I accept or reject the mode of being symbolized by viscosity. And the same is true for any other quality of food or drink: bitter, sweet, hard, salty or gaseous. Each quality presents to us a specific type of existence; and we will swallow it with pleasure or spit it out with nausea, not according to the structure of our stomach or some allergy, but according to our "original project." One cannot say that Existential psychoanalysis lacks imagination.

> It is thus by no means insignificant to like oysters . . . or snails, or shrimps, if we only are able to unravel the existential significance of these kinds of food. In a general way, there is no taste and no inclination which would be irreducible. They all represent a certain appropriative choice of being.[10]

Up to now it was only considered dangerous for a person to tell his dreams in a group where there might be a Freudian psychoanalyst. From now on it also becomes dangerous to dine where there might be a Sartrean Existential psychoanalyst.

Viscosity, to Sartre, is the perpetual danger of, and threat to, consciousness and freedom, and no victory over it is definite. As a citizen of two worlds—the one of consciousness and freedom, the other of thinghood and determinism—man has always to fight in order to keep the higher part of his existence from being sucked up and swallowed by the lower part. This perpetual fight is masterfully described in Sartre's novels and dramas, and Robert Campbell is right when he calls Sartre "the painter of human viscosity."[11] Since in Sartre's eyes viscosity is the antivalue, he

9 *L'Etre et le Néant*, p. 707.
10 *Ibid.*
11 *Jean-Paul Sartre ou une Littérature philosophique*, p. 40.

has to paint it with the ugliest colors. This explains why, in his novels, the kisses are given between attacks of diarrhea and love is made between vomitings, as one of Sartre's critics put it, unfortunately without exaggeration. The French magazine, *France au Combat*, was even more violent and called Sartre's Existentialism an "Excrementalism." And Sartre himself quoted another similarly scatological remark by one of his critics, which involves a pun that can hardly be translated: *"Nous avions le mouvement dada, voici maintenant, le mouvement caca."*[12]

Of course, vomits and excrements are repugnant. But in Sartre's work the viscosity they symbolize is even more repugnant: the loss of human dignity, man's debasement to thinghood. We doubt that this symbolism is a real objective structure of the world, as Sartre would have us believe. We would prefer to consider it as Sartre's very personal way of symbolizing moral relations.

We still remember his statement that man's fundamental project is to become God by possessing the whole world in the form of certain qualities. Only by uniting himself with the world possessed, can man achieve that being-in-itself-for-itself, which would be its own foundation, the *ens causa sui*, which religion calls God. We have also seen that viscosity symbolizes man's being possessed by the world and thus is diametrically opposed to the fundamental human project.

But even if man's project to become God by possessing the world were not thwarted by the opposite tendency of viscosity, the project would nevertheless be condemned to failure, for, as Sartre states, the idea of God is "contradictory." Thus man is a "useless passion."[13]

[12] *Pour et contre L'Existentialisme*, Paris, 1948, p. 187.
[13] *L'Etre et le Néant*, p. 708.

Existential Psychoanalysis and Ethics

ONE OF THE CHARACTERISTIC FEATURES of Existentialism is the mixing of scientific, epistemological and moral concepts, disregarding the ideal of a value-free science which modern thought has tried to establish. While Freud's empirical psychoanalysis is such a value-free science, a psychological investigation which abstains intentionally from any value judgment, any moral condemnation or approbation, Sartre's Existential psychoanalysis wants to be considered as a "moral description, because it reveals to us the ethical sense of the different human projects." [1]

This new discipline vacillating among psychology, ontology, and ethics, tried, at first, to detect the origin of the concept of value, and found it in that which the being-for-itself lacks, in order to be in-itself-for-itself and to be its own foundation. Revealing thus the ideal significance of all human attitudes, Existential psychoanalysis rejects any utilitarian interpretation of human behavior and is the enemy of the psychology of interest. Even while stating that "to be in the world means to project to possess the world," Sartre rejects all utilitarian ideas and thinks only of man's quest for being and justification. And although all this looks very much like egoism, Sartre would not admit it. He even suggests the opposite interpretation: that man loses himself so that the absolute may exist.

The main ethical purpose of Existential psychoanalysis is to make man renounce the "spirit of seriousness." We already know

[1] *L'Etre et le Néant*, p. 720.

that the latter means ascribing more reality to the world than to man and considering man as a result of the world, a part of the tangible world. The main consequence of this spirit of seriousness is that under its domination man will consider values as transcendent data independent of human subjectivity, and will transfer the valuable qualities of things from their onto-logical structure to their material constitution. But, claims Sartre, the possession of a thing is not desirable because we like or need it, but because ownership of it symbolizes the ideal value of a unification of the being-for-itself with the being-in-itself. The result of the spirit of seriousness, which governs the world, is that the symbolic values of things are sucked up "as if by a blotter." Things themselves, in their opacity, are considered as an irreducible desirability. Thus the spirit of seriousness implies an ethics of bad faith, which helps man to hide from himself his own aims, in order to escape from anxiety. For the spirit of seriousness objects are "mute exigencies" requiring a passive obedience.

Now Existential psychoanalysis will reveal to man the true aim of his search, which is a kind of synthetic merger of the being-for-itself he is, with the being-in-itself he recognizes and wants to possess. Sartre thinks that many men have applied this Existential psychoanalysis to themselves. Knowing that the aim of their search is being, they would not appropriate things to themselves for the things' sake, but would try to realize a symbolic appropriation of their being-in-itself.

But even then, as long as men are governed by the spirit of seriousness and believe that "their mission to make exist the in-itself-for-itself is written in the things," they are condemned to despair, for they discover that "all human activities are equiva-lent. . . . Thus to take to solitary drinking or to lead nations amount to the same thing." [2]

The terrifying practical consequences of such an axiology of equivalence have been painted by Albert Camus, in his tragedy *Caligula.* "This world is without importance," the tyrant says, "and he who recognizes it conquers his freedom." [3] And he uses

---

[2] *Ibid.,* p. 721.
[3] *Op. cit.,* p. 121.

his freedom in order to humiliate, terrorize, and kill his subjects ad libitum, since "a person is always free at the expense of another person" and "all actions are equivalent." [4]

Sartre thinks that Existential psychoanalysis will save us from the despair of nihilism by teaching us that man is the being through whom values exist, that values are not written in things but that we are writing them into things. But with this Sartre is again only expressing Nietzsche's wisdom, and again without mentioning his name Nietzsche wrote:

> All beauty, all sublimity we have ascribed to things real and imaginary, I reclaim as the property and creation of man, as his most beautiful adornment and justification. Man as a poet, as a thinker, as God, as might, as compassion: with what royal generosity has he enriched things in order to impoverish himself and to feel miserable. It is his greatest abnegation to admire and venerate, without knowing or wanting to know that he has created what he admires. [5]

In our chapter on "Freedom and Values: Sartre and Nietzsche" we showed that Sartre's "spirit of seriousness" is only a new edition of Nietzsche's "spirit of gravity."

There is a very strange element in Sartre's discussion of the ethical aspects of Existential psychoanalysis: he considers it a great merit that it unfolds to man the true aim of his strivings and that this aim is the synthetic merger of the being-for-itself which he is, with the being-in-itself he wants to possess. But had not Sartre stated before that the idea of this merger, the idea of God, is self-contradictory, and that man is a "useless passion"? Thus in revealing to man the true aim of his strivings, Existential psychoanalysis only shows him that even ontologically his projects are senseless, contradictory, and unattainable. I do not see how man is more advanced than before by this knowledge.

Here is one of the reasons why the optimistic interpretation Sartre has tried to give to his Existentialism during these last years appears to be an optimism of defiance, an optimism in

[4] *Ibid.*, pp. 142, 179.
[5] *Gesammelte Werke* (Munich, 1924), Band XI, p. 277.

spite of a desperate situation. To be sure, the ethical implications of Existential psychoanalysis have only been sketched by Sartre, and he has reserved their development to a new theoretical work which has not yet been published. But Simone de Beauvoir, Sartre's collaborator, tried, in her book *The Ethics of Ambiguity*, to clarify some of the questions left open in *Being and Nothingness*.

She states that only a person possessed by the "spirit of seriousness" would try to achieve the impossible synthesis of the for-itself and the in-itself called God, and that the "authentic" man would be willing *not* to "be," in order to "exist." We know that existence is basically man's lack of coincidence with himself and with external being. Madame de Beauvoir thinks that our only salvation is "to accept the lack and to side with a man who exists, against the idea of a God who does not exist." [6]

To be sure, we cannot truly "possess" the snowfield we glide over on skis, but this does not prevent us from enjoying it with a feeling of triumph. "In his vain attempt to be God, man makes himself exist as man," Simone de Beauvoir says,[7] and she insists that man should not seek a foundation for his existence outside himself, since he alone can provide such a foundation. She demands that the "joy of existence" be affirmed at every moment, and seems to be opposed to Sartre's affirmation that "man is a useless passion," since she admits that the concepts, "useless" and "useful" have no meaning outside human existence.

Finally, she denies the equivalence of all human activities, affirming the privileged character of some of them: those which serve the freedom of other people. With Sartre she thinks that man's liberty can be achieved only through other people's freedom, so that the struggle for the former becomes one for the liberation of our fellow men. But since liberty is never definite, it must be conquered again and again. In this sense Madame de Beauvoir, like Sartre, adopts explicitly Trotzky's idea of "permanent revolution." [8] But, as we remarked earlier, this idea implies the contradiction that the revolutionary would never be able

---

[6] *Pour une Morale de l'Ambiguité*, p. 80.

[7] *Ibid.*, p. 19.

[8] *Ibid.*, p. 166.

to enjoy the freedom for which he fought, because he would have to overthrow it by a new revolution, and so on *ad infinitum*.

Since freedom is the source of all values, Sartre says, man cannot want anything but freedom. But this Existentialist freedom is very problematic. Let us recall another consequence of the revelation by Existential psychoanalysis that values are not offered ready-made to our consciousness but are the product of our active, creative freedom. Since nothing justifies us in adopting this value rather than that, this hierarchy rather than that, and since nothing prevents us from revoking our choice of values and replacing it with another, we are entirely responsible for the values we have chosen. We have already seen that this explains man's "ethical anxiety." Now we see that we owe its revelation to Existential psychoanalysis. And through this revelation the new discipline leads us to an "authentic" existence, which is an existence conscious of our freedom and responsibility and, consequently, an existence in permanent anxiety.

In *The Flies*, Sartre gave us an impressive picture of such an authentic existence in the character of Orestes. Having had the sudden revelation of his freedom, Orestes joyfully accepts all its consequences. He recognizes that he is the source of all values, that there is neither good nor evil unless he invents them, and he accepts the terrifying responsibility and ethical anxiety linked to his free choice of values.

When I asked Sartre if Existential psychoanalysis had found any practical application, he answered in a letter, dated October 3, 1948: "I tried to apply it twice: once to the study of an individual (*Baudelaire*), the other time to the study of a collective problem (*Réflexions sur la Question juive*)." The latter appears in an English translation under the title *Anti-Semite and Jew*.[9] To these two masterful psychological essays Sartre in 1952 added a disproportionately large volume of 578 pages devoted to an Existential analysis of Jean Genet which seemed to give too much importance to a subject matter of doubtful value.

The writer Jean Genet, abandoned by his parents as a child, chooses God as a substitute for his missing mother. God becomes

[9] *Anti-Semite and Jew*, New York: Shocken, 1948; Grove Press, 1960.

the witness of his secret life. But from time to time "God turns his head away," and then the boy Genet begins to steal. Just as God replaces the absent mother, stealing replaces the absent property.

According to Sartre, Genet was not interested in the stolen object itself. It only lent substance to his desperate longing to possess. Finally, Genet chose deliberately to be the criminal which society had made of him, became and remained a jailbird until the discovery of his literary talents allowed him to abreact symbolically. In Sartre's words: *"En nous infectant de son mal, Genet s'en délivre. Chacun de ses livres est une crise de possession cathartique, un psychodrame"* [10]—by infecting us with his ailment, Genet frees himself of it. Each of his books is a crisis of cathartic possession, a psychodrama.

In his study of Baudelaire, Sartre tries to show in a concrete way that what one calls a man's destiny is always identical with his free choice of himself. Baudelaire always chose to exist for himself as he appeared to the look of other people. "Baudelaire is the man who has chosen to see himself as if he were another self: his life is only the history of his failure." [11]

We are reminded of the passage in *The Reprieve* in which Daniel cries out his need of being seen, so that his essence would be congealed and he would be relieved of his responsibility for what he is. "To be a homosexual, just as the oak is an oak. Why can't I be what they see?" [12] So Daniel becomes religious, in order to be seen permanently by God.

As Sartre's Existential psychoanalysis of Baudelaire tries to show, the great French poet's life was under the spell of a similar passion for coincidence with himself and for being justified by the gaze of other persons.

At first it was through the gaze of his adored mother that Baudelaire sought definition and justification of his essence. Later it had to be other persons, especially beautiful frigid women, whose gaze he needed in order to know what he was and be justified in his being. In his worst debauches with whores he imagined himself to be under the severe gaze of a goddesslike

---

[10] *Saint-Genet, Comédien et Martyr* (Paris 1952), p. 501.
[11] *Baudelaire*, p. 31.
[12] *The Reprieve*, pp. 133–134.

woman, who would see him as he was and relieve him of the responsibility for his free acts. In his poems, Baudelaire seemed often to identify himself with Satan; and Sartre's Existential psychoanalysis finds that this too served the same purpose. "For what is Satan basically if not the symbol of disobedient children who ask to be petrified in their peculiar essence by the paternal gaze?" [13]

Just as Baudelaire's destiny was his free choice, so is that of the anti-Semite in Sartre's application of Existential psycho-analysis to a collective problem.

> The anti-Semite has chosen to be a criminal, and a criminal pure of heart. . . . Anti-Semitism is only a justification of his existence. His futility is such that he will eagerly aban-don this justification for any other, provided that the latter is more distinguished. . . . In espousing anti-Semitism, he does not simply adopt an opinion, he chooses himself as a person. He chooses the permanence and impenetrability of a stone, the total irresponsibility of the warrior who obeys his leaders. . . . He is a man who is afraid. Not of the Jews, to be sure, but of himself, of his own conscious-ness, of his liberty, of his instincts, of his responsibilities, of solitariness, of change, of society, and of the world—of everything except the Jews. . . . The existence of the Jew merely permits the anti-Semite to stifle his anxieties at their inception by persuading himself that his place in the world has been marked out in advance, that it awaits him, and that tradition gives him the right to occupy it. Anti-Semitism, in short, is fear of the human condition. The anti-Semite is a man who wishes to be a pitiless stone, a furious torrent, a devastating thunderbolt—anything except a man.[14]

In his brilliant story, "*L'Enfance d'un Chef,*" which he might equally well have called "The Making of an Anti-Semite," Sartre has individualized this type in the person of young Lucien Fleurier, who takes his way into the viscosity of an unauthentic existence, away from freedom and responsibility.

[13] *Baudelaire*, p. 88.
[14] *Anti-Semite and Jew*, pp. 50–54.

Besides being a fascinating psychological portrait of the poet, Sartre's *Baudelaire* also outlines the general scheme of man's moral evolution as seen by Existential psychoanalysis: The child considers its parents as gods. They embody the universal reason, the world of absolute values. When the parents look at the child, it feels justified. Since the parents cannot be mistaken, the child is as its parents see it. As a true essence among true essences, the child has its place in the world. Everything it meets is already classified for it, each object has a kind of label, on which the parents have written its value.

However, as the child grows, it loses this absolute security in the realm of values. The boy or the girl becomes taller than father and mother, goes to school and discovers one day that father and mother do not know everything, that they can be mistaken, that they are not infallible, but are just ordinary people. Suddenly, the child sees them in their normal size, unjustified and unjustifiable, their majestic ideas degraded to the rank of personal opinions.

Now the adolescent realizes that the whole system of values he has received must be reconstructed, and that the severe look of his parents no longer fixes and justifies his essence. The child loses its truth: "Unjustified, unjustifiable, it suddenly experiences its dreadful freedom. Everything has to be redone; the child emerges suddenly in its solitude, and in nothingness." [15]

In Jean Anouilh's tragedy *Antigone,* young Hemon says to King Creon: "Father, it is not true! it is not you. . . . You are still as powerful as you were when I was a child. . . . I am too lonely and the world is too naked if I can no longer admire you." But Creon replies: "People *are* entirely alone, Hemon, the world *is* naked. And you have admired me too long. Look at me! To become a man means to see some day one's father's face as it is!" [16]

In Arthur Miller's *Death of a Salesman,* an adolescent's life is broken the day he realizes that his father is not the paragon of perfection he had imagined.

When the adolescent has lost his childhood paradise, two ways

[15] *Baudelaire,* p. 61.
[16] *Antigone* (Paris, 1946) , p. 109; English edition, *Two Plays,* London, Methuen, 1951.

are open to him. He can try to find substitute gods for the gods called mama and papa, and thus find a new paradise. Robert Campbell calls them god-society, god-the-other-person, god-people, god-gaze.[17] The young person would then feel himself justified in the eyes of these new gods. They would give him ready-made patterns of values, which he could accept blindly, and he would be relieved of the necessity of choosing his values for himself, under his own responsibility and with all the anxiety which such responsibility entails. This new paradise is obviously one of bad faith, of unauthenticity, a running-away from freedom, a solidification of consciousness into viscosity and thinghood.

The other way open to the adolescent who has lost his childhood paradise is that of authenticity. The authentic man will accept his freedom, will realize that values are not transcendent entities which he can receive ready-made, that he has to invent and to choose them, free, without help, without excuse, condemned to decide without any possible recourse, with the whole responsibility for his choice resting on his shoulders and, in his heart, all the terrifying anxiety that it entails. The authentic existence is chosen by Sartre's Orestes, who exclaims:

> Suddenly freedom dashed upon me and penetrated me. . . .
> There was no longer anything in heaven, neither good nor
> evil, nor anybody to give me orders. . . . I am condemned
> to have no other law than my own. . . . For I am a man,
> Jupiter, and each man has to invent his own way.[18]

This portrait of Orestes is that which Existential psychoanalysis offers to man as the only moral ideal. It is a great and terrifying image—terrifying, because its basic tonality is anxiety. Trying to convert his beloved sister Electra also to authenticity, Orestes admits this anxiety by saying: "The anxiety which devours you, do you think that it will ever cease to gnaw me? But what does it matter? I am free!"

We may legitimately doubt whether this Sartrean freedom has kept any resemblance to human happiness with which it was always supposed to be closely associated. In Camus' *Caligula*, the

---

[17] *Jean-Paul Sartre ou une Littérature philosophique*, p. 273.
[18] *Les Mouches, Théâtre*, pp. 100–101.

Roman tyrant is asked by his mistress: "Is this dreadful freedom still happiness?" And the emperor answers: "Be sure, Caesonia, that without it I would have been a satisfied man. Thanks to it, I conquered the divine clear-sightedness of the solitary man."[19]

There is no doubt that in seeking freedom Sartre's heroes do not seek happiness. This is obvious also in Sartre's play *Les Mains sales* (Dirty Hands), presented in New York under the title of *Red Gloves*. Trying to explain why he killed the Communist leader Hoederer, whom he admired deeply, Hugo, a young idealist similar to Orestes, says: "I found myself too young. I wanted to hang a crime around my neck, like a rock. And I was afraid it would be too heavy to carry. What a mistake! It is light, horribly light!"[20]

To understand the strange psychology of Sartre's characters, we have to consider it as what it truly is: a reflex of his axiology. To be sure, Hugo surprised Hoederer kissing his (Hugo's) wife, Jessica, and even though Hugo admits that he is no longer in love with Jessica, he nevertheless shoots Hoederer to death. "For a long time I had been living in tragedy. I shot, in order to preserve the tragedy."[21] These words of Hugo's show a conception very close to that of the celebrated Spanish Existentialist Miguel de Unamuno, who taught that we should welcome suffering and anxiety, for through them we become more conscious of the tragic sense of life.

In *The Flies* Sartre suggests that the first step toward an authentic life is to defy God, all gods who want to impose upon man another law than that which he would give to himself by choosing it, including the god-society. In a powerful scene of the play (influenced by Giraudoux' *Electra*), Sartre's Orestes defies Jupiter by exclaiming:

> You are the king of the gods, Jupiter, the king of the stones and of the stars, the king of the waves of the sea. But you are not the king of men. . . . Men are free, and human life begins on the other side of despair![22]

[19] *Op. cit.*, p. 209.
[20] *Les Mains sales*, p. 247.
[21] *Ibid.*, p. 244.
[22] *Op. cit.*, 99–102.

One almost believes that one hears not Orestes but Prometheus, especially the Prometheus of Goethe's wonderful poem, who exclaims:

> Here I sit, forming mankind
> In my own image,
> A race resembling me
> To sorrow, to weep,
> To taste, to have pleasure
> And to have no need of thee,
> Even as me![23]

> Hier sitz ich, forme Menschen,
> Nach meinem Bilde,
> Ein Geschlecht, das mir gleich sei,
> Zu leiden, zu weinen,
> Zu geniessen und zu freuen sich,
> Und Dein nicht zu achten,
> Wie ich!

At the end of Sartre's tragedy, Orestes decides to deliver his people of their complexes of guilt for crimes they have not committed, by freeing them from all the false values which had been imposed on them from outside, by their despotic king Egistus. The sticky flies which attack the citizens of Argos and torture them symbolize these false values imposed on the individuals from outside. The most rotten among these values were those which—at the time the play was written and produced—were imposed on Sartre's compatriots by the Nazis occupying France. As an authentic and victorious resistant, Orestes carries with him this viscous swarm of flies, viscosity being the antivalue of Existential psychoanalysis, symbolizing the absorption of the being-for-itself by the being-in-itself. When Orestes leaves Argos, he is bowed under the "precious burden" of his freedom and responsibility and followed by the howling crowd of Furies, symbols of his anxiety.

Thus we see that while Freud's empirical psychoanalysis tries to *deliver us from anxiety*, Sartre's Existential psychoanalysis

[23] Goethe, *Gedichte*, in *Werke* (Basel, 1944), I, pp. 256–258; American edition, *Poetical Works*, Boston, A. Niccolls and Co., 1902, Vol. I.

tries to *give us anxiety,* the anxiety of an authentic life. Consequently, I do not consider Sartre's Existential psychoanalysis a
psychotherapy in the traditional sense. The present movement
in psychotherapy called Existential psychoanalysis is not based
on Sartre, but on Heidegger's *Daseinsanalyse,* or analysis of existence, and tries to see the patient in his concrete world in which
he lives and moves.

And yet, in one way—not in a medical sense but in a moral
sense—we may consider Sartre's Existential psychoanalysis a
therapy: for it tries to cure man of the infantile disease of unauthenticity and lead him to the *age of reason* of maturity, where
he can stand alone, able to assume his freedom, his autonomy,
and the responsibilities it implies.

At the end of World War II, Sartre depicted the image of a
man who has reached his age of reason in the following words:
"War leaves man naked, without illusions, abandoned to his own
forces, and having finally understood that he can rely only on
himself."[24]

In his play *Le Diable et le bon Dieu* (*The Devil and the Good
Lord*), published in 1951, Sartre gave another, even more forceful
expression to his ideal of the sovereign man who, having liberated
himself from all supranatural illusions, accepts proudly and
joyfully his human task as the only legislator of good and evil
on earth. It is a Nietzschean ideal and also again reminds us of
Goethe, for the hero of *The Devil and the Good Lord* is the same
Goetz von Berlichingen who had been immortalized by Germany's greatest poet. At the moment of his conversion to atheism,
Sartre's Goetz exclaims:

> God is silence! God is absence! God is the loneliness of
> men! There is nobody but me: I alone have decided about
> evil. I alone have invented the good. . . . I alone am accusing
> myself today. I alone can absolve myself. I, the man! If God
> exists, man is nothingness! . . . God does not exist! . . . Joy,
> and tears of joy! . . . No more heaven, no more hell: nothing
> but the earth.[25]

[24] "La Fin de la Guerre," *Les Temps Modernes* (October 1945) , p. 167.
[25] *Le Diable et le bon Dieu,* pp. 228–230.

One almost believes one can hear Nietzsche's admonition to man to be faithful to the earth. Turning toward his beloved Hilda, Sartre's Goetz uses Nietzsche's words to announce to her that "God is dead!"

Unlike Orestes, Sartre's Goetz is not followed by the howling crowd of Furies. But if he is an "authentic" man, he will not escape ethical anxiety, which is the price of liberation.

The reader may remember the passage in Goethe's *Faust* where Mephistopheles writes into the student's album the biblical words: *"Eritis sicut Deus, scientes bonum et malum,"* you will be like God, knowing good and evil. Modern man, as depicted by Sartre, *is* such a god. He knows good and evil because he determines these concepts by his autonomous choices and decisions, realizing that he is the only moral lawgiver in the world. Let him be aware of the tremendous responsibility involved in this high office.

Existentialism and Psychiatry

We HAVE SAID that Sartre's Existential psychoanalysis, by offering anxiety to man, cannot be considered therapy. Empirical psychoanalysis, unlike the Existential kind, undertakes to free man from anxiety—and in many cases, succeeds. We feel, however, that before coming to a final conclusion we must consider the opinions of some psychiatrists. The French mathematician, Robert Campbell, one of the most penetrating and enthusiastic votaries of Sartre's philosophy, declared in an article in 1950, that some psychiatrists ascribe a certain "therapeutic value" to Existential psychoanalysis.[1] Campbell refers especially to the study of Dr. Paul Abély on "Bad Faith in Delirious Persons."[2] We have read this study, but we do not find that this psychiatrist actually ascribes a "therapeutic value" to Existential psychoanalysis. What Dr. Abély really did was to reveal that in many cases of hallucinatory psychosis the patient tries to escape into "bad faith," as defined by Sartre, in order to evade his anxiety. Dr. Abély quotes Sartre and comments:

> I use the term "bad faith" in a philosophical sense. It is not a question of a cynical lie . . . but a negation of his own truth; the subject lies to himself, he is more the deceived one than the deceiver, "his bad faith is faith." He tries to escape from himself, to flee from himself and also to dis-

[1] "L'Existentialisme en France depuis la Libération," *L'Activité philosophique contemporaine en France et aux Etats-Unis*, Paris, 1950, II, pp. 149–163.
[2] "La mauvaise Foi chez les Délirants," *Annales médico-psychologiques* (Paris, 1948), II, 5, pp. 620–624.

place his original responsibility, to project it into the external world. It is a question . . . of . . . escaping at any cost from his own psychic danger, of changing it into an exterior danger . . . and this is *another way of trying to recover his freedom*: to become able to defend himself against something. By this circuitous process arises the delirium of persecution, of demoniac possession, the dilirium of influence, the echo and flight of ideas, auditive, coenesthopathic, psychic, olfactic, genital, and other hallucinations . . . *this ensemble of phenomena is nothing but the effective echo of bad faith.*[3]

Dr. Abély believes that this Sartrean concept of bad faith can be applied in the majority of the cases of delirious persons and that it is particularly important in the cases of the so-called chronic delirium. He concludes by saying:

For the moment I tried to introduce the new concept of "bad faith" in the analysis of these states of delirium, its clinical and physiological modalities. I believe it is able to shed some light on these syndromes, which are still very controversial and badly elucidated.[4]

These opinions of the French psychiatrist are certainly very interesting and may prove that the pictures of certain psychological mechanisms as sketched by Sartre are basically correct. But do they affirm a "therapeutic value" of Existential psychoanalysis? I do not think so. In the only concrete case described by Dr. Abély, he found bad faith as a *symptom* of the hallucinatory delirium; but he says that the recovery of his patient was achieved by shock therapy. The same is true in all other cases to which this psychiatrist refers in a summary way. In all of them bad faith appears as a symptom of the mental illness and Existentialist psychoanalysis as a means to *uncover*, but *not to cure*, either this symptom or the whole psycho-pathological condition. We may conclude that the concept of bad faith introduced by Sartre's Existential psychoanalysis is part of the psychiatric *symptomatology* but not, as Campbell's remark suggests, of psychiatric *therapy*.

---

[3] *Ibid.*, p. 622.
[4] *Ibid.*, p. 624.

As far as therapy is concerned, Dr. Abély proposes different methods, such as prefrontal lobotomy, shock, lowering of the patient's blood pressure—everything but Existential psychoanalysis. And this seems very obvious to us, since all the methods mentioned are able to give the patient *freedom from anxiety*, while Existential psychoanalysis offers him only *freedom with anxiety*.

In the previous chapter we intimated that if Sartre's Existential psychoanalysis is not a medical therapy, it might be considered a moral therapy, trying to cure man of the infantile disease of unauthenticity and leading him to the age of reason, where he can stand alone, free, independent and responsible. From the point of view of psychiatry it turns out, however, that this moral therapy of Existential psychoanalysis can be very dangerous. This is the opinion expressed in an interesting study by a Swiss psychiatrist, Louisa Duss of Geneva. It was published in the same volume of the *Annales médico-psychologiques* as Dr. Abély's report. It cannot have escaped the attention of Robert Campbell, for it covers forty-three pages of the issue, while Dr. Abély's report covers only five. Nevertheless, Campbell mentioned only Dr. Abély's study. Could it be because the Duss study is less favorable to Sartre? Whatever the case, the Duss study deserves careful consideration. Its title is *"Critique psychiatrique de l'Existentialisme"* ("Psychiatric Criticism of Existentialism") and its sub-title *"Expérience existentialiste chez un Schizophrène"* ("An Existentialist Experience of a Schizophrenic").[5] Mme Duss studied the case of a schizophrenic girl named Renée and found a strange relationship to Existentialist philosophy. Three years after the publication of Mme Duss's study, Renée's case became known in the United States, but only under its psychiatric and psychoanalytical aspects, without any reference to its philosophical implications. In 1951 an English version of Renée's autobiography was published in this country,[6] and, in another book, her analyst, Marguérite Sechehaye, a leading Swiss authority, gave the American reader an account of the method, "symbolic

[5] "Critique psychiatrique de l'Existentialisme," *Annales médico-psychologiques* (December, 1948) , II, 5, pp. 553–595.

[6] M. Sechehaye, *Autobiography of a Schizophrenic Girl*, New York, Grune & Stratton, 1951.

realization," by which she cured Renée.[7] Neither of these volumes referred to Existentialism, even though Mme Duss's article about Renée pays special attention to the Existentialist aspects of the girl's schizophrenia. A comparison between Mme Duss's analysis and Mme Sechehaye's books shows that Mme Duss must have had some additional information on the case that does not appear in the two books published in America. In part it came from personal conversations between Mmes. Sechehaye and Duss.

Renée, daughter of a French mother and a Swedish industrialist father, was brought up in Geneva. She combined a remarkable intelligence and a keen logical sense with certain mystical tendencies. A devout Catholic, filled with religious exaltation, she rose each morning at five to attend mass. She had an unhappy childhood, suffering from the mental cruelty of her father and a lack of love from her mother. At the age of thirteen she suffered a deep shock when her mother told her she had been an unwanted child. She suffered from mental illness (hebephrenia), linked with her puberty, and at the age of nineteen developed a delirium, accompanied by autodestructive tendencies, which necessitated her confinement in an institution.

During the years of the development of her schizophrenic condition Renée retained a strange lucidity which allowed her to observe and, after her recovery, to describe her mental and emotional experiences in a remarkable autobiography. Freud thought that such patients, having turned away from outer reality, are more aware of their inner reality, about which they make astounding revelations. Renée's case proves it. Examining her reports and those of her analyst, Mme Duss found that the mental experiences of this young schizophrenic were, in many respects, those reported by the Existentialists, and, especially, by some of the characters in Sartre's novels. Examining this material myself, I agree with many of Mme Duss's interpretations and conclusions, but not with all of them. Her study seems to be based mainly on Foulquié's interpretation of Existentialism[8] rather than on a close study of Sartre and Heidegger. I also have the impression that Mme Duss's final conclusions are too radical,

---

[7] *Symbolic Realization*, New York, Internat. University Press, Inc., 1951.
[8] P. Foulquié, *L'Existentialisme*, Paris, 1947.

because they neglect the emotional factors, which Madame Seche-haye recognized and analyzed in her successful treatment of the girl. For these reasons, I shall first present some results of my own examination of Renée's confessions from the point of view of Existentialist philosophy, and then consider them in the light of Mme Duss's interpretations.

According to Renée's autobiography, her mental illness started with feelings of unreality. Describing these feelings, Renée says that suddenly the outer world seemed to be

> limitless, unreal, mechanical and without meaning. . . . Pupils and teachers were puppets revolving without cause, without objective. I recognized nothing, nobody. It was as though reality, attenuated, had slipped away from all these things and these people. Profound dread overwhelmed me. . . . I looked around desperately for help. . . .[9]

This slipping away of reality and the accompanying dread are known to readers of Existentialist literature. They have been described by Heidegger in abstract terms and concretized by the principal character of one of Sartre's novels. Heidegger wrote:

> In anxiety . . . all things and we with them sink into a state of indifference. This happens, however, not in the sense of a mere disappearance; rather in moving away from us things turn toward us. This moving away of the real in its totality, which, in the state of anxiety, crowds round us, oppresses us. There remains nothing to hold on to. What alone remains and overwhelms us in this slipping away of the real is this "nothing." . . . We are "floating" in anxiety. Anxiety makes us float, because it brings about the slipping away of the real in its totality.[10]

Experiencing Heidegger's "anxiety" concretely, Roquentin in Sartre's *Nausea* describes his feelings in terms which strongly recall those of Renée. Sitting in the reading room of a public library, Roquentin reports the following experience:

[9] *Autobiography*, p. 7.
[10] *Was ist Metaphysik?* 8. Aufl., Frankfurt a. M., V. Klostermann, 1960, p. 32.

I strongly pressed in my hands the volume I was reading. But the most violent sensations were dulled. Nothing looked real. I felt myself surrounded by a scenery of cardboard which, suddenly, could be displaced.[11]

Renée continually speaks of her "dread," "anguish," or "anxiety," which always had the indefiniteness and objectlessness described by Kierkegaard, Freud, Heidegger, and Sartre, and which, as we know, is the dominating pathos of Existentialism. It is also, as we see now, the dominating pathos of schizophrenia. Often Renée's anguish—which "no resolve could allay" and which "squeezed" her heart—was accompanied by the impression that something terrifying, something awful, was about to take place —a catastrophe which, in fact, never did occur. Walking in a street of Geneva, Renée suddenly felt that

> . . . everything seemed to stop, to wait, to hold its breath, in a state of extreme tension. . . . Something seemed about to occur, some extraordinary catastrophe. An overpowering anxiety forced me to stop and wait.[12]

On another occasion Renée "had the impression that some dreadful thing was about to occur . . . something horrible, overwhelming. I waited, holding my breath . . . but nothing happened." [13]

These experiences were much like those of Sartre's Roquentin who, while walking through the streets of Bouville, says to himself, again and again:

> Everything may occur, everything may happen. . . . I ran along the docks . . . the houses with their gloomy eyes watched me fleeing. I repeated to myself in anxiety: Where shall I go, where shall I go? Everything may happen.[14]

In *Symbolic Realization*, Mme Sechehaye reports that, as a child, Renée "sucked the rust of fences in order to 'become stiff like iron' and sucked stones to 'become cold and hard' like

---

[11] *La Nausée*, p. 105.
[12] *Autobiography*, p. 11.
[13] *Ibid.*, p. 25.
[14] *La Nausée*, pp. 105–106.

them."[15] I do not know whether Mme Sechehaye ever read Sartre's novels. If she did, she must have noticed the strange analogy between her patient's wish to become hard like stone and similar wishes of Sartre's characters. The most typical example is Daniel in *The Reprieve*, who exclaims: "If I had been an insensible stone figure, incapable of sound and movement, blind and deaf. . . ." [16] Also Mathieu Delarue, in the same novel, longs for melting into a stone, "to fill himself with its opaqueness and repose." [17]

The common motive of these strange longings of Sartre's heroes is the hidden wish to escape from the responsibilities of human existence. There is no doubt that this is also Renée's dominating motive. Her analyst describes her retreat into autism as "a refusal of life's responsibilities." [18]

Renée's discovery of the "existence" of things was just as awe-inspiring to her as it was to Roquentin. Renée writes:

> When, for example, I looked at a chair or a jug, I thought not of their use or function . . . but as having lost their names, their functions and meanings; they became "things" and began . . . to exist. This existence accounted for my great fear. In the unreal scene, in the murky quiet of my perception, suddenly "the thing" sprang up. The stone jar . . . was there facing me, defying me with its presence, with its existence. . . .[19]

Roquentin underwent similar experiences:

> Existence revealed itself suddenly. It had lost its inoffensive aspect of an abstract category. . . . The diversity of things, their individuality, was nothing but an appearance, a varnish. This varnish had melted. What was left were monstrous soft masses in disorder, naked in frightening nudity.[20]

---

[15] *Symbolic Realization*, p. 25.
[16] *Le Sursis*, p. 133.
[17] *Ibid.*, p. 362.
[18] Sechehaye, *Symbolic Realization*, p. 73.
[19] *Autobiography*, pp. 34–35.
[20] *La Nausée*, p. 166.

Roquentin's discovery of his own existence and its gratuitousness is so terrifying to him that it gives him nausea:

> To exist is simply to be there; the existing beings appear but can never be deduced. . . . Everything is gratuitous, this garden, this town, I, myself. When we realize this, then it turns our hearts, everything begins to float . . . that is nausea.[21]

Renée too felt this nausea when she discovered her own existence in its complete gratuitousness.

> I think that I could be not I: I am appalled at the thought that I could have been in another person's place. . . . Then things would not exist for me as they exist.[22]

Madame Duss, who did not make such a detailed comparison as I am trying to present here, spoke of the "Existentialist experience of a schizophrenic." My inclination, however, is to see in the analogies some *schizophrenic experiences of Existentialists.* Conditions like those described in Heidegger's "floating" or in Sartre's "nausea" can hardly be encountered in normal individuals; they have a definite pathological tinge, and the fact that they are also the most striking symptoms of Renée's schizophrenia can be considered a proof of this contention. Some of Renée's symptoms could be designated as manifestations of a "Heidegger-complex" (the anguished sliding away of reality); some as those of a "Sartre-complex" (the awe-inspiring discovery of existence); and some could be called a "Kafka-complex." By a Kafka-complex I mean a guilt obsession, without the subject knowing wherein his sin lies. Kafka, who twenty years after his death in 1924 was proclaimed a great Existentialist writer, described this unreal guilt in many stories, and especially in *The Trial.* The hero of this gloomy novel, Josef K. (read "Kafka") is accused and found guilty of a crime of which he knows nothing and which nobody will define for him. But his ignorance of the evil of which he is accused does not prevent a profound feeling of guilt. He writes letters of entreaty to the unknown prosecutor,

[21] *Ibid.*, p. 171.
[22] Duss, *op. cit.*, p. 561.

but in vain. His feeling of guilt and his ignorance of its cause remain unchanged to the end of this nightmarish novel. Although some of Kafka's enthusiastic partisans have called *The Trial* a "supra-human work," [23] one has the impression that the unreal world in which Joseph K. moves—a world of unmotivated events, of strangest confusions of places and persons—is that of a schizophrenic. In Renée's *Autobiography of a Schizophrenic Girl,* her Kafka-complex is as clear as noonday. For example:

> I was guilty, abominably, intolerably guilty, without cause and without motive. . . . Indeed, I knew not wherein lay my sin, but the ignorance did not prevent a profound feeling of guilt. . . . One day I wrote a letter of entreaty to the unknown author of my suffering, to the Prosecutor, asking him to tell me what evil I had done, that I might finally know. But because I did not know where to send my letter, I tore it up.[24]

With the development of her schizophrenia, Renée became aware, step by step, of all the basic principles of Existentialism and tried to live up to their rigorous requirements: she realized the problems of choice, freedom, commitment, total responsibility, ethical anxiety, existence as conflict, subjectivity of values, the gaze of other people, etc. For example, she wrote: "People wish me to behave like a poor person, because I am poor. . . . But I decide, I wish, I *choose* to behave like a rich person. . . . Who has the right to judge me?" [25] Evidently nobody; for according to the Existentialist doctrine, there are no standards of good and evil as long as each of us has not set them up in his own way. In the American edition of her memoirs Renée writes that at the psychiatric hospital a doctor asked her how she liked the hangings in her room. "Awful," she replied, and she adds:

> In saying this, I didn't have the least intention of being disagreeable. But at that time, according to my concept of the world, things did not exist in and of themselves, but each person created a world after his own fashion. There-

[23] See M. Brod, *Franz Kafka's Glauben und Lehre,* Munich, 1948, p. 70.
[24] *Autobiography,* pp. 28–29, 54.
[25] Duss, *op. cit.,* p. 563.

fore it seemed natural that the doctor should find the hangings pretty, the nurse find them interesting, and I find them awful.[26]

The "concept of the world" of which Renée speaks is exactly that of Existentialism, which teaches that things become realities only by the fact that man takes interest in them and includes them in his projects. Each man sets up certain relationships among things, and as soon as he loses his interest in them they fall back into the condition of brute existents. The last quotation from Renée's autobiography also expresses the doctrine of the subjectivity of values, the negation of all universal essences and general norms, which, as we know, is likewise an integral part of Sartre's Existentialism.

The same is true of the necessity for commiting oneself, for choosing and assuming a total responsibility for one's choice, which is not sanctioned by a general norm or objective essence. And also Sartre's doctrine that each individual act engages the whole of mankind [27] is incorporated in Renée's pathological philosophy, and the responsibility springing from this principle was taken by her most seriously. It became "obsessional" to her, Mme Sechehaye writes. The girl "did not dare buy herself a roll or a piece of bread when hungry. The two pennies it cost might have satisfied the hunger of some poor man who might otherwise kill someone because of hunger." [28] Explaining the theoretical suppositions of this idea, Renée writes: "Since every man was responsible for all other men, each of his acts had a repercussion on other things." [29] It is almost as if she had read Sartre's sentence: "If we say that man is responsible for himself, we do not want to say that he is responsible for his strict individuality, but that he is responsible for all men." [30] And yet we cannot believe that Renée had read Sartre when she was obsessed by the notion of total responsibility for all men, for the events she describes took place during a period of years ending in January 1938.

[26] *Autobiography*, pp. 54–55.
[27] *L'Existentialisme*, pp. 24–27.
[28] *Symbolic Realization*, p. 26.
[29] *Autobiography*, p. 28.
[30] *L'Existentialisme*, p. 24.

At the time none of Sartre's basic theoretical works had been published. Is it not strange that many of his philosophical positions should appear to have been anticipated by a schizophrenic girl? This we have to admit, however, when we read the following passage of Renée's memoirs, reported by Dr. Duss:

> Everything I do has an incredible importance, because it has unforeseen consequences, which follow every action. I feel myself already committed by the mere fact that I am in the world. . . . Also, to do nothing involves my integral responsibility, which I cannot escape. For if I do not do anything, *I choose* to do nothing, and everything which will result from my decision. What can I do in order to do well? [31]

All this is also taught by Sartre, who, as the reader will remember, wrote that "freedom is freedom to choose, but not freedom not to choose. For not to choose is to choose not to choose." [32]

Sartre's theme of the existence of "the other" self and its tendency to "enslave" him by "gaze" occurs again and again as an obsession in the schizophrenic mental experiences of Renée. Mme Sechehaye told Mme Duss that Renée suffered terribly from the fact of being "looked at" by other persons, that she felt that by this gaze the other person took possession of her subjectivity, degrading her to the condition of an object, trying to "enslave" her, and that in order to defend herself against this tendency she tried to enslave the other person's freedom through her gaze, trying to change him into an object. All this is well known to the reader, from our analysis of Sartre's theories and from the experiences of characters in his novels, especially those of Daniel in *The Reprieve*.[33]

We also remember the Existentialist thesis of guilt and conflict by the mere fact of our existence. "Conflict is the original sense of the being-for-others," Sartre says, for each of our projects limits the other person's freedom. From this springs the concept of guilt. By my mere existence in a world where other persons exist,

[31] Duss, *op. cit.*, p. 562.
[32] *L'Etre et le Néant*, p. 561.
[33] See earlier chapters: Ch. 14, "Our 'Being-for-Others' and Their 'Gaze' "; Ch. 20, "Sex and Love in Existential Psychoanalysis."

I am guilty toward the other person. . . . The original sin is my springing up in a world where the other self exists, and whatever my later relations toward him may be, they will be nothing but variations of the original theme of guilt.[34]

It is like a paraphrase of these Sartrean theses when Renée writes:

Every moment and without intentions we enter into conflicts with other persons. It is a struggle, silent and terrible, in order to resist their "grasp" and to stay in the authenticity of one's being. . . . And I do the same with my neighbors. I am committed by the mere fact of being in the world, etc.[35]

According to Dr. Duss, it was the feeling of total responsibility and guilt of everybody for everything and toward everybody which finally drove Renée to complete insanity. Sartre wrote: "With each of my acts the meaning of the world is at stake and the place of man in the universe. . . . And one wishes that we be not seized with awe before such total responsibility?" [36] Renée draws exactly the same inference with her pitiless logic, when she writes: "Each of my actions leaves a commotion behind it, which will indefinitely change by the repercussion of my initial act, so that future individuals will have to suffer the consequences of my acts. . . . To think of this is appalling!" [37]

Renée's analyst reports that once, on the bank of a river, the girl threw a few stones into the water, but suddenly stopped and exclaimed:

The least gesture involves the whole universe. This stone I am throwing now ricochets and leaves behind it a wake of waves; it may contribute to cause a shipwreck in the ocean. Consequently I shall be the cause of the shipwreck, and I will have to assume the total responsibility. . . . I am guilty of everything, of absolutely everything! . . . By my mere existence I am guilty and I involve the whole world

[34] *L'Etre et le Néant*, p. 481.
[35] Duss, *op. cit.*, pp. 562, 565, *passim*.
[36] Quoted by Duss, *op. cit.*, p. 563, from *Action* (Paris, 1947).
[37] Duss, *op. cit.*, p. 563.

in my disgrace. . . . How terrible this eternal load on our human shoulders! To be sure of nothing, to be unable to rely on anything, and, nevertheless, to be obliged to commit oneself always totally. . . .[38]

These terrifying requirements, pointed out by Existentialist philosophy, went beyond Renée's strength. "How much would I have wished to be relieved from my responsibility, only for a second!" she exclaimed.

In her despair Renée sometimes uttered these unconscious and shocking words: "I should prefer to escape into madness to avoid this consuming fear." [39] She finally did escape into madness, and although she declared later that her hope of finding there relief from her sufferings was vain, Mme Duss thinks that Renée found a pseudo-equilibrium in her delirious construction which she called "the system" and that it helped to reduce her anxiety. The "system" imagined in Renée's delirium was a kind of mechanical organization responsible for the world, thus relieving her from responsibility.

To be sure, in the system we are equally guilty, but not in the same way as in life. Everything is mechanical in it. . . . If one raises his arm, one is guilty; if one puts it down, one is guilty. . . . But if I am guilty, abominably guilty, I am, at least, no longer responsible, either for myself or for the world. For the true chief of the world is the system, the mechanical organization.[40]

However, this pseudo-equilibrium of Renée's delirium did not last long. It was followed by a violent crisis of hebephrenic, catatonic restlessness and a crisis of accentuated stupor. "Except for moments of agitation or intense crises of guilt, I fell . . . into complete apathy. The world was a moving picture, taking place without my participation." [41] Renée's delirium became incoherent, she fell into infantilism, into automatism, echolalia, caducity, interrupted by aggressive and auto-destructive impulsions,

[38] *Ibid.*, pp. 563–571.
[39] *Autobiography*, p. 23.
[40] Duss, *op. cit.*, p. 572.
[41] *Autobiography*, p. 68.

until Mme Sechehaye saved her from definitive insanity by applying her new method, called "symbolic realization."

The conclusions that Mme Duss draws from this case are crushing and, it may be, even too radical. She thinks of Renée as a person who tried earnestly to live up to rigorous principles which exactly paralleled those of Existentialism and, as a consequence, became insane. In order to escape the terrifying responsibility of the individual in a world deprived of universal norms for good and evil and of general categories or logical essences, she returned, in a pathological form, to a world of essences, classes, norms, universal categories—the world of her delirium, which she called "the system." The Existentialists would say that she exchanged her freedom for security, and would despise her for it. From all this Mme Duss infers that the principles of Existentialism are not consonant with life. Man is unable always to use his free will and judgment without being able to rest upon any universal principle and without being directed by any general norm. For a person who wishes to carry out this principle of freedom to the utmost in his individual choice, without being guided by general norms and with the total individual responsibility required by Existentialism, there is only one alternative left, according to Mme Duss: suicide or escape into insanity. Renée avoided suicide only because she escaped into insanity. This was the only way to evade the terrifying responsibility which her Existentialist-like philosophy tried to load upon her shoulders. By her psychotic construction of a universal "system" into which she could discharge her responsibility for the world, Renée was able to reduce her anxiety so that it did not totally crush her.

Trying to apply the Freudian psychoanalytic technique to Existential psychoanalysis itself, Mme Duss thinks that the latter constitutes a return to the sado-masochistic state of our psyche. This fixation, she thinks, explains the apparent need of the Existentialist philosophers to crush their disciples under a terrifying responsibility; it also explains the kind of morbid pleasure the masters of Existentialism seem to feel in developing the irrational, almost inhuman consequences of this responsibility, which, after all, is exaggerated.

Does this mean that Existentialism is a philosophy of lunatics?

From reading the confessions of Sartre's Roquentin or of Kafka's Joseph K., one truly has this impression. But such a conclusion would go too far. Mme Duss thinks that the difference between a normal Existentialist philosopher and a pathological Existentialist, like Renée, is that the former dissociates himself emotionally from his intellectual thesis and does not truly apply it to his own life. This "bad faith" of the Existentialist philosopher is in a certain way his self-defense against his mental self-destruction by this philosophy of despair and nothingness. But the pathological Existentialist, like Renée, is deprived of this kind of self-defense through bad faith. She is sincere, and follows her version of the requirements of Existentialist philosophy to the end, trying to test to the utmost the thesis of total responsibility in a normless world. The result is total madness.

There might be a good portion of truth in Mme Duss's conclusions, but it seems to me that they do not follow cogently from Renée's case. Mme Duss presents the case of this schizophrenic girl as if her main unsatisfied mental need had been of an intellectual, epistemological character: the need of a system of categories and norms of universal validity. But from reading Mme Sechehaye's extremely interesting *Symbolic Realization,* and her "analytic interpretation" of Renée's autobiography, one understands clearly that the girl's psychic needs were mainly *emotional.* The crux of her mental illness was that as an infant she had been deprived of maternal love. Mme Sechehaye explains:

> Renée could not love herself, since her mother had refused to nourish, hence, to love her. When the ego is no longer charged with libidinal energy produced by the introjection of maternal love, destructive forces soon pervade it. As Freud has shown, there is a complication of drives. When the libidinal drives are frustrated, the drives to self-preservation lose their defensive energy and abandon the ego to self-destruction. He sees in the latter one aspect of the death-instinct linked to primary masochism.[42]

[42] *Symbolic Realization,* p. 118.

We understand now the true purpose of Renée's delirious construction called "the system." Renée's mother had seemed to condemn her desire for nourishment and had created in the child the idea that it was bad to want to eat. Consequently, the desire to live was also blameworthy. Therefore, Renée refused food and often had to receive nourishment through artificial means. Yet her irrepressible desire for food created in her terrifying feelings of guilt. "These guilt feelings," explains Mme Sechehaye, "were alleviated by *self-punishment which attended the System.*" [43] Here is the true purpose of Renée's delirious "system," which is very far from Mme Duss's supposition that it provided for the universal categories and norms which Renée had lost by her "Existentialist philosophy." Having not been loved by her mother, having, symbolically, been condemned to death by her mother, Renée felt guilty about her wish to live. "These guilt feelings demanded punishment and punishment consisted in having guilt feelings." [44] Thus, "the system," which forbade her to eat and gave her feelings of guilt for whatever she did or omitted doing, was well adapted to her condition.

As we saw, Renée's basic need was love, maternal love. Among her delirious constructions was one in which she believed herself to be the Queen of Tibet, "a country where one finds all the necessities of life, especially heat [!] and where one no longer suffers from not being loved." [45]

Mme Sechehaye's brilliant approach to a solution was to offer her patient a *symbolic realization* of her frustrated emotional demands. Once she gave her apples, but Renée refused them, pointed to her analyst's breasts and said: "I want apples from Mummy like that." Realizing that the apples meant maternal breasts, maternal milk, maternal love, Mme Sechehaye took an apple, cut it in two, offered the halves to Renée and said: "It is time to drink the good milk from Mummy's apples." [46] Renée, who at this period was twenty-one years old but in regression to the infantile stage of magic participation, leaned toward Mme

[43] *Ibid.*, p. 135.
[44] *Ibid.*, p. 136.
[45] *Ibid.*, p. 45.
[46] *Ibid.*, p. 51.

Sechehaye's shoulder, pressed the apple upon her analyst's breast, and began to eat.

The girl describes the almost miraculous effects of this symbolic realization of her frustrated emotional need of maternal love by writing:

> I ate, or rather, I drank, my milk. A nameless felicity flowed into my heart. . . . I was fully content, with a . . . contentment of a tiny baby, quite unconscious. . . . I left with the nurse . . . and when we were outside I realized that my perception of things had completely changed. Instead of infinite space, unreal, where everything was cut off, naked, and isolated, I saw Reality, marvelous Reality, for the first time. . . ! [47]

The complete success of Mme Sechehaye's symbolic realization of maternal love shows that Renée's true need was emotional and not intellectual. Were Mme Duss's supposition correct— that what Renée needed was a new belief in universal essences, which she had lost through her "Existentialist philosophy"— then Mme Sechehaye would have been compelled to offer her patient a symbolic realization of Plato's world of ideas. Of course, one may be of the opinion that there is no love and security without essences. Mme Duss's judgment may contain a certain portion of truth, for there is little doubt that Renée's "Existentialist" concept of total responsibility of the individual in a normless world had very bad effects on her mental condition; it certainly increased her pathological anxiety.

The analysis of the psychiatric aspects of Existentialism has not shaken, but rather strengthened, our conviction that Sartre's Existential psychoanalysis cannot be regarded as a *therapy* since it gives *freedom with anxiety,* while a true mental therapy would give *freedom from anxiety.* And if Existentialism is to be used as a *moral therapy,* it cannot be in the form of a metaphysical thesis, as in Sartre, but only in that of a moral fiction, an ethical "as if." We shall try to explain this in the next chapter.

Before closing the present analysis, still one more fact must be taken into consideration: Renée's case seems to give some

[47] *Autobiography,* pp. 79–80.

confirmation of Sartre's psychoanalysis of foods. As explained in a previous chapter,[48] Sartre thinks that each kind of food has a symbolic significance, that each represents being in a different symbolic way. To a certain extent, this idea seems to be substantiated by Mme Sechehaye's method of "symbolic realization." We have seen already that apples truly symbolized maternal love. "On the mantelpiece were always two beautiful apples representing maternal breasts, given me by Mama to protect me. At the least anxiety I ran to them and at once was reassured," Renée recounts.[49] On another occasion she describes how her analyst —in whom she had found a new mother—tried to assuage the girl's terrible feeling of guilt by bringing her whipped cream and placing a spoonful of it in her (the girl's) mouth. "Take some white snow," Mme Sechehaye said to her patient, "it will purify Renée. When Mama gives Renée snow, the crime will disappear; Renée will be pure again." [50] And the girl describes how, while she was swallowing the whipped cream, symbol of moral purity, her pervasive feeling of guilt and unworthiness was at once tempered.

Thus a definitive symbolic character of whipped cream was revealed by its positive therapeutic effects, just as, in the other case, the symbolic meaning of the apples had become obvious. These experiences seem to me a confirmation of Sartre's ideas on the psychoanalysis of foods, but, certain qualifiers are necessary: Sartre's Existential psychoanalysis considers the symbolic significance of foods as their "metaphysical coefficient," [51] permanent and unchangeable. This rigid, metaphysical concept of the symbolic significance of foods has not been confirmed by Mme Sechehaye's experiments in symbolic realization. Without referring to Sartre's psychoanalysis of foods (which she seems not to know), Mme Sechehaye recounts how she tried to satisfy symbolically Renée's wish to retreat into her analyst-mother's body. Freud had already spoken of man's nostalgia for his prenatal life, the life of the foetus, passive and free from responsibilities. In order to give symbolic realization to this emotional demand

[48] Ch. 23, "The Psychoanalysis of Qualities and Foods: Viscosity and Nausea."
[49] *Autobiography*, p. 82.
[50] *Ibid.*, p. 90.
[51] *L'Etre et le Néant*, p. 695.

of Renée, her analyst had her lie down in a room whose green shades had been pulled down so that it was filled with green light. Mme Sechehaye gave her patient a sedative, hot compresses, and herb infusions, which represented symbols of maternal refuge. Renée says that she felt wonderfully relieved, and her moral pain was assuaged in that state of perfect passivity. But one difficulty arose when this experiment was repeated: Renée suffered from nausea (physiological as well as Existential) which increased with the hot drinks she was taking in her mother-analyst's symbolic body. To counteract this nausea the doctor ordered ice cream. Now, ice cream is cold, and the contrary of the symbol of maternal warmth. Madame Sechehaye says that Renée was completely bewildered to see that the heat which she had desired so much made her suffer and that she had to eat cold ice cream to relieve her nausea when resting in her mother's body. The analyst got around this difficulty by saying to the girl that she was going to take away her nausea with a liquid that was "a mother's liquid." She was then able to give Renée the ice cream, which relieved her.

Thus the symbolic character is shown not to be a permanent "metaphysical coefficient" of a given food, but as psychologically variable and dependent on the ideas with which one associates it. Although Mme Sechehaye's experiments do not substantiate Sartre's metaphysical conceptions of symbolism, they seem to confirm his general psychoanalytical theory of the symbolic character of food.

xxvi
Critical Considerations and Conclusions

EXISTENTIAL PSYCHOANALYSIS tries to investigate certain mental data which empirical psychoanalysis and individual psychology considered as irreducible. To push back the limits of apparently irreducible data means to expand the field of scientific investigation, and in this sense Sartre's Existential psychoanalysis may have some scientific merit, which only the future can confirm. For the time being, it is only a rough draft. Sartre himself says that Existential psychoanalysis has not yet found its Freud, but there is little doubt that he will be its Freud.

What seems to me defective, is his method of psychoanalytical investigation; for it is the method of Husserl's phenomenology. Sartre considers qualities like viscosity, fluidity, solidity, etc., "objective natures," or essences in Husserl's sense, and tries to discover their meaning through Husserl's phenomenological "intuition." However, intuition is always subjective, in spite of the phenomenologists' protestations. Basing this discipline on intuition, Husserl, nevertheless, pretended to give philosophy the character of a *"strenge Wissenschaft,"* a rigorous science. And so does Sartre with his Existential psychoanalysis, when he says, for instance: "The sweet . . . *expresses* viscosity, when we eat a spoonful of honey or molasses, just as an analytical function expresses a geometric curve." [1] But is not this relation between sweetness and viscosity, to which he wants to give the objective

[1] *L'Etre et le Néant*, p. 707.

character of a mathematical function, merely a subjective one? Is there more than a personal, subjective "intuition" in the following statement? "If I am eating a pink cake, the taste is pink; the slight sweet perfume and the unctuousness of the butter cream *are* pink." [2]

In order to become a true science, Existential psychoanalysis must, in my opinion, become independent of the phenomenological method, which, according to its creator, Husserl, wants to make decisive discoveries "without the apparatus of syllogisms and proofs." [3] But there *is* no science without proofs.

The difference between Freud's and Sartre's psychoanalysis in their attitudes toward therapy has already been discussed. While Freud's empirical psychoanalysis belongs to the realm of *mental* hygiene, Sartre's Existential psychoanalysis belongs rather to that of *moral* hygiene, which, as we have seen, sometimes lives at the expense of mental health. Philosophically speaking, Freud's psychoanalysis is a rationalism, directly in the line of Spinoza's. In Spinoza's rationalism suffering is revealed as an error, arising from the limited understanding of individual existence; but in recognizing things *sub specie aeternitatis* we are relieved from our suffering. Thus Spinoza's ethics is tantamount to a liberation of man from his sufferings through knowledge. I think Freud's psychoanalysis also can be considered a liberation of man from his sufferings through knowledge, for in recognizing our repressed tendencies under the guidance of the psychoanalyst, we are delivered from the sufferings they once caused us. In this sense Spinoza's and Freud's teachings are rationalistic. Reason appears as the great liberator.

Sartre's Existential psychoanalysis, on the contrary, gives us not liberation from suffering, but more suffering. It does not give us *liberation* at all. It gives us *liberty*. And that is different. For liberty is a gift of Danaë. We cannot embrace the beautiful goddess of freedom without accepting her Siamese-twin sister, anxiety. They are joined to each other by an unbreakable bond, as we have seen in Sartre's philosophy, in his novels, and, most impressively, in his tragedy *The Flies*. Clearing the way for

[2] *Ibid.*, p. 707.
[3] "Philosophie als strenge Wissenschaft," *Logos* I (1910), p. 341.

recognition of our freedom, Existential psychoanalysis does not free us from our suffering but brings us the suffering of an existence in *authenticity*. Ascribing to this authenticity an absolute positive value, considering it an absolute ideal which would justify the sufferings of our anxiety, Sartre's Existentialism can be interpreted as an absolute "ethical idealism" and, at the same time, an "irrationalism"; for the acceptance of the sufferings of an authentic existence cannot be justified by reason. On the contrary, reason shows us that all those persons who lead an unauthentic life do not suffer at all. They live in bad faith, running away from the admission of their freedom and thus escape from responsibility for their choice of values. Trying to evade anxiety, they live comfortably in bad faith, accepting values as ready-made things and considering themselves as justified by their little functions within a society for whose values they are not responsible.

A life in authenticity, as preached by Sartre, gives us only *one* reward for the sufferings it imposes upon us: the moral satisfaction of living no longer in bad faith, of being sincere, of being no longer *salauds*. But only an irrationalist approach to existence can consider this moral satisfaction an adequate reward for the sufferings of anxiety; only an irrationalist idealist like Sartre's Orestes can praise "the freedom of the prisoner loaded with chains on the floor of his dungeon, and of the crucified slave." [4]

Sartre's Existentialism *is not a nihilism,* as it seems to many people, but a kind of absolute ethical Idealism, although we realize that Sartre himself would reject this designation with horror. By absolute ethical idealism we mean the attitude of affirming an idea merely for the sake of the values bound up with it, without any regard to the advantages or disadvantages flowing to the agent from the realization of that idea. While Sartre's unconditional affirmation of an "authentic existence" merely for the sake of the values bound up with it, without regard to subsequent sufferings, is a typical example of absolute ethical idealism, it is obvious that the absolute value he ascribes to authenticity and sincerity cannot be justified by his own philosophy; for we know that the latter does not admit any value

[4] *Les Mouches,* in *Théâtre,* p. 94.

of supra-individual validity, given before an individual choice, since Sartre thinks that each individual has to choose his values freely and may even revoke his choice and replace it with another. According to this view, the acceptance of the absolute value of authenticity could even be characterized as a manifestation of unauthenticity, that is of the spirit of seriousness, which considers values as transcendent data, independent of human subjectivity. Yet it is in this way that Sartre accepts the absolute value of authenticity and sincerity; so it would seem that only through a fortunate inconsequence his philosophy avoids nihilism and becomes an irrationalist absolute idealism. Like Nietzsche's philosophy, that of Sartre passes through nihilism in order to overcome it.

It seems to us that Sartre's striving against the comfort of an unauthentic life in bad faith, and his preaching of an authentic life in sincerity, with all the sufferings linked to it, is a new form of the message brought to us in the second half of the nineteenth century by Ibsen. There is no doubt that the great Norwegian, too, preached against the ease of an unauthentic existence in bad faith and summoned us to accept an authentic existence in sincerity and to suffer for it. In *The Wild Duck*, Hjalmar Ekdal lives in bad faith, entirely satisfied with his unauthentic existence built on a lie, the lie which Ibsen calls "life-lie" (*Livslögnen*). Sartre has defined bad faith as a lie, a lie to oneself, and Ibsen's life-lie, or life-illusion, is also a lie to oneself. Ibsen calls it "the stimulating principle" of life; [5] Sartre's "bad faith" has exactly such a strong stimulating function.

Gregers Werle, the idealist, tries to pull Hjalmar out of "the poisonous marsh" of an unauthentic life. In the name of the "claim of the ideal" he wants Hjalmar to accept an authentic life built on sincerity, with all the suffering it involves. And Hjalmar does suffer: his family life is destroyed, his daughter commits suicide.

In *An Enemy of the People* we find a similar message. Dr. Stockmann wishes to free a whole town from bad faith and lead it to authenticity. In the end he stands alone, consoling himself by saying that "the strongest man in the world is he who stands

[5] *The Wild Duck*, New York, Charles Scribner's Sons, 1911, p. 432.

alone." [6] Sartre's Orestes also stands alone in his authenticity, suffering the attack of the Furies.

But Ibsen's Peer Gynt, whose existence is entirely unauthentic, lives happily in bad faith and does not stand alone. By means of elaborate lies he helps his mother to a mild death and spares her an awakening to the authenticity of Heidegger's mortal anxiety. Peer Gynt is the embodiment of unauthenticity, which is also symbolized in the playwright's trolls.

In *Brand* a pastor fights the ease that comes with bad faith and tries to convert his community to an authentic Christendom. He accepts all the sufferings of an authentic life, sacrifices his happiness, his wife and child, and finally, his own life in order to uproot the dominance of bad faith, the comfortable lies in the traditional way of practicing religion. "All or naught!" is Brand's battle cry in his fight against bad faith and for authenticity. It was also the battle cry of his model, Søren Kierkegaard, the founder of Existentialism, whose whole life was a striving for authenticity in the realm of Christian faith, a struggle against the bad faith of those who lie to themselves by pretending to be Christians without trying to live up to the severe and austere requirements of an authentic Christianity.

Miguel de Unamuno, the great Spanish writer and Christian Existentialist, calls *Brand* "*el reflejo de Kierkegaard en el arte dramático*" ("Kierkegaard's reflection in dramatic art"); and he adds: "*Cuanto dure* Brand *durará Kierkegaard*" ("Kierkegaard will last as long as *Brand*").[7]

And yet it seems to us that Kierkegaard was of bad faith. He was engaged to a lovely girl, Regine Olsen, who adored him. But suddenly he broke with her, brutally accusing her of being on a lower religious level, accusing the Church of bad faith in making terms with marriage, which he called "sinful." For woman is the supreme enemy of the spirit; she is the devil who draws young men to her snare. In some of his writings Kierkegaard turned sentimental, declaring, in an obvious allusion to his behavior toward Regine, that "each man must offer up his Isaac, his best."

---

[6] *An Enemy of the People*, New York, Charles Scribner's Sons, 1911, p. 216.
[7] *Mi religión, y otros ensayos* (Buenos Aires-Mexico, 1942), p. 55.

The question of eroticism in Kierkegaard's life is still controversial, and the opinions expressed here are our own conjecture. It seems to us that the reasons Kierkegaard gave for his breach with Regine were lies to the world and to himself, and the Copenhagen magazine *Korsar* appears not to have been wrong when it accused Kierkegaard of odious behavior toward Regine and an indelicate exploitation of this behavior in his books. From Kierkegaard's conversations with Emil Boesen during his last illness, we are led to believe that the "authentic" reason for his rupture with Regine Olsen might have been the incurable physical disability, for which, in vain, he had sought medical help. In his interesting book on Kierkegaard, E. L. Allan writes:

> One cannot but think in this whole connection of some form of sexual impotence, so that it would finally be of a lack of virility that he accused himself. May this be a case in which Adler's analysis applies, and a life-long mental conflict can be traced back to some organ inferiority? [8]

We entirely agree with Allan's assumption and are inclined to think that the striving for authenticity by the pope of modern Existentialism was a manifestation of bad faith. Kierkegaard's case seems to be explained not by Sartre's Existentialist psychoanalysis but by Adler's Individual Psychology.

As for literary form, Sartre adopted Schnitzler's "interior monologue," in which the principal character sets down his thoughts as they are actually formulated in his mind, with all of the seemingly irrelevant associations of ideas. Those who read Schnitzler's *Leutnant Gustl* and *Fräulein Else* or James Joyce's *Ulysses* will not be astonished by the form in which Sartre's Mathieu and Boris express their thoughts.

To be sure, in his essays on literature Sartre criticized Schnitzler's interior monologue, but this did not prevent him from using it.

And what of the literary form Sartre employs in *The Reprieve?* In this novel we are told what is taking place in Paris, Prague, Godesberg, Morocco, and elsewhere, jumping from place to

[8] *Kierkegaard, His Life and Thought* (London and New York, Harper & Brothers, 1935) , p. 30.

place abruptly, often in the same sentence and with no transitions. The antecedents of personal pronouns are not identified. When Sartre writes "he," we are not always told which "he" is meant—a character in Paris or another thinking and acting at the same time in the Sudetenland or in Africa. The effect is often bewildering. The device is only the extension of the ideas André Gide expressed but did not develop in his novel *Les Faux-Monnayeurs* (*The Counterfeiters*). Speaking of the reform of the novel, Gide criticized the naturalistic school, which sought to present "a slice of life" (*une tranche de vie*), but would always cut it longitudinally, in time. Why not cut it transversely, in width, that is to say, make a cross-section through simultaneous events? Sartre tried it out, violating Lessing's sensible laws, and not with the best results.

Yet it would be wrong to consider Sartre an eclectic writer. For the foreign elements he uses are deeply enriched by the synthesis in which he unites them. Sartre's is a syncretic talent, a genius of synthesis. In his short story "La Chambre" ("The Room"), when he describes a woman who tries to enter the world of insane ideas and feelings of her beloved but lunatic husband and thus to pierce "the wall" between reason and madness, Sartre certainly carries out an idea hinted at in Balzac's novel *Louis Lambert*. But what in Balzac was only a light sketch of amazing inspiration became in Sartre's story a master painting carried out with the deepest, gloomiest, and most powerful colors of human passion.

And so it is also with Sartre's philosophy and Existential psychoanalysis. Everywhere the ideas or germs of ideas of his predecessors are developed, seen from new angles, brought to interesting conclusions. Sartre's power of synthesis, his imposing dialectic, the penetrating subtlety of his novels, and his forceful dramatic genius all proclaim him one of the most fascinating personages of our time.

What is the final result of Sartre's philosophy? He has examined all human projects: love, desire, hate, indifference, the enslavement of other persons, the appropriation of inanimate objects; and all these projects turned out to be failures. To be sure, one may not share Sartre's opinion that love is nothing but the wish to be loved, amounting to an endless mirror game.

I am of the opinion—and I have developed this idea elsewhere —that of all human projects love comes closest to overcoming the opposition between subject and object.[9] Love, consequently, may to a certain extent free the individual from his cosmic loneliness. I have also tried to show that love is the only human attitude which ties man to the present and thus redeems him for moments from his everlasting projection toward the future.[10]

However, in Sartre's philosophy love is a failure, and so is man's fundamental project to be God by possessing the world. "For the idea of God is contradictory and we lose ourselves in vain; man is a useless passion." [11]

Closing his main philosophical treatise on this gloomy note, Sartre seems to have achieved what Camus and Juin reproach him for: rationalizing the absurdity of existence.[12] *Being and Nothingness* really demonstrates the necessity of the absurdity and contingency of our existence, which Roquentin, the hero of *Nausea*, had only felt irrationally. *Being and Nothingness* is a logical demonstration that man's existence cannot be demonstrated logically; it gives an ontological foundation to the fact that man's existence has no ontological foundation. It is a justification of man's not being justified. It is a most intelligent demonstration of absurdity.

And yet, in spite of proclaiming the failure of man's project to become God and thus to find a foundation of his existence, Sartre's philosophy finally gives man the attributes of divinity and a foundation—in the form of freedom. In commenting on Descartes, Sartre describes the concept of freedom as defined by the father of modern philosophy. But in Descartes, absolute freedom, which invents reason and values and has no limits other than itself, is a divine prerogative, while Sartre affirms that absolute freedom is human freedom. He concludes by writing:

> We do not reproach Descartes for having given to God what belongs to us (man); we admire him rather for having . . .

[9] See A. Stern, *Die philosophischen Grundlagen von Wahrheit, Wirklichkeit, Wert*, Munich, E. Reinhardt, 1932, pp. 404–421; *La Filosofía de los Valores*, Segunda edición, Buenos Aires, 1960, pp. 169–173.
[10] See A. Stern, *Philosophie du Rire et des Pleurs*, pp. 186–193.
[11] *L'Etre et le Néant*, p. 708.
[12] See Ch. 6, above.

developed to the end the requirements of the idea of autonomy and for having understood, a long time before the Heidegger of *Vom Wesen des Grundes,* that the unique foundation of being is freedom.[13]

To be sure, in looking more closely we realize that this divine freedom, which Sartre so proudly proclaims as our human patrimony, is reduced to miserable remnants. What is left of this boundless human freedom, "not limited by an order of truths nor values which would be offered to our consent as eternal things," [14] when Sartre later restricts it, by our facticity, our situation, and finally admits that it is only a freedom of choosing and not of obtaining? I do not think a God would be satisfied with that type of freedom. Sartre says that a slave in his chains is as free as his master, adding: "The life of the slave who revolts and dies in the course of the uprising is a free life." [15] In many cases Sartre's freedom is reduced to the choice between bearing chains or dying. The idea has been expressed before, in Schiller's *Wilhelm Tell,* when Gertrud Stauffacher exclaims:

> None are so weak but one last choice is left.
> A leap from yonder bridge—and I am free.[16]

Nothing shows better the extreme impoverishment of Sartre's proud, godlike human freedom than his words, "We were never more free than during the German occupation." [17]

Sometimes Sartre's insistence on man's sovereignty and godlike freedom, in spite of the most oppressing situation, sounds willy-nilly almost as ironical as Voltaire's comments on Leibniz's idea of freedom. As a soldier in the Bulgarian (read Prussian) army, Voltaire's hero Candide is asked whether he would rather be

---

13 "La liberté cartésienne," *Situations I,* pp. 334–335.

14 *Ibid.,* p. 335.

15 *L'Etre et le Néant,* p. 635.

16 *Wilhelm Tell,* in *Schillers Werke,* Stuttgart, 1885, III, Sc. 2, p. 9:
    Die letzte Wahl steht auch dem Schwächsten offen,
    Ein Sprung von dieser Brücke macht mich frei.
American edition, "William Tell," *Works,* Boston, A. Niccolls and Co., 1902, Vol. IV.

17 *Republic of Silence,* New York, Harcourt, Brace & Co., Inc. 1947, ed. A. J. Liebling, p. 498.

thrashed thirty-six times by the whole regiment or receive a dozen lead bullets at once in his brain.

> Although he protested that man's will is free and that he wanted neither one nor the other, he had to make a choice; by virtue of that gift of God which is called liberty, he determined to run the gauntlet thirty-six times. . . .[18]

Voltaire's Candide, having to choose between being thrashed to death or shot to death has about the same freedom of choice as Sartre's slave, who must choose between dying in his chains in prison, or dying in a jailbreak. Voltaire, however, recognized that a choice between two destructive necessities is no freedom at all, but its bloody caricature, while Sartre stubbornly maintains that it is godlike freedom. The inconsistency of this attitude is reflected in the fact that, as far as freedom of will is concerned, the skeptic atheist Sartre is much closer to the optimistic creator of the *Theodicy*, Leibniz, than to the skeptic deist Voltaire.

During the Korean War, when Sartre violently disagreed with the United States position he became aware of some very definite limits of human freedom. We know this thanks to Simone de Beauvoir, who, in 1963, published some notes written by Sartre twelve years before. There he said: "That liberty which I was, implied that of everybody. And everybody was not free. . . . I could not be free alone." [19]

Yet it is on this concept of freedom that Sartre bases the final optimism of his Existentialism. For if people are vile, feeble, wicked, cowardly, it is not because of their biological inheritance, or the influence of their environment, or any other organic or social determinism, but because they freely choose themselves as vile, feeble, wicked, cowardly. Thus they are responsible for their vices. But this implies also that "it is always possible for the coward not to be a coward." [20] His becoming a hero only depends finally on his free choice to become heroic.

---

[18] *Candide*, in *Oeuvres choisies*, Paris, 1878, II, p. 49. American edition, *Candide*, New York, Hermitage House, 1949.
[19] S. de Beauvoir, *La Force des Choses*, p. 262.
[20] *L'Existentialisme*, p. 62.

We may reply that genetics and psychology have established the fact of inheritance and that sociology has proved the influence of environment. To this Sartre would answer that science is only one among many projects of existence, which presupposes existence and freedom, and that "human freedom is not limited by any order of truths," for "reason comes into being by freedom." [21] Finally, he probably would retort that the biologists and sociologists, who insist on the factors of inheritance and environment in order to explain man's moral character, are themselves of bad faith in trying to escape from their moral responsibilities under the pretext of a scientific determinism.

Thus Sartre's strategic position in his defense of freedom appears to be impregnable. And yet the foundations of his concept of freedom are not of the solidest. He has told us that "freedom coincides . . . with the nothingness which is in the heart of man." [22] But he is not able to tell us what nothingness is, because it is undefinable. Any definition of it would have to say "nothingness is . . . this or that," but this would be a *contradictio in adjecto,* by which the verb affirms what the noun denies. Sartre's nothingness, which he inherited from Heidegger, is almost a mystical entity, and yet it is the basis of his concept of freedom.

Perhaps Sartre himself feels the logical weakness of his demonstration of freedom, for he relies now more on Descartes' principle: We know our freedom without any proof, by the sole experience we have of it.

But even if we granted Sartre that, thanks to freedom, there is always a chance for the cowardly to become courageous and the vile to be noble, would this be a sufficient reason for optimism? Not for Existentialism, because for it the world even then would continue to wander aimlessly, still devoid of purpose. And —what is even more important—Existentialism cannot recognize the superior value of courage and nobleness, for, according to its own presuppositions, there are no values of universal validity. Each individual has to invent his own system of values and can

---

[21] "La liberté cartésienne," *Situations I,* p. 333; *L'Etre et le Néant,* p. 567.
[22] *Ibid.,* p. 516.

revoke and replace it with another as soon as he wants to make another choice. Values, we have been told by Sartre, are valid only within a definite, individual *project.*

Consequently, if by his free choice the coward has a chance to become courageous and the vile man to become noble, it would not indicate the world's progress toward a higher degree of moral perfection, for only the "rotten spirit of seriousness" can ascribe to the values of courage and nobleness a superior rank of universal and everlasting validity. Thus if Sartre's Existentialism wants to be optimistic *in spite* of having dried up all sources of optimism, its optimism seems to be an *optimism of defiance.*

But the strange thing is that Sartre really believes in the superior value of courage and nobleness independent of any definite project, although his system excludes this belief. As a result of the ruthless German behavior in occupied France, Sartre affirmed the absolute character of good and evil [23] in open violation of his axiological relativism. If that is so, then Sartre's philosophy is both more moral and more dogmatic than he is either theoretically able or emotionally willing to admit.

In spite of the vague nature of Sartre's nothingness as the basis of human freedom, this freedom seems to have certain citizen-rights within human consciousness, although no such absolute rights as Sartre's grants it. For there is no doubt that the subject feels himself free and responsible. But as soon as he tries to *think* of himself, he has to think of himself as determined by long chains of causes and effects. To be thinkable as absolutely free, man would have to be outside space and time. But being an object in space and time, man can think of himself only as determined by other objects and thus as subjected to necessity.[24]

Thus, I should say that subjectively man's existence is felt and lived as free, but objectively he must be thought of as determined. This position, although more restricted than Sartre's, would nevertheless enable philosophy to draw most of the ethical benefit from his theory of freedom. Since the subject feels and lives himself as free, although he cannot think himself as free, I believe

[23] *What Is Literature?* p. 219.
[24] See A. Stern, *Pensée transcendantale-logique et Pensée anthropologique-psychologique-cérébrale, Travaux du IXe Congrès International de Philosophie* (Paris, 1937), VII, pp. 44–51.

that he may adopt the thesis of moral freedom at least in the sense of an "as if," a fiction in Vaihinger's sense. Fiction is a "legitimized error," whose reason of being has to be justified by its success.[25] In this sense I should say that the individual should act "as if" he were free, for he feels that he is free and responsible, although this freedom cannot be conceived theoretically with the categories of the mind.

Considered not as a metaphysical reality but as an ethical "as if," Sartre's concept of freedom certainly could fulfill its whole moral mission by helping to prevent biological and sociological determinism from becoming a pretext for moral laziness and fatalism. The drunkard has to act "as if" he were free to become a sober man, although alcoholism runs in his family. The coward has to act "as if" he were free to choose to be courageous, although his education and environment may not have given him much chance to develop heroic feelings and attitudes.

The same is true of responsibility. The subject feels that he is responsible for his choices, although when thinking of himself he appears as an object determined by so many outside factors that almost no place is left for responsibility.

In considering responsibility as an absolute postulate, Sartre certainly goes much too far. The tragic experience of young Renée, brought into a desperate psycho-pathological condition by the obsession of her total individual responsibility for all the evils in the world, has clearly shown that the idea of an unlimited responsibility cannot be upheld as an absolute imperative.[26] With persons of weak mental equilibrium it will lead to a psychosis, and with sane people it simply will not work because of its extreme character. "If I am mobilized in a war," Sartre writes, "this war is my war. . . . I deserve it, because I could have evaded it by suicide or desertion. Not having evaded this war, I chose it." Thus I am "as responsible for the war as if I myself had declared it." [27] I think that this thesis of Sartre's perverts the moral meaning of the idea of responsibility. *Summum jus,*

---

[25] H. Vaihinger, *Die Philosophie des Als-Ob,* Cap. XXV, p. 190; American edition, *The Philosophy of As-If,* New York, Harcourt, Brace, 1935.
[26] See Ch. 25, "Existentialism and Psychiatry."
[27] *L'Etre et le Néant,* pp. 639–641.

summa injuria ("The highest justice is the greatest injustice"), the Romans said. Likewise, we may say that when driven to extreme, the idea of responsibility refutes itself. No decent man will try to evade his military obligations if his country is implicated in a war for its survival. Are we therefore entitled to say that any man who complies with his civic duty has "chosen" the war and is "responsible" for it? By taking this position we mock the ideas of choice and responsibility.

But as soon as we consider the Sartre-Dostoyevsky idea—everybody is responsible for everything to everybody—not as a metaphysical principle but as an ethical fiction, as a moral "as if," we can harvest all its benefits for ethics. If we had said to a French citizen during the German occupation that he "is" responsible for the war Hitler had started, he would have rejected this accusation as false. But if we had said to him that he ought to act "as if" he were responsible for the war, our suggestion might have enhanced his sense of responsibility.

There is still another element of great ethical importance in Sartre's philosophy. His Existential psychoanalysis has called our attention to the fact that many persons—among them even a genious like Baudelaire—have a tendency to see themselves as they are seen by other people. To be sure, sometimes we need another person to see through his eyes how we are, who we are. But we already know that, according to Sartre, under the gaze of other people the self changes from a subject, which is in the making, into an object, which *is* what it is, which coincides with itself and is petrified. And in this Sartre certainly is right. As long as he lives, every coward is a coward *en sursis,* on reprieve, who can become a hero. But under the gaze of other people the coward is no longer on reprieve, he is definitely a coward, his essence has been fixed and pinned down by the other person's gaze as though he were dead.

Now, if a person always sees himself through the eyes of other people, he sees himself as petrified in his essence, as definitely a coward, a drunkard, a miser, who is no longer in the making, who is not on reprieve and therefore cannot change. And if he cannot change, why should he make any moral effort to try? A person who sees himself through the eyes of other people exists no longer for himself, but only for others. He transposes the center of gravity of his existence from himself into the consciousness of other people, he ceases to a certain extent to be an ego. And seeing himself through the eyes of other people as a drunkard or a homosexual, in the same way that an oak is an oak, he will say to himself that he can cease being a drunkard or a homosexual as little as an oak can cease being an oak. And this would kill in him all moral effort to change, to make himself into something more worthwhile.

I think a bridge leads from this deep insight of Sartre's Existential psychoanalysis across to Adler's Individual Psychology with its superiority goal. In the latter we can discern a lack of being-for-itself. An individual possessed by the goal of superiority always looks at himself in the mirror of other people's consciousness, where he appears as a petrified thing. In Sartre's story "L'Enfance d'un Chef" (The Childhood of a Leader), when Lucien Fleurier, a fascist in the making, is introduced to a young Jew during a party in a friend's home, he wants at first to shake the hand the Jew extends to him. But suddenly Fleurier remembers that his fascist friends consider him as somebody who mortally hates Jews and would kill them all if he could. Thus he suddenly sees himself through the eyes of other people; and immediately he gives up his first gentle impulse, refuses the young Jew's hand, puts his own hands in his pockets, and leaves the party. And when, the next day, his friend, toward whom he feels guilty, tells him that he respects his "conviction" without sharing it, Lucien Fleurier again sees himself proudly through the eyes of other people, who see in him somebody who "has a conviction" which has to be respected. Seeing himself through the eyes of other people, he feels himself justified by their gaze and from now on is lost as a being-for-itself, as a consciousness in the making. He feels himself "full of respect for himself." Through the gaze of other people he has acquired the unchangeable, impenetrable character of a rock, and in this respect he resembles Mauriac's Bernard Desqueyroux. Finally, seeing himself through the eyes of these other people, Lucien is a rock for himself, a dead thing from which noble initiatives can never be expected.

On the other hand, we have Herostratus in Sartre's short story "Erostrate," whose basic project is not, as Robert Campbell believes, only hatred but that of being exclusively for-others and not for-himself. He wants to have a permanent place in other people's consciousness; and because he sees himself only through the eyes of others he lives entirely under the gaze of other people. Therefore, his only obsession is to amaze them, by any means, even a crime. *"Voilà ce que je voudrais, les étonner tous,"* he says to himself.[28] He, too, is lost as a being-for-itself, as a man, for he has become entirely a being-for-others.

Now it seems to me that Adler's "vanity" or "will to superiority" is closely related to the tendency of certain of Sartre's characters to exist only for others, to see themselves only through the eyes of other people. We designate a person as conceited when he is concerned only with the image he offers to the gaze of other people. He has his center of gravity outside himself and is half a man and half a thing, the half which is looked on. Only weak personalities need to exist in the consciousness of other people in order to exist for themselves. Vanity is certainly a form of Adler's inferiority complex.

There is a very valuable imperative we can draw from Sartre's analysis of those persons who exist only through the gaze of other people and therefore exist according to these gazes. We may formulate it in this way: Let us be for-ourselves and not for-others, let us not be petrified things, existing through the judgment of other people, but selves! Let us be not viscous substances, but action, with the fluidity of water. This imperative "let us be for-ourselves and not for-others" should not be confused with egoism, of course, just as the vain dependency on the opinion of others is not to be mistaken for true community feeling or social interest, which is the criterion of mental and moral health.

I think that these ethical principles which we can draw from Sartre's Existentialism, even without sharing his ontological presuppositions, are valuable enough to justify it. We saw that Sartre created a place for "conscience," "guilt," and even "sin," in spite of his atheism. "We are cast into the world, already face to face with the other person; our springing up in it is a free limitation of his freedom. . . . It is from this strange situation that the

28 "Erostrate," *Le Mur*, p. 77.

concept of guilt and sin originates. It is vis-à-vis the other person that I am guilty." [29]

All this explains that, in spite of the fact that Sartre's books have been put on the *Index librorum prohibitorum* of the Vatican, some Catholic thinkers have adopted a favorable attitude toward his philosophy. Even Maritain is not entirely negative, and in Marcel and Mounier we find more preparedness to understand Sartre and to agree with certain of his theses. Although rejecting the conclusions of the author of *Being and Nothingness*, Gabriel Marcel admits "fully the validity and power of some of Sartre's premises" and calls his anthropology "irrefutable." [30] And the late Emmanuel Mounier even accepted certain Sartrean conclusions, as can be seen from the following:

> What is important for an existing being is . . . the authentic life, the perpetual liberation of my freedom, the perpetual breaking away from the inertia of things. . . . That transcendence of human existence with relation to life and matter, that rebellious character of spiritual affirmation . . . that sovereign empire of creative freedom which turns man into a kind of god, this intimate link between man and matter, and this threatening which, nevertheless, he finds in it—with all this we are, as it seems, wholly in a *Christian universe*.[31]

And Mounier adds that Sartre cannot be unaware of the fact that, in certain respects, he is a Christian, in spite of his atheism.[32] It seems to us that these affirmations are correct. Sartre's philosophy expresses man's eternal struggle to free life from the chains of matter and mechanism, from natural and social pressure, and to come to an individual, self-dependent, free ethical existence. Sartre has these tendencies in common with Bergson, Lecomte du Noüy, and Teilhard de Chardin, who were theistic

---

[29] *L'Etre et le Néant*, pp. 480–481.
[30] *The Philosophy of Existence*, New York, Philosophical Library, 1949, pp. 32–33.
[31] "Perspectives existentialistes et perspectives chrétiennes," *Pour et contre l'Existentialisme* (Paris, 1948), p. 135.
[32] *Ibid.*, p. 138.

thinkers. There is in the whole of Sartre's Existentialism, in the persons of his novels and dramas, the theme of the gnawing conscience, which is a Christian theme. In all of his writings, his characters perpetually scrutinize their consciences, and this is a typical Christian attitude. It is perhaps not a pure coincidence that Renée, the girl who tried to live up to all the moral requirements of a Sartrean Existentialism, had been a devout Catholic, trained by a rigorous education in the art of pitilessly scrutinizing her conscience. Many of Sartre's characters are concerned with only one thing: that at the moment of their death their essence may enter eternity in nobleness, courage, purity—although Sartre's type of Existentialism does not provide such eternal values and even definitely excludes them. Why are the characters of Sartre's great tragedy *The Victors* concerned only with their eternal essence, since, being atheists, they do not believe in a Last Judgment? A true iconoclast, like the late Communist philosopher Politzer, once said to Sartre: "I do not give a penny for your eternal essences!" Yet one has the impression that Sartre would give his life for them.

In spite of his atheism and the pornographic character of a part of his work, Sartre—to use the words by which Nietzsche characterized Zarathustra—is the most pious of all those who do not believe in God.

POSTSCRIPT ON EXISTENTIALISM AND MARXISM

IF WE CLOSED our analysis on this spiritualist, individualist note, we would not do justice to the Sartre that has developed in the two decades following the liberation of France. Since that time he has struggled to overcome the contradiction between the subjectivism and individualism inherent in his Existentialist ontology and the collectivism required by his ethics of *"engagement"* or commitment. Commitment requires a struggle for the freedom not only of himself, but of all men, especially of those who need it most urgently: the underprivileged. This conflict between subjectivism and collectivism inherent in his philosophy is rooted in a deeper conflict within Sartre's personal being and existence. It came into the open in his drama *The Devil and the Good Lord,* published in 1951. Its hero, Goetz, is a "bastard," like Sartre's friend Genet, whom he analyzed existentially in a voluminous book. Sartre himself feels to be a bastard, as a bourgeois by birth and education, and an advocate of the proletariat by choice. Insisting on the deep symbolic significance of *The Devil and the Good Lord* as a reflection of Sartre's ideological evolution since the liberation, Simone de Beauvoir writes: "In 1944 he (Sartre) thought that every situation could be transcended by a subjective movement. In 1951 he knew that sometimes the circumstances rob us of our transcendence. Against them no individual salvation is possible, but only collective struggle." [1] Goetz ends up by becoming the leader of the muti-

[1] S. de Beauvoir, *La Force des Choses,* p. 261.

nous peasants in the German peasants' war of the sixteenth century, accepting the discipline necessary for collective action, without renouncing his subjectivity. Sartre's ideal is no longer Orestes, the isolated, individual hero, but Goetz, the man of action, who was able to achieve the synthesis of individualism and collectivism. As Sartre himself wrote in some unpublished notes, quoted by Simone de Beauvoir: *"J'ai fait faire à Goetz ce que je ne pouvais pas faire"*—I made Goetz do what I was not able to do. And he continues: "The contradiction was not in the ideas, it was in my being. For that liberty which I was, implied that of everybody. And everybody was not free. I could not, without breaking down, submit to the discipline of all. And I could not be free alone." [2]

What Sartre alludes to here is the basic contradiction between subjectivist Existentialism and collectivist Marxism, the two philosophies he tries to synthesize. If he has, admittedly, been unable to perform this synthesis practically, in his own existence, he tried at least to achieve it theoretically, in his last great theoretical work *Critique de la Raison dialectique*, which he published in Paris in 1960. It is a gigantic work; the first volume has 755 pages, each of 50 lines, and one still does not know the size of its second volume, which is in preparation. It is thus larger than Sartre's main work, *L'Etre et le Néant*, with its 722 pages in one volume. In addition, the *Critique de la Raison dialectique* is a very abstract work and no easy reading. The Parisian critics, all of them trained philosophers, sociologists or economists, reproached it for the great number of neologisms it introduces, for the length and involvement of its sentences, and on other grounds. Simone de Beauvoir admits that in reading the manuscript she had to advance struggling and groping through long "obscure tunnels." It would be too bold perhaps to try to summarize such a work in a short postscript. But it is also unnecessary, because the book does not modify the basic contents of his Existentialist philosophy as developed in his earlier books, but only complements it, by means of a thorough clarification of its relations to Marxism.

As we have seen in earlier chapters, Sartre's relations to Marx-

[2] *Ibid.*, p. 262.

ism have been full of dramatic peripeties. It consisted of an alternation of friendly rapprochements and hostile withdrawals. There was one very characteristic episode in this perpetual counter-dance: during the fall of 1954 an important Viennese theater prepared the staging of Sartre's tragedy *Les mains sales* (in two different English versions, *Dirty Hands* and *Red Gloves*), the most anti-Communist of his plays, inspired by the murder of Trotzky. After its Parisian performance a Russian critique had called Sartre a Judas, who had been bought by thirty American pieces of silver. But the planned Viennese performance of that play coincided with a new honeymoon between Sartre and the Communists and besides, with an International Peace Congress organized by them in the Austrian capital, to which Sartre was invited. Sartre went to Vienna and tried hard to prevent the performance of the play since its anti-Communist outlook no longer corresponded to his ideology. The director of the theater (the Deutsches Volkstheater) had acquired the play legally through Sartre's publisher and refused to cancel the production. The production was a success, to Sartre's great embarrassment. Two years later, the Hungarian rebellion and its suppression by Russian tanks changed Sartre's attitude again and converted him into a severe critic of the Communists. This ill feeling, however, did not last long and soon after, friendship was restored and his bitter resentments about Budapest were erased.

In his theoretical work of 1960, Sartre designates Marxism as *"l'indépassable philosophie de notre temps"* [3]—that is, the unsurpassable philosophy of our time. Why is that so? Well, according to Sartre, Marxist philosophy is unsurpassable because the historical and economic situations which it expresses have not been overcome. Basing himself on Marx's historical materialism, Sartre declares that a philosophy is efficient as long as the "praxis" which created it, remains alive.[4] This happens with Marxist philosophy, dialectical Materialism. For this reason, Sartre says, every so-called overcoming of Marxism is only a falling-back into pre-Marxism.

---

[3] *Critique de la Raison dialectique*, p. 9.
[4] *Ibid.*, pp. 16, 29.

With these affirmations Sartre remains faithful to the philosophy of the creator of modern dialectics—Hegel—who declared that every philosophy is its epoch, expressed in thoughts[5] and to Marx's idea of the primacy of action over knowledge.

But if Marxism is the unsurpassable philosophy of our time, what, then, is the *raison d'être,* the justification of Sartre's own philosophy, i.e., of Existentialism? This is one of the questions which his new theoretical work tries to answer. "It would seem natural under these conditions," Sartre writes, "that Existentialism, this Idealistic protest against Idealism, has lost all its usefulness . . ." [6] and he himself calls it a "parasitical system." [7]

Marxist philosophers attack Sartre's Existentialism as an ideological expression of the decadent bourgeoisie in the period of the breakdown of capitalism. One of these Communist philosophers, Auguste Cornu, declares that Existentialism translates this decadence into an escape from reality, the isolation of the individual, and the affirmation of the ego's absolute autonomy and superiority to the world.

Sartre admits these criticisms with respect to the Existentialism of Kierkegaard, this "reaction of Christian Romanticism against the Rationalistic humanisation of faith," and especially with respect to Jaspers' *Existenzphilosophie* which he condemns as *"molle et sournoise"* (soft and sullen).[8]

Sartre acknowledges Kierkegaard's merit in having affirmed—against Hegel—his own reality, his subjectivity. But from these reactionary Existential philosophies Sartre distinguishes another type of Existentialism, which developed not against Marxism, but beside it, at its margin. It is his own. He is convinced that Marxism offers the only valid interpretation of history, but that his own Existentialism is the only way which leads to concrete reality. As long as Marx lived, history not only developed but also knew itself, it was interpreted, reflected in thought. Yet during these last decades Marxist theory stopped in its development, it became "sclerotic." Sartre accuses contemporary Marxists of the same error of which they accuse him: the error of idealism,

---

[5] G. W. F. Hegel, *Sämtliche Werke* (edit. Glockner) , Band, VII, p. 35.
[6] *Op. cit.,* p. 21.
[7] *Ibid.,* p. 18.
[8] *Ibid.,* pp. 19, 22.

that is to say of a separation of theory from practice. He writes: "There are two ways of falling into Idealism: the one consists in dissolving reality into subjectivity, the other in denying all real subjectivity for the benefit of objectivity." [9]

The Communists are accusing Sartre of practicing the first type of Idealism, while Sartre accuses them of applying the second type. Normally this latter would not be called "idealism," but Sartre justifies this designation by insisting that today's Communistic bureaucracy tends to subject, *a priori*, men and things to *ideas*. If experience does not verify these ideas, it is "wrong." And with caustic irony Sartre gives the following example of "Marxist idealism," a combination of words which should enrage every dialectical materialist: "The subway of Budapest was real in the head of Rakosi; if the soil of Budapest did not permit its construction, the reason was that the soil was counter-revolutionary." [10]

When Marx wrote that "the materialistic world view simply means the conception of nature such as it *is*, without any foreign addition," he eliminated the ego, he suppressed subjectivity, and moved into a purely objective world, without a subject, that is into a fictitious world. That is what Sartre cannot accept.

What he accepts without restriction, is however, Marx's definition of historical materialism in *Capital*: "The mode of production of material life dominates, in general, the development of social, political and intellectual life." According to Sartre, this formula will be valid as long as the transformation of the production relations within society and the progress of technology have not liberated man from the yoke of "scarcity" (*rareté*). The "leap" from the realm of necessity into a realm of liberty, which Marx and Engels announced as a future ideal,[11] will, according to Sartre, mark the end of Marxism and the beginning of a philosophy of freedom.

This future ideal is, however, far away. In the meantime Marx-

9 *Ibid.*, p. 31.
10 *Ibid.*, p. 25.
11 K. Marx, *Das Kapital* (Berlin, 1953), III, p. 873; F. Engels, *Die Entwicklung des Sozialismus von der Utopie zur Wissenschaft* (Berlin, 1920), p. 51; American edition, F. Engels, *Socialism Utopian and Scientific*, New York, International Publishers, 1935, p. 72.

ism is in danger of degenerating into an "inhuman anthropology," [12] unless it reintegrates living man as its foundation. And it is his Existentialism, which, according to Sartre, can give Marxism this subjective, human, existential foundation it needs. It was exactly that "expulsion of man" from the purely objective world of Marxism which had to produce the renaissance of Existentialism. The concepts used by Marxism—work, exploitation, alienation, reification—require an investigation of their existential foundation. Sartre insists that human work—this basic concept of Marxist theory—is meaningless if its fundamental structure is not a human project, which is a basic concept of Existentialism. Therefore, Sartre thinks that "the comprehension of existence presents itself as the human foundation of Marxist anthropology" [13]—a foundation which is still missing.

This shows how Sartre justifies the reason of being of Existentialism besides or inside Marxism. As long as Marxism bases its doctrine on a dialectic of nature, which, in Sartre's eyes is "a dogmatic metaphysics," instead of grounding it on the comprehension of existing man and his "praxis," Existentialism will continue its investigations. But Sartre himself announces the future abdication of Existentialism in favor of Marxism, with the following decisive sentence: *"A partir du jour où la recherche marxiste prendra la dimension humaine (c'est à dire le projet existentiel) comme le fondement du Savoir anthropologique, l'existentialisme n'aura plus de raison d'être"* [14]—from the day on which Marxist research will take the human dimension (that is to say, the existential project) as the foundation of anthropological knowledge, Existentialism will no longer have any reason for being.

The clarification of the relations between Existentialism and dialectical materialism is one of the basic problems of Sartre's last theoretical work. But it examines many other problems, as well. Sartre wishes to know, for example, whether the positivistic reason of physical sciences suffices for the comprehension of man and his history or whether this comprehension requires another type of reason: a specific historical reason which is dialectical.

[12] Sartre, *Critique de la Raison dialectique*, p. 109.
[13] *Ibid.*, p. 108.
[14] *Ibid.*, p. 111.

Sartre seems to ignore the fact that José Ortega y Gasset already raised this question and answered it affirmatively, by establishing his theory of "vital" or "historical" reason. Also Sartre's answer is affirmative. Refusing to reduce man to nature and the cultural order to natural order, Sartre tries to maintain his Existentialist concept of human liberty, in spite of his adoption of historical materialism. Communist philosophers, however, like the leading Polish theoretician Adam Schaff, see total failure in Sartre's attempt at blending indeterministic Existentialism with deterministic Marxism. "Materialism and idealism cannot come together, and no kind of 'dialectic' can unite them," writes Professor Schaff.[15]

The major part of the first volume of Sartre's latest work is devoted to the establishment of the elementary structures of human "praxis." Work, for example, is a "praxis," the aim of which is the satisfaction of human needs in the prevailing condition of "scarcity." It is the latter which explains class struggle and, in general, violence, since due to the scarcity of goods not all human needs can be satisfied. In this situation of "scarcity" to live means to survive, and the existence of every individual implies the risk of the nonexistence of another individual. Here again the Marxists object. With his theory of "scarcity," says Professor Adam Schaff, Sartre replaces Marxism with a version of social Darwinism.

In Sartre's eyes, dialectical reason is the movement of history in the making and in becoming conscious of itself. And history is the "totalization of all the practical multiplicities and of all their struggles."[16] In his conception of dialectical reason, which he shares with Hegel and Marx, Sartre is, however, in disagreement with Marxism. The latter derives dialectic from nature. In *Dialectics of Nature* Engels considers the three fundamental laws of Hegel's logic—the law of conflict, interpenetration, and unity of opposites, the law of the transformation of quantity into quality, and the law of the negation of the negation—as laws of nature itself. Although even some Western scientists, like the Englishman Haldane, believe in Engels' dialectic of nature, Sartre con-

15 A. Schaff, "A Philosophy of Man" in G. Novack, *Existentialism versus Marxism*, New York, Dell Pub. Co., 1966, p. 314.
16 *Critique de la Raison dialectiques*, p. 754.

siders it rightfully only as a metaphysical hypothesis and as one which has no epistemological foundation, since it is, in a way, a knowledge without a knower, without an existing and thinking man "in situation," to whom dialectic is revealed through his "praxis." *"La loi n'engendre pas d'elle-même la connaissance de la loi"*[17] says Sartre correctly—the law does not engender by itself the knowledge of the law. According to Sartre, dialectical reason is to be found only in the *historical* and *social* world, and it is discovered only by the praxis of men "situated" in a certain society.

Nevertheless, Sartre remains convinced that Marxism is the history of our time becoming conscious of itself and that it is the only valid philosophy of history of this time. Thus the whole new theoretical work of Sartre's rotates around Marxism. Just as Jacob struggled with the angel of God, telling him I "will not let you go, unless you bless me," so Sartre struggles with the god of modern socialism. Yet, judging from the way Marxist reviewers received Sartre's work on dialectical reason, this god still denies him his blessing.

[17]*Ibid.*, p. 127.

Selected Bibliography

Sartre's Works

L'Imagination (Paris: Alcan, 1937; Presses Univ. de France, 1956); Amer. ed., *Imagination* (Ann Arbor: Univ. of Michigan Press, 1962).

La Nausée (Paris: Gallimard, 1938, 1957); Amer. ed., *Nausea* (Norfolk, Conn.: New Directions, 1949, 1959).

Esquisse d'une Théorie des Emotions (Paris: Hermann et Cie., 1939, 1960); Amer. ed., *Existence and Human Emotions* (New York: Philosophical Library, 1948; Wisdom Library, 1957).

Le Mur (Paris: Gallimard, 1939, 1955); Amer. ed., *The Wall and Other Stories* (New York: New Directions, 1948); *Intimacy and Other Stories* (New York: Berkley Corp., 1960).

L'Imaginaire; Psychologie Phénoménologique de l'Imagination (Paris: Gallimard, 1940, 1956); Amer. ed., *The Psychology of Imagination* (New York: Philosophical Library, 1948).

Les Mouches (Paris: Gallimard, 1943).

Théâtre (*Les Mouches, Huis Clos, Morts sans Sépulture, La Putain Respecteuse*) (Paris: Gallimard, 1947); Amer. ed., *No Exit and Three Other Plays* (*No Exit, The Flies, Dirty Hands, The Respectful Prostitute*) (New York: Alfred A. Knopf, 1947, 1955; Vintage Books, 1960).

L'Etre et le Néant; Essai d'Ontologie Phénoménologique (Paris: Gallimard, 1943, 1948, etc.); Amer. ed., *Being and Nothingness; An Essay on Phenomenological Ontology* (New York: Philosophical Library, 1956).

Les Chemins de la Liberté (Paris, Gallimard)
  I. *L'Age de Raison* (1945, éd. recomposée 1949, 1960); Amer.

ed., *The Age of Reason* (New York: Alfred A. Knopf, 1947; Bantam Books, 1959).

II. *Le Sursis* (1945); Amer. ed., *The Reprieve* (New York: Alfred A. Knopf, 1947).

III. *La Mort dans l'Ame* (1949); Amer. ed., *Troubled Sleep* (New York: Alfred A. Knopf, 1951).

Morts sans Sépulture (Lausanne: Marguerat, 1946), and in *Théâtre* (see above); Amer. ed., *The Victors* in *Three Plays* (New York: Alfred A. Knopf, 1949).

L'Existentialisme est un Humanisme (Paris: Nagel, 1946, 1954); Amer. ed., *Existentialism* (New York: Philosophical Library, 1947); Engl. ed., *Existentialism and Humanism* (London: Methuen, 1957).

Réflexions sur la Question juive (Paris: Morihien, 1946; Gallimard, 1954); Amer. ed., *Antisemite and Jew* (New York: Schocken, 1948; Grove Press, 1960).

Les Jeux sont faits (Paris: Nagel, 1947, 1955); Amer. ed., *The Chips Are Down* (New York, 1948); Amer. French ed., *Les Jeux sont faits* (New York: Appleton-Century-Crofts, 1952).

Baudelaire (Paris: Gallimard, 1947); Amer. ed., *Baudelaire* (Norfolk, Conn.: New Directions, 1950).

Situations I, II, III (Paris: Gallimard, 1947, 1948, 1949); Amer. ed., *Literary and Philosophical Essays* (tr. of *Situations* I and III), (New York: Philosophical Library, 1957); *What Is Literature?* (tr. of *Situations* II) (New York: Philosophical Library, 1949); *Literature and Existentialism* (New York: Citadel Press, 1962).

Le Diable et le bon Dieu (Paris: Gallimard, 1951, 1958); Amer. ed., *The Devil and the Good Lord and Two Other Plays* (New York: Alfred A. Knopf, 1960).

Saint-Genet, Comédien et Martyr (Paris: Gallimard, 1952); Amer. ed., *Saint Genet: Actor and Martyr* (New York: Braziller).

L'Affaire Henri Martin (Paris: Gallimard, 1953).

Existential Psychoanalysis (New York: Philosophical Library, 1953).

Kean (Alexandre Dumas). *Adaptation de Jean-Paul Sartre* (Paris: Gallimard, 1954); Amer. ed., *Kean,* based on the play by Alexandre Dumas, in *The Devil and the Good Lord and Two Other Plays* (New York: Alfred A. Knopf, 1960).

Sartre par lui-même, Images et Textes présentés par Francis Jeanson (Paris: Ed. du Seuil, 1954).

Nekrassov (Paris: Gallimard, 1956); Amer. ed., in *The Devil and the Good Lord and Two Other Plays* (New York: Alfred A. Knopf, 1960).

The Transcendence of the Ego (New York: Noonday Press, 1957).

Critique de la Raison dialectique, précédé de *Question de Méthode* (Paris: Gallimard, 1960).

Les Séquéstrés d'Altona (Paris: Gallimard, 1960); Amer. ed., *The Condemned of Altona* (New York: Alfred A. Knopf, 1961).

Ouragan sur le Sucre (Paris: France-Soir, 1960); Amer. ed., *Sartre on Cuba* (New York: Ballantine Books, 1961).

Les Mots (Paris: Gallimard, 1964); Amer. ed., *The Words* (New York, G. Braziller, 1964).

Most of Sartre's articles have been published in the magazine *Les Temps Modernes* (Paris), which he has been directing since 1946, and many have been reproduced in the three volumes of *Situations.* Besides, see especially, "La Republique du Silence," *Eternelle Revue I* (Paris, 1945); Amer. ed., *The Republic of Silence,* ed. A. J. Liebling (Harcourt Brace: New York, 1947).

Collateral Readings

ADLER, A., *The Practice and Theory of Individual Psychology* (New York, 1929).

ANSBACHER, H. L. and R., eds., *The Individual Psychology of Alfred Adler* (New York, 1956).

—— *Superiority and Social Interest* (Evanston, Ill., 1964).

ASTRADA, C., *Existencialismo y Crisis de la Filosofía* (Buenos Aires, 1964).

BACHELARD, G., *La Psychanalyse du Feu* (Paris, 1938).

—— *L'Eau et les Rêves* (Paris, 1942).

BARRETT, W., *What Is Existentialism?* (New York, 1964).

BARNES, H. E., *The Literature of Possibility: A Study in Humanistic Existentialism* (Lincoln, Neb., 1959).

BEAUVOIR, S. DE, *Pyrrhus et Cinéas* (Paris, 1945).

—— *Pour une Morale de l'Ambiguité* (Paris, 1946); Amer. ed., *The Ethics of Ambiguity* (New York, 1949).

—— *Le Sang des Autres* (Paris, 1947); Amer. ed., *The Blood of Others* (New York, 1948).

—— *Mémoires d'une Jeune Fille rangée* (Paris, 1958); Amer. ed., *Memoirs of a Dutiful Daughter* (Cleveland, 1959).

—— *La Force de l'Age* (Paris, 1960); Amer. ed., *The Prime of Life* (Cleveland, 1962).

—— *La Force des Choses* (Paris, 1963); Amer. ed., *Force of Circumstance* (New York, 1965).

BEIGBEDER, M., *L'Homme Sartre* (Paris, 1947).

BENDA, J., *Trois Idoles Romantiques: le Dynamisme, l'Existentialisme, La Dialectique Matérialiste* (Geneva, 1948).

BERGER, G., *Existentialism and Literature in Action* (Buffalo, 1948).

BLACKHAM, H. J., *Six Existentialist Thinkers* (New York, 1952).

BOBBIO, N., *La Filosofía del Decadentismo* (Torino, 1944); Engl. ed., *The Philosophy of Decadentism* (Oxford, 1948).

BOROWITZ, E. B., *A Layman's Introduction to Religious Existentialism* (Philadelphia, 1965).

BOUTANG, H. J., *Sartre est-il un Possédé?* (Paris, 1946).

BUGENTAL, J. F., *The Search for Authenticity* (New York, 1965).

CAMPBELL, R., *Jean-Paul Sartre or Une Littérature Philosophique* (Paris, 1947).

CAMUS, A., *L'Etranger* (Paris, 1942); Amer. ed., *The Stranger* (New York, 1946).

—————— *Caligula* (Paris, 1943); Amer. ed., *Caligula and Three Other Plays* (New York, 1958).

—————— *Le Mythe de Sisyphe* (Paris, 1943); Amer. ed., *The Myth of Sisyphus and Other Essays* (New York, 1955).

—————— *La Peste* (Paris, 1947); Amer. ed., *The Plague* (New York, 1948).

—————— *L'Homme Révolté* (Paris, 1951); Amer. ed., *The Rebel* (New York, 1954).

CHAMPIGNY, R., *Stages on Sartre's Way 1938–1952* (Bloomington, Ind., 1959).

CHIAROMONTE, N., *Il Tempo della Malafede* (Rome, 1953).

COLLINS, J. D., *The Existentialists* (Chicago, 1952).

DEMPSEY, P. J., *The Psychology of Sartre* (Westminster, 1950).

DESAN, W., *The Tragic Finale: An Essay on the Philosophy of Jean-Paul Sartre* (New York, 1960).

—————— *The Marxism of Jean-Paul Sartre* (New York, 1965).

ESTIÚ, E., *De La Vida a la Existencia en la Filosofía Contemporanea* (La Plata, 1964).

FOULQUIÉ, P., *L'Existentialisme* (Paris, 1947); Engl. ed., *Existentialism* (London, 1948).

FREUD, S., *Die Traumdeutung* (Leipzig, Vienna, 1914).

—————— *The Problem of Anxiety* (New York, 1936).

—————— *The Basic Writings of Sigmund Freud* (New York, 1938).

—————— *Gesammelte Werke* (London, 1942).

—————— *An Outline of Psychoanalysis* (New York, 1949).

GILSON, E., *L'Essence et l'Existence* (Paris, 1948).

GRENE, M., *Introduction to Existentialism* (Chicago, 1959).

GREENE, N. N., *Jean-Paul Sartre, The Existentialist Ethics* (Ann Arbor, 1964).

HARPER, P., *Existentialism, A Theory of Man* (Cambridge, 1948).

HEGEL, G. W. F., *The Logic of Hegel* (Oxford, 1874).

HEIDEGGER, M., *Sein und Zeit* (Tübingen, 1949); Amer. ed., *Being and Time* (New York, 1962).

—— *Was ist Metaphysik?* (Frankfurt, 1960); Amer. ed., *Existence and Being* (Chicago, 1951).

—— *Einführung in die Metaphysik* (Tübingen, 1958); Amer. ed., *An Introduction to Metaphysics* (New Haven, Conn., 1959).

—— *Platons Lehre von der Wahrheit, mit einem Brief über den Humanismus* (Bern, 1947, 1959).

—— *Vom Wesen der Wahrheit* (Frankfurt, 1949, 1954, etc.); Amer. ed., *Existence and Being* (Chicago, 1951).

—— *Holzwege* (Frankfurt, 1950).

HUSSERL, E., *Gesammelte Werke* (The Hague, 1950).

—— *Ideas; General Introduction to Phenomenology* (New York: Macmillan, 1958).

JASPERS, K., *Vernunft und Existenz* (Munich, 1960); Amer. ed., *Reason and Existence* (New York, 1959).

—— *Tragedy Is Not Enough* (Boston, 1952).

—— *Philosophie* (Berlin, 1956).

JEANSON, F., *Le Problème moral et la Pensée de Sartre* (Paris, 1947, 1965).

JOLIVET, R., *Les Doctrines Existentialistes de Kierkegaard à J.-P. Sartre* (Paris, 1948).

JUIN, H., *Jean-Paul Sartre ou La Condition Humaine* (Brussels, 1946).

KAELIN, E. F., *An Existentialist Aesthetic: The Theories of Sartre and Merleau-Ponty* (Madison, Wisc., 1962).

KERN, E. G., *Sartre, A Collection of Critical Essays* (Englewood Cliffs, N.J., 1962).

KIERKEGAARD, S., *Gesammelte Werke* (Jena, 1911–1922).

—— *Concluding Unscientific Postscript* (Princeton, 1941).

—— *Philosophical Fragments* (Princeton, 1962).

KUHN, H., *Encounter With Nothingness* (Chicago, 1949).

LAMBRE, M., *L'Ange Exterminateur* (Paris, 1949).

Lavelle, L., *De l'Acte* (Paris, 1946).

Lehan, R. D., *Existentialism and the Modern American Novel* (Ann Arbor, 1959).

Luijpen, W. A. M., *Existential Phenomenology* (Pittsburgh, 1960).

Lefebure, H., *L'Existentialisme* (Paris, 1946).

Lefèvre, L. J., *L'Existentialiste est-il un Philosophe?* (Paris, 1946).

Lévinas, E., *De l'Existence à l'Existant* (Paris, 1947).

Lukács, G., *Existentialisme ou Marxisme?* (Paris, 1948).

Marcel, G., *Journal Métaphysique* (Paris, 1927, 1935, 1958); Amer. ed., *Metaphysical Journal* (Chicago, 1952).

———— *The Philosophy of Existentialism* (New York, 1956, 1961).

Maritain, J., *Court Traité de l'Existence et de l'Existant* (Paris, 1947); Amer. ed., *Existence and the Existant* (New York, 1948, 1964).

McElroy, D. D., *Existentialism in Modern Literature* (New York, 1963).

Merleau-Ponty, M., *La Phénoménologie de la Perception* (Paris, 1945); Amer. ed., *The Phenomenology of Perception* (New York, 1962).

———— *Sens et Non-sens* (Paris, 1948).

———— *Les Aventures de la Dialectique* (Paris, 1955).

Möller, J., *Absurdes Sein? Eine Auseinandersetzung mit der Ontologie J.-P. Sartres* (Stuttgart, 1959).

Molina, F., *Existentialism as Philosophy* (Englewood Cliffs, N.J., 1962).

Morales, D. M., *El Existencialismo y la Creación de la Personalidad* (Cochamba, Bolivia, 1963).

Mounier, E., *Introduction aux Existentialismes* (Paris, 1947); Amer. ed., *Existentialist Philosophies, An Introduction* (New York, 1949).

Murdoch, E., *Sartre, Romantic Rationalist* (New Haven, Conn., 1959).

Natanson, M., *A Critique of Jean-Paul Sartre's Ontology* (Lincoln, Neb., 1951).

Naville, P., *Les Conditions de la Liberté* (Paris, 1947).

Nicol, E., *Historicismo y Existencialismo; La Temporalidad del Ser y la Razón* (Mexico, 1950).

NOVACK, G., ed., *Existentialism versus Marxism* (New York, 1966).

ODAJNYK, W., *Marxism and Existentialism* (New York, 1965).

ORTEGA Y GASSET, J., *Obras Completas* (Madrid, 1950–1952).

—— *La Idea de Principio en Leibniz* (Buenos Aires, 1958).

—— *El Hombre y la Gente*, I, II (Madrid, 1962).

PFLEGER, K., *Kundschafter der Existenztiefe* (Frankfurt, 1959).

PONTALIS, G. B., et al., *Pour et contre l'Existentialisme* (Paris, 1948).

QUILLES, I., *Sartre y su Existencialismo* (Buenos Aires, 1952).

RUGGIERO, G., *Existentialism, Disintegration of Man's Soul* (New York, 1948).

STERN, A., *Philosophie du Rire et des Pleurs* (Paris, 1949).

—— *Philosophy of History and the Problem of Values* (The Hague, 1962).

THODY, P., *Jean-Paul Sartre, A Literary and Political Study* (New York, 1961).

TRUC, G., *De J.-P. Sartre à L. Lavelle, ou Désagrégation et Réintégration* (Paris, 1946).

UNAMUNO, M. de, *Del Sentimiento trágico de la Vida* (Madrid, 1913; New York, 1959); Amer. ed., *The Tragic Sense of Life* (New York, 1954).

USHER, A., *Journey Through Dread* (London, 1955).

VELA, F., *Ortega y los Existencialismos* (Madrid, 1961).

VARET, G., *L'Ontologie de Sartre* (Paris, 1948).

WAHL, J., *Etudes Kierkegaardiennes* (Paris, 1938).

—— *Petite Histoire de l'Existentialisme* (Paris, 1946); Amer. ed., *A Short History of Existentialism* (New York, 1949).

WEISMAN, A. D., *The Existential Core of Psychoanalysis* (Boston, 1965).

WOLFF, W., *Values and Personality, An Existential Psychology of Crisis* (New York, 1950).

Index